Bit Tyrants

Load Screen

Let me start by saying I use all these corporations' services constantly. This book was written on Apple devices, using Microsoft Word software, employing an enormous number of Google searches, with some of the research material purchased from Amazon affiliates. And I will irritate my friends by promoting it on Facebook.

So I'm not pretending to be above using these services. Indeed, I probably couldn't have written this book without them. And that's the point—it's not just me.

In 2017 the world was on the edge of global confrontation over the clusterfuck of a chess game that was the Syrian Civil War, and a number of times the United States and Russia came dangerously close to a full confrontation, which could have gone all the way to nuclear conflict. Preventing that scenario is the hotline system, maintained by the two countries' military bases in the region, which allows both sides to inform one another of their flight paths and attack plans, so that the air forces don't accidentally target one another or risk an unintentional near-collision. A mainstay in US-Russia relations since the Cold War era, the hotline is a pawn in disputes between the countries, but rarely is it actually deactivated.

It was reported at the time that a backup exists to the conventional phone-based hotline. It is a declassified Gmail account.[1]

This book is not about whether the towering corporate empires of Silicon Valley make useful products—few people would try to deny that. It's about the fact that I have little choice but to rely on these huge firms in order to carry out a project like producing a book, much like the American and Russian air forces in running a war. Our economy now largely relies on these tech companies, giving them incredible power. It's not the first time capitalism has evolved a new ruling core of networked companies that eventually dominate the entire system, but it may wreak the deepest changes yet.

And exploring these new, powerful institutions of capital is the purpose of this book.

Bit Tyrants

The Political Economy of Silicon Valley

ROB LARSON

Haymarket Books
Chicago, Illinois

Published in 2020 by
Haymarket Books
P.O. Box 180165
Chicago, IL 60618
773-583-7884
www.haymarketbooks.org
info@haymarketbooks.org

ISBN: 978-1-64259-031-9

Distributed to the trade in the US through Consortium Book
Sales and Distribution (www.cbsd.com) and internationally
through Ingram Publisher Services International
(www.ingramcontent.com).

This book was published with the generous support of Lannan
Foundation and Wallace Action Fund.

Special discounts are available for bulk purchases by organizations and institutions. Please call 773-583-7884 or email
info@haymarketbooks.org for more information.

Cover design by Matt Avery.

Printed in Canada by union labor.

Library of Congress Cataloging-in-Publication data is available.

10 9 8 7 6 5 4 3 2 1

Contents

INTRODUCTION

Bitatorship

What this book is for

It might seem weird that so many people are turning against Big Tech. After all, we spend much of the day on our phones, log long hours on Facebook and YouTube, and for many years the great innovators of Silicon Valley and its CEOs have been toasted on TV and praised by presidents. Apple CEO Steve Jobs became a global icon of the visionary genius, even becoming a basis for the *Iron Man* movies. Barack Obama was extremely close to the industry, and especially to Google, with 250 people moving between his administration and the company.[1] During his first presidential meeting with tech CEOs, even Donald Trump said, "We want you to keep going with the incredible innovation. There's nobody like you in the world. . . . Anything we can do to help this go along, we're going to be there for you."[2]

Many liberal and conservative figures have celebrated the tech industry's fun and useful new services, often available for free, and for decades praised the disruptive instincts of Silicon Valley. Libertarian economist Tyler Cowen, for example, writes that the tech companies "have placed so much of the world's information at our fingertips, and more often than not it is accessible within minutes or even seconds. . . . The benefits of the tech companies still far outweigh their costs, as evidenced by how few Americans are trying very hard to opt out."[3] There are whole books of this shallow, religious ball-fondling.

But despite this bottomless ocean of mainstream ass-kissery, the reality is that Big Tech towers over us and has incredible influence over our lives. So much of our daily work, commerce, and socializing happens on their systems or relies on their data. All the feverish worship of Innovation can't hide the fact that the technology companies have largely taken over the economy, hoarded our data, played dirty to crush challengers, and utterly reshaped our lives to their advantage. The companies are typically run by bullying tyrant CEOs, who abuse their corporate subordinates and have structured their companies so as to maintain their sole power over major decisions. No vision for fundamentally changing our society can succeed without seriously thinking about how to deal with today's tech companies, which have arguably become the central industry in capitalism altogether. And all using technology the bastards didn't even invent!

Holding a magnifying glass up to the monumental tech corporations is the purpose of this book, and it won't conform to the conventional picture of Big Tech as friendly giants with free software—a picture that's finally wearing thin anyway. I wash my brains of it! We'll be looking head-on at the different forms of stupefying, world-changing power wielded by today's biggest corporate titans over the man in the street.

And you don't have to take my work for it. Consider a little-noticed report in the conservative *Wall Street Journal*, titled "Giants Tighten Grip on Internet Economy," focusing on the major tech corporations, which were represented in the article's art design as a huge flying saucer covered in corporate logos, apparently beaming people aboard.[4] "The Internet economy is powered by an infrastructure . . . controlled by a small handful of tech giants," it declared, describing Google, Microsoft, Apple, Amazon, and Facebook as "established companies [that] dominate in essential services that both fuel and extract value from the rising digital economy."

The centrality of these firms to the functioning of the Internet means whole "ecosystems" of users are gradually built around these corporate nodes, so that "anyone building a brand, for example, can't ignore Facebook's highly engaged daily audience of 1 billion. Anyone starting a business needs to make sure they can be found on Google. Anyone with goods to sell wants Amazon to carry them." And the same goes for mobile apps (dominated by Google and Apple's stores) and video (Google's YouTube).

As of this writing, the five biggest companies in the world by market value are Microsoft, Amazon, Apple, Google, and Facebook. It's very unusual for the world's five biggest corporations to all lie in a single sector of the economy. It reflects the fact that the technology markets are especially prone toward winner-take-all outcomes.

The short version is that the tech sector is especially monopoly-prone because of an economic phenomenon called "network effects." Network effects occur when the value of a good or service increases as more people use it—like a telephone. As more people joined the early phone network, the value of a telephone in your house grew, since you could potentially call more people and businesses with it. The same principle applies to other markets that operate on networks, like web search engines and social media.

Network effects tend to create monopolies because the first one or two companies to gain a large mass of users tend to attract more users—success breeds success in network markets. This means that early market leaders tend to become almost magnetically irresistible and grow extremely quickly as the network gains value from more users, leading to yet more users. This economic process tends to leave a single hugely dominant company, like YouTube, with gigantic user numbers due to the overwhelming attractiveness of a network that has everyone on it. This kind of dominance, where users are attracted *because* of the existing presence of many users, makes a company into a "platform."

In other networked markets, a full monopoly isn't reached but still there are at most two companies dominating, as with Google's and Apple's smartphone software. But even there monopoly power is present, as seen in the laborious process involved in switching from an Apple to an Android phone. It's an enormous headache, requiring the movement of tons of personal data like music and pictures, re-changing many settings, and recognizing that some apps are only available on one smartphone platform, or must be repurchased. This creates a barrier to entry known as "lock-in," where users face real costs to switching.

Network effects are discussed more fully in the next chapter, but one fascinating point to raise here is that several of the Big Tech CEOs knew about network economics back when they first created their companies, or early on in their history. Consider this recounting from a *Fortune* journalist describing Facebook cofounder and CEO Mark Zuckerberg and his friends in the early days of their company:

> They loved to talk about how Thefacebook showed what economists call "network effects." And it did, just as have many of the great communications and software innovations of the last hundred years. . . . Since every incremental user thus in effect strengthens the service, growth tends to lead to more growth, in a virtuous cycle. That was surely the case with Thefacebook, just as it was with instant messaging, AOL, the Internet itself, and even the telephone.[5]

So Zuckerberg and company knew the deck was stacked in their favor. So did Bill Gates, the cofounder and longtime CEO of Microsoft, who exploited similar network effects to dominate computer operating system software. As we'll see, Microsoft's Windows platform became dominant once its early success attracted more developers and users than smaller upstarts could, making Windows an industry standard for productivity apps and games to work on users' computers. Since almost all apps thus ran on Windows, that created an application-based barrier to entry for other software companies, and meant "lock-in" on an industry-wide scale and insane growth for Microsoft. A senior Microsoft executive wrote in a confidential email to billionaire investor Warren Buffett that applications create "the 'moat' that protects the operating system business," a recognition of the entrenched power of platform economics.[6]

And to top it off, besides these companies often seeing their own monopolies coming, almost all of the crucial basic research that created the gigantic platforms' technologies, essential hardware, and even the Internet itself came from the public sector, not from the tech industry's tyrannical kid CEOs. Despite a surging river of bullshit that worshiped Apple CEO Steve Jobs and other slick tech front men, the long-term research into the dirty work of making mobile tech and fancy software platforms came from Cold War R&D investments by the military and the US university system.

In short, the towering tech platform corporations and their heavily celebrated CEOs are a bunch of phony, power-mongering, monopolist douchebags and the new core of the global ruling class. As we'll see, their power is truly incredible, and the growing techlash against them will likely fail to seriously limit their influence. They must be understood.

Gilded Rage

The dominance of Big Tech over major chunks of world commerce might smell pretty familiar. Similar levels of market power were held by previous network monopolies, like the railroads; and actually, the pro-business *Wall Street Journal* reporters draw the point directly: "Put another way, they own the digital equivalent of railroad lines just as the Web enters a new phase of growth."[7]

Indeed, in trying to anticipate the possible futures of our online giants, the early era of railroad network monopolization can be pretty instructive. For example, consider the cruel monopolies that were dominant in the late 1800s, during the US Industrial Revolution and the "Gilded Age." Historians describe the railroad monopolist Cornelius Vanderbilt as wanting "to make himself a dictator in modern civilization" by buying up railroad routes, since "trade now dominates the world, and railways dominate trade."[8] Railroads were the circulatory system of the Industrial Revolution, and the Gilded Age capitalists built them into continent-spanning empires with tremendous influence.

The robber barons—the big capitalists of the 1800s—held enormous power over their different domains, but also fought bitterly to undermine or corner one another's monopolies. This include monopolies that arose from markets without the boost of network effects—John Rockefeller tried using the thundering income from his Standard Oil monopoly to buy up iron ore in order to force the steel magnate Andrew Carnegie into paying him for it. Later, the Wall Street kingpin J. P. Morgan maneuvered Carnegie into accepting a buyout so he could more fully "Morganize" steel into the supposedly more "rational" US Steel monopoly, as he eventually did for other corporate titans from American Tobacco to General Electric.

Fascinatingly (and horrifyingly), the barons also fought by buying up major railroads—the equivalent of today's interstate highways. When Morgan's various railroad networks doubled their freight rates simultaneously in order to twist Carnegie's arm, the city of Pittsburgh's very economic life was threatened until Carnegie's giant fortune paid for a hastily built new rail line to reach the coastal networks.[9] Carnegie himself had made similar moves to push back against smaller railroads in the past, as Matthew Josephson's great history *The Robber Barons* recounts. These kinds of epic battles among gigantic, annoyed capitalists are happening right now, although on very different digital platforms, like when Google pulled YouTube from Amazon's smart speaker devices after Amazon wouldn't carry Google's Pixel phones. These twisted battles of the giants will appear throughout this book.

Ultimately, that historic rail-network battle led to the climax of the Gilded Age epoch of unregulated capitalism, when the growth of Rockefeller's encroaching Union Pacific–based south-western rail network threatened the Eastern Seaboard–centered system owned by Morgan and his allies. The banker had endeavored to Morganize the industry for years, buying up bankrupt rail lines in transactions that always created great paper wealth on Wall Street, and by the McKinley era Morgan was estimated to control as much as half the total US rail mileage—a truly impressive level of network concentration.

But the Rockefeller-aligned network fought back, and soon the two sprawling rail octopuses came into direct conflict over the important Northern Pacific line, held by Morgan allies. The two trust giants battled through proxies to buy a direct controlling interest in the line, and in the process they unintentionally triggered an enormous crash in the stock market—the 1901 "Northern Pacific Panic." Morgan kept control, and Rockefeller's proxies got board seats, but the collateral damage of the crash to the economy was enormous. In the aftermath Morgan famously told a journalist, "I owe the public nothing."[10]

Again today, while conservative figures insist that the government regulation of rail networks during the midcentury New Deal period was unnecessary and stifled the competition that must arise in free markets, after railroad deregulation in the 1980s, the industry went through a predictable merger binge. Eventually, as *Fortune* magazine reported, "since freight railroads were deregulated in 1980, the number of large, so-called Class I railroads has shrunk from 40 to seven. In truth, there are only four that matter. . . . An estimated one-third of shippers have access to only one railroad."[11]

Wow, that sounds very slightly similar to our new online economy! Even pro-business columnists like the *Wall Street Journal*'s Christopher Mims recognize that the tech giants "Tiptoe Toward Monopoly," as a headline of his went. Fittingly, the paper's editors playfully illustrated that article with tech company CEOs dressed up like their Gilded Age forbears.[12]

User's Guide

Having reviewed the basics of network effects, the prominent views celebrating the Silicon Valley giants, and some historical networks, we can now outline this book's more critical views of the tech titans.

The first chapter dissects the nature of networks, their particularly strong tendency toward monopoly, and mainstream views of these subjects. Chapter 2 takes up Microsoft, a company that clearly owes its monopoly to network effects. To quote the *Financial Times*, "Microsoft worked hard through the 1980s to win over software developers. This ensured there was a steady supply of Microsoft-compatible applications and helped to establish MS-DOS and Windows as industry standards."[13] Its monopoly is better known than those of its newer tech compatriots because of its long history of monopoly-related legal trouble, from the ongoing European Union competition inquiries to the aborted 2001 US antitrust suit. The latter complaint alleged that Microsoft used its overwhelming dominance in commercial operating system software to crush competitors in other markets, and to entrench its network hub status.[14] The company's heavy reliance on permanently "temporary" workers, to whom they deny benefits, also deserves attention.

Apple is the subject of chapter 3, which examines the gigantic success of what is now among the world's largest companies by market value. Since Apple primarily produces hardware—iPhones, Mac desktops, and laptops, along with the software to run them—some have suggested that Apple has not benefited from network effects. But Apple products and services, like Microsoft's Windows and Facebook's services, also constitute a platform because they are a nexus of network effects. Beyond being a network hub, a platform is a group of related services that allow others to create and use content and applications, as Facebook and Google's Android phone system do. Developing a successful platform is the holy grail of network effects, as it can create an ecosystem of users and services organized around it. Apple's open (but curated) App Store meets these criteria. Labor conditions in the plants of Apple's contractors have become a scandal too, the most frontline picture of the company's network monopoly power.

Chapter 4 takes up the colossal Amazon, which is fast growing beyond being simply the online Walmart. Amazon has benefited from the same network effects that have helped the other web giants, and from its current status as a platform for a broader ecosystem of commerce. Consider Amazon's enormous network of third-party sellers, representing merchandise producers who sell through Amazon's site. The *Financial Times* observes that Amazon "acts as e-commerce platform for an increasing number of retailers," with the power of network effects.[15] Also, author Nicholas Carr reminds us that "much of Amazon.com's early appeal came from the book reviews donated by customers," which also demonstrated a network effect as avid readers were attracted to the site's large number of reviewers and reviews, showing the classic positive feedback pattern.[16] Satisfying Amazon's flood of orders has also required a giant "fulfillment" workforce, sweating away their hours in Amazon's warehouse network.

Chapter 5 examines Google. Although its reputation is far sunnier than the other giants, Google too has benefited pivotally from network effects. Investor Arun Rao and consultant Piero Scaruffi's *History of Silicon Valley* finds that

> [s]earch was a classic network service. The more people that used a search engine and clicked on results, the better a search engine could be at optimizing results and so have more relevant results, attracting more users. . . . On the technology side, it was impossible for most companies to enter search. Because most search algorithms optimized based on past users' searches, network effects prevent new engines from being as powerful as the dominant few.

The authors conclude that Google's "terabytes of data" from past searches and emails constitute "an enormous barrier to entry."[17] Furthermore, the *Financial Times* quotes a Citigroup analyst describing YouTube, the hugely popular video-sharing platform Google purchased in 2006, as "a network effects business" itself.[18]

Chapter 6 explores the great time consumer, Facebook. The company has perhaps the clearest version of the network effect: everyone wants to join a social network that their friends are on, not one with none of their friends. And, as more and more users become subject to this effect, the value of the network and its attraction to others grows and grows. We now know its founder, Mark Zuckerberg, was aware of this dynamic, and it's such a classic case that it's become literally a textbook example, with prominent economists citing it as an easy-to-understand example of network effects creating a platform.[19] The company's giant market capitalization, the fifth-biggest in the world, reflects the monopoly potential of even a trivial-seeming company, with a rather durable market position despite an endless parade of scandals like the livestreaming of capital crimes and a series of data breaches.

After these profiles in power, chapter 7 explores the battles over net neutrality—the principle that all online data should receive the same treatment. This issue involves the telecommunications companies, like Verizon, Comcast, and AT&T, in conflict with the Silicon Valley web giants, although the latter have moderated their views. The telecom firms lost on net neutrality in 2015 but won in 2017, partially because of waning support for the neutrality cause from the tech empires themselves.

Chapter 8 reviews the history of the marvelous technology these companies all rely on, and explores the little-known fact that almost all of it, from the early Internet to the tech in your smartphone, was developed by various public, government, and military entities. Chapter 9 confronts the relationship between the tech sector and major governments, including the Trump administration, which the tech titans have criticized but have mostly continued to work for.

Finally, chapter 10 explores possibilities for stripping these firms of their huge power by socializing the industry, through a combination of user activism, workforce organization, and political action. This could create a version of the Internet over which users and programmers actually share influence, rather than following the dictates of CEOs and their Wall Street investors. The acute need for online socialism is suggested by the words of Tim Berners-Lee himself, the computer scientist who invented the World Wide Web: "The problem is the dominance of one search engine, one big social network, one Twitter for micro-blogging. We don't have a technology problem, we have a social problem."[20] Or more specifically, an economic problem. The Internet, so famously free and quirky in the early days of the 1990s, is becoming enclosed by colossal giants of online monopoly capital.

Irony loves company!

CHAPTER 1

The Flaw of Gravity

The network origins of tech monopolies

The nineteenth-century railroad regulator Charles Francis Adams observed that "gravitation is the rule, and centralization the natural consequence, in society no less than in physics."[1] And indeed, markets for goods and services have a long history of becoming dominated by giant companies, from Standard Oil to Ticketmaster. But today's globalized information networks have taken the perennial trend even further.

The 1 percent's technology corporations are reaching new heights in the drive to accumulate capital, and they are conquering our newest industries. Even the liberal *New York Times*, for example, in 2017 ran a business-section analysis of Silicon Valley's dominance over our information networks, calling giants like Google and Facebook the "undisputed rulers of the consumer technology industry."[2] Its author, the reliable technophile Farhad Manjoo, writes that the "Frightful Five," as he calls the tech behemoths, "lord over all that happens in tech" and are "better insulated against surprising competition from upstarts." At turns rivals and partners, they are "inescapable" and "central to just about everything we do with computers," and together they "form a gilded mesh blanketing the entire economy." Elsewhere in the piece, Manjoo describes the giants as "the warden of a very comfortable corporate prison. . . . It's too late to escape."[3] The paper, usually happy to celebrate Silicon Valley, now finds that its corporations aim to "own every waking moment," to quote its technology blog.[4]

Elsewhere, the sober *Financial Times* of London has said of Apple that "Steve Jobs' legacy is the omniscient tech company," with its galaxy of data on our reading and listening and viewing habits, along with a giant scale of operation "that smaller rivals cannot match," leaving the company with "huge power."[5] Investment bankers, quoted in the *Wall Street Journal*, suggest that the tech monopolies will last because "scale is rewarded," and that entering these markets requires "a very high level of capital intensity." Another important factor in the fast-evolving online landscape is how "the giants can spend more money than rivals to improve their services."[6] However, despite having highlighted Silicon Valley's monopoly power in their own coverage, the business press plays along by focusing on the tech giants' sunny stock futures and their ability to "extract extraordinary market value," rather than examining the ethical or political ramifications of this incredible monopoly power.

And it's not just the economy that relies on these platforms—it's society. These corporations own the major systems for music sharing, web video, and online social interaction, the latter taking up larger portions of the world's waking hours each year. And due to the gatekeeper status they hold, other apps for music and social media must meet the terms of Big Tech to appear on their platforms. National media often note the sheer difficulty of boycotting the companies because of their sprawling reach alone.[7] These monopolies raise profound questions about how much influence corporate-curated online environments have on our day-to-day lives, and our connections with our fellow men and women.

So the question is, why are these crucial new markets "straight out of the box" monopolies, as the *Economist* once described them?[8] If the Internet is such a rich landscape, with a broad diversity of sites and interests and sources of information, why are so many of the markets related to it utterly dominated by great monopolists? The answers lie mainly with a phenomenon known as network effects.

Siliconopoly

By their nature, some goods and services are distributed through networks, in which the service moves from hubs to users, or from one user to the next. The classic example is telephone service—you and anyone else with a cellular phone is a participant in the telecommunications network, and when you call a friend, your conversation travels through nodes in the network between the two of you, like cell phone towers.

Markets for services that are provided through networks have a number of special features. A crucial one is the network effect, which illustrates a basic fact about this kind of service: the more users a network has, the more valuable it becomes. In other words, when you enter a given market—for example by buying a smart-phone and signing up for a cell service package—you slightly increase the value of the service for everyone else on the network, since your number is one more that can be dialed. So the more people that join the network, the more valuable it becomes for each of us as its potential reach expands.

These network effects have several ramifications. One is that markets for services distributed through networks tend to get monopolized—meaning a single company produces all, or almost all, of the market's product. Since the value of a network grows as more users join it, it means that firms with early success in the market can experience a positive feedback cycle, where a large number of users attracts yet more users, leading one or two firms to enjoy runaway growth, swamping their rivals.

Many other markets have strong tendencies toward monopoly for more common reasons, such as the advantage offered by economies of scale, where large up-front investments in a business can be "spread out" over large amounts of output. This cost pattern, common in manufacturing and other industries with big startup costs, also encourages companies to become big in order to exploit the scale economy and improve their profitability. At the same time, the large up-front costs act as a barrier that discourages new startups from entering the market. The result tends to be an "oligopoly," a market dominated by a few big firms, or sometimes a straight monopoly.

Microsoft, one of the firms reviewed in this book, is a great example of both network effects and scale economies. Its Windows operating system (OS) was adopted by IBM for an influential PC model, and as it came to be used on a large number of commercial computers, its OS attracted more software coders to write their applications to run on Windows so they could have access to the biggest possible market. Through Windows' popularity among programmers, Microsoft attracted more PC users, who desired the OS with the most useful tools and games. This cycle creates a need for "interoperability"—the ability of parts of a system to work together. A crucial factor in the development of networked services that can talk to each other, interoperability requires a standard system that everyone agrees to adopt so that new applications can be widely used. This standard system, once it becomes widely accepted, is often said to be "locked in"—so dominant that it's almost impossible to break away from. This dynamic explains the origin of the awkward "QWERTY" keyboard configuration, which is far from optimal; but after it became widespread in hardware around the world, and with so many generations of workers having trained on it, changing to a new standard would have unacceptably high costs.

Of course, giant companies and monopolies are common in other markets too, including those that don't rely on networks for the value of the product or service. The Western world has monopolies in eyewear, emergency adrenaline packs, and beer, and in the past had them in huge sectors like oil, steel, and cigarettes.[9] These giant monopolies (or oligopolies) arise from common market phenomena such as economies of scale. But when network effects and the need for technical standards are present on top of economies of scale, we observe this particularly strong drive toward capitalist monopoly.

Albert-László Barabási, a Romanian physicist and network science pioneer, has developed many of our core ideas about how networks behave, which can help us understand how they evolve in information markets such as those for telephone service or Internet access. Barabási observes that the network of connections among sites on the Internet doesn't resemble a road map, where each city has about the same number of highways connecting it to other cities. Rather, information networks resemble maps of airline service, with most cities having just a handful of connections, while a few cities, the major hubs of the airline system, have a giant number of connections. In network science, most of these connected entities, whether cities or Internet users, are referred to as "nodes," which are connected by links to the major "hubs." In this structure, there is no meaningful average number of connections among the nodes, since most have just a few links while a handful are hugely connected, so these networks are considered "scale free," meaning they have no representative scale of connectivity among them.[10]

This network structure applies directly to the online sites that we surf through web browsers, since a small minority of sites— Google, Facebook, Amazon, and others—are enormous "hubs," with gigantic numbers of visitors and tons of connections to other websites. Barabási observes that as networks grow over time, there is a common behavioral pattern called "preferential attachment," in which new nodes favor linking to other nodes that already have many links—the hubs of the system. As he explains in his absorbing book *Linked*, this creates "a clear advantage for the senior nodes" since in many networks, "popularity is attractive." This creates a "rich-get-richer phenomenon" for the senior nodes that have become hubs.[11] Preferential attachment plays a major role in the growth of a huge variety of networks, from phone and Internet systems to networks of proteins that control how genes are expressed in living organisms.[12]

Importantly, Barabási also found that seniority is not the only factor determining whether a network node becomes a hub—there is also the question of each node's actual inherent value. Some nodes, even if they aren't yet heavily linked to, are still very attractive for the valuable services or content they provide. Barabási finds that the nodes' "fitness," along with whatever preferential attachment they already enjoy, determine which nodes attract more links and become hubs. Google's excellent search algorithm software, for example, ensured it was "fit" relative to its early search competitors. (Its software was developed heavily by public institutions like Stanford University—see chapter 8.) But "if two nodes have the same fitness . . . the older one still has an advantage."[13]

Economists have occasionally recognized that networked markets differ in major ways from others, even in the very constrained formal models they often focus on. In the early days of personal computing in the 1980s, economists Joseph Farrell and Garth Saloner concluded in the prestigious *American Economic Review* that network industries have "a socially excessive reluctance to switch to a superior new standard" as users resist being cut off from other network users, and that early incumbents may have "an insurmountable advantage of installed base" that enables their predation on newcomers.[14] Furthermore, as Stanford economist W. Brian Arthur observed, once a dominant tech format "begins to emerge it becomes progressively more 'locked in,'" and in that context "laissez-faire gives no guarantee that the 'superior' technology . . . will be the one that survives."[15] These are painful admissions from economists, who usually admit to few flaws in the marketplace.

Experts on the guts of the Internet are also well aware of these issues, which not only apply to the network structures of the World Wide Web but also to the technical standards that allow us to view the information on any online service. Writing in the tech industry magazine *Wired*, Steve Steinberg observes that for the basic systems used to send information through the Internet, there's "incredible resistance to change," because "existing standards have simply become too pervasive for us to even think about changing them."[16] Since network-based services "put a premium on compatibility," eventually technology like Internet Protocol, or IP, which is used to send packets of information through the global network, reaches lock-in. Steinberg laments this basic reality: "Network effects are depressing—they allow bad standards to win."

And what's true on the technical end is true on our user end. As the conservative magazine the *Economist* observes, "Customers, once they have chosen a program, tend to 'groove in'; learning to use software takes time, and information is often saved in proprietary file formats, so switching programs is painful." This explains "the tendency of market leaders to get even further ahead. . . . The winning firm can invest that money in developing new products, lengthening its lead." In the end, "monopoly power becomes pervasive."[17]

This network reality shapes the web we browse every day, along with the mobile apps we often use as shortcuts to specific Internet services. The results are recognized across the spectrum of opinion, from the conservative business experts quoted above, to more liberal ones like communications scholar Tim Wu, who writes in his eminent book *The Master Switch* that "over the long haul, competition in the information industries has been the exception, monopoly the rule." He observes that "no one joins a social network like Facebook without other users . . . a network that everyone uses is worth fantastically more than the sum value of one hundred networks with as many users collectively as the one great network."[18]

Further to the left, Marxist media critic Robert McChesney writes that network effects explain why "monopoly [is] so much more pronounced and so much more impervious to direct competitive challenge on the Internet than in the balance of the economy."[19] And even mainstream investor and business writer Arun Rao, while recognizing their established importance, calls network effects "the most overhyped concept in Silicon Valley." In his analysis, tech startups heavily cite the network effect as a way to draw in investors with the promise of a company's domination of a new market.[20]

Furthermore, the web giants themselves are on the record more or less agreeing with this interpretation. Speaking to the *Financial Times*, Hal Varian, Google's own chief economist, explained that "network effects unleashed by digital technology tend not to spawn free competition among equals but a 'winner takes all' effect in which a single company emerges with all the spoils. In the software era, that company was Microsoft; in the internet era, it is Google."[21] And eBay founder Pierre Omidyar agrees his giant site has benefited from network effects, where "the more people that use them, the more useful they are," as the business press summarized.[22]

Antitrustworthy

Of course, not everyone supports this negative picture of the monopoly-like power of the network hubs. Indeed, most commentary on the web giants celebrates their fun technology and accepts their size and power as the price of our electronic conveniences. In fact, a good deal of the coverage of these giants insists they don't actually have that much power at all.

Returning to the *Economist*, consider its discussion of the question "Should digital monopolies be broken up?"[23] Despite its own reporting on the network-based power of the web giants, the magazine answers in the negative, claiming that its central example, Google, "is clearly dominant . . . but whether it abuses that dominance is another matter." While network effects mean Google has few serious competitors, the author claims that the huge company

> is not in the same class as Microsoft's systematic campaign against the Netscape browser in the late 1990s: there are no emails talking about "cutting off" competitors' "air supply." What's more, some of the features that hurt Google's competitors benefit its consumers. Giving people flight details, dictionary definitions or a map right away saves them time.

Similarly, defenders of Silicon Valley have held that "network effects and advantages of scale do not in themselves amount to barriers to entry. Facebook was not the first social media company, and did not have unique access to network effects. . . . Whatever barriers Google may enjoy, they are clearly not sufficient to put off all comers."[24] This argument is used by most defenders of monopoly—since it's not inconceivable for a new firm to win against the odds, the monopoly can't really be that powerful. But this is weak-sauce ideology, as the point isn't that barriers are 100 percent effective; it's just that they strongly *discourage* new market entrants and limit the potential pool of new competitors to gigantic firms from other industries, which might have enough resources to punch in.

Nevertheless, this argument does raise an interesting issue, which is that many of today's dominant tech titans did have earlier competition that they beat out before rising to their current unassailable positions. Google was preceded by AltaVista and other search engines, and Facebook grew in the shadow of Myspace. However, the basic dynamic of network effects leading to locked-in monopoly is still in effect here—the key issue is which firm can first reach a tipping point, where the site's rich body of users itself begins to gravitationally attract new users. The *Financial Times* reported that while Internet firms "thrive on network effects. . . . They also atrophy rapidly when users turn to the next new thing and let their free accounts become dormant." Thus the accumulation of network effects to Facebook's advantage allowed it to eclipse Myspace, which indeed went into rapid decline. For networked markets, "when growth stalls, or even slows, they tend to implode as the network effect goes into reverse."[25]

And indeed, the *Economist* does concede that its usual sunny free market portrayal "paints too rosy a picture. . . . The internet giants rarely compete strenuously on each other's home turf. Instead they scuffle for position in markets that are less important to them while trying to build up defenses around their core businesses. . . . All the big internet companies 'own a space.'"[26]

Other prominent defenders of Silicon Valley monopolies include Robert Bork, a former circuit judge of the US Court of Appeals and failed Supreme Court justice candidate. Writing with economist J. Gregory Sidak in the *Journal of Competition Law and Economics*, Bork mounted a vigorous defense of Google, insisting that mere "possession of monopoly power in the relevant market" isn't enough to justify government action to break the monopolist apart. Rather, the existing law only prohibits "the willful acquisition or maintenance of that power as distinguished from growth or development as a consequence of a superior product, business acumen, or historic accident."[27]

So simply being a monopoly with no effective competition doesn't justify any legal charge in the US; it must be proven in court that the company was actively scheming to evily crush its competitors. The fact that network effects make early market leaders magnets for new users, which increases their edge and leads toward their company achieving "lock-in," is totally irrelevant in the eyes of these conservative legal experts. And for good reason—one may note the disclosure in the Bork report's fine print: "Google commissioned this report, but the views expressed are solely our own."[28]

Bork and Sidak also claim "Google has no incentive to foreclose competitors from search because doing so is unlikely to offer additional profit at the potential cost of driving away consumers."[29]

But as discussed in the business press, consumers do get "grooved in" to using software that takes time to learn to use, and as a result of network effects they tend to become entrenched and attract more users. And despite the eminent paid research of former justice Bork, the conservative *Wall Street Journal* openly reports its findings that "Google Searches Boost Its Own Products." Specifically: "Ads for products sold by Google and its sister companies appeared in the most prominent spot in 91% of 25,000 recent searches related to such items. In 43% of the searches, the top two ads both were for Google-related products."[30]

The monopolists themselves are sometimes more open about and indeed proud of, their uncontested power, taking a brazen "might makes right" position. Exhibit A is eBay cofounder Peter Thiel, who has claimed "we tend to confuse capitalism with competition," as David Brooks paraphrased in the *New York Times*. Brooks adds, "When Thiel is talking about a 'monopoly,' he isn't talking about the illegal eliminate-your-rivals kind. He's talking about doing something so creative that you establish a distinct market, niche and identity."[31] The end result, however, is still a gigantic monopolist, regardless of its snowflake uniqueness. Like many others, from those of Rockefeller to today's drug makers, their monopoly is often a point of pride.

Beyond the writers who defend the Silicon Valley giants as either powerless, not abusing their power, or deserving of their monopolies, many observers—both liberal and conservative—say that all this talk about "economic power" and monopolies is overblown in the face of US antitrust laws and European competition laws, which prohibit any "restraint of trade." For example, New America Foundation fellow Barry Lynn—who promotes a regulated capitalism—claims that antitrust law puts "checks on the autocratic power of the corporate managers and the labor bosses."[32] And indeed, in his book *Cornered*, Lynn argues that anti-monopoly laws "prove [Charles] Adams wrong" about the gravitational principle of capitalism.[33]

Yet antitrust law has been attacked aggressively over the last forty years. In the lead-up to President Reagan's inauguration, business reporters at the *New York Times* observed that "the Reagan Administration appears likely to aim at a more relaxed and flexible approach to antitrust policy," with the new head of the program favoring a "policy based on efficiency considerations."[34] Later, the Obama administration promised a return to aggressive antitrust action, but it only blocked the very biggest horizontal tie-ups, like Comcast's attempted purchase of Time Warner Cable, or AT&T's pass at buying T-Mobile. The *Wall Street Journal*'s Brent Kendall attributed this reluctance to a view that "antitrust enforcers, once in office, also want to avoid unfairly penalizing companies that earned their dominance on the merits."[35]

But this allegedly merit-based dominance is difficult to square with the conclusions of Harvard business professor Alfred Chandler Jr., who in books like *Scale and Scope* details the monopolization incentives. According to Chandler, even in traditional manufacturing, and even without the added incentives of network structures, economies of scale still meant the presence of giant companies and limited competition across the economy:

> Production units achieved much greater economies of scale. . . . In many industries the throughput of plants of that scale was so high that a small number of them could meet the existing national and even global demand. The structure of these industries quickly became oligopolistic. . . . In many instances the first company to build a plant of minimum efficient scale and to recruit the essential management team remained the leader in its industry for decades.[36]

But enforced or not, Chandler explains the inherent limits of antitrust policy's ability to fix the fundamental problem of market concentration: "The existence of the Sherman Act discouraged monopoly in industries where integration and concentration had already occurred. It helped to create oligopoly where monopoly existed and to prevent oligopoly from becoming monopoly."[37] In other words, antitrust prevents full monopolization but leaves many huge, vertically integrated firms in place to continue dominating the marketplace.

And today even this pattern has declined, especially since the Justice Department's attempt in the 1990s to break up Microsoft, to the point that antitrust policy's sole function is to block the most outright monopolistic network mergers. After all, as the right-wing *Economist* observed, even if one of the Big Tech giants were broken up in an antitrust action, "in all likelihood" one of the smaller resulting firms "would eventually sweep all before it as the inexorable logic of network effects reasserted itself."[38] In other words, network economics drives many markets to monopoly again and again, as in the case of the telecom giant AT&T, which had its landline monopoly broken up by antitrust action in 1982, but then completely rebuilt its grip on landline service through subsequent mergers.

Other similarly reformist steps have sometimes limited the monopoly power of the telecom networks that bring you net access, like AT&T. An example is 2015's Title II net neutrality ruling, which outlawed these telecom companies' favoring of certain online content or slowing some of its delivery—although it was overturned in 2017.[39] But while net neutrality requires that the owners of the data "pipes" to our phones don't get to charge for extra speed or throttle holdouts, it doesn't limit the development of the web *itself* into ecosystems built around privately owned platforms, like Amazon and Google.

So these reforms, which regulate particular expressions of power, are valuable but limited in scope—and under constant assault by industry. Antitrust law arose partially as a concession to populist agitation against the great industrial and rail network trusts of the late nineteenth century, but it was recognized then as a relatively small surrender of the most naked forms of monopoly, leaving untouched the foundations of the system. As President Theodore Roosevelt—considered to be a great champion of trust-busting—once exclaimed to J. P. Morgan, "If you don't let us do this, those who will come after us will rise and bring you to ruin!"[40] So competition laws leave in place gigantic companies owned by their stockholders, who are usually the richest citizens of an economy—connecting today's towering corporations to the economic ruling class. These competition laws have been further weakened since their heyday, thanks in part to heroic intellectuals like the former circuit judge Bork.

This all means that antitrust law won't change the fact that large chunks of the United States and world economies are heavily reliant on Big Tech. The Department of Justice and Federal Trade Commission may investigate the platform giants, impose hearty fines, or even order limited sell-offs of big acquisitions, but their gigantic social role isn't going anywhere. The coming chapters will dissect each of the Big Five platforms, revealing similar stories of network effects and user/developer lock-in. But while the stunning raw size and power of the online titans was fated in the nature of networks, our failure to regulate them, break them up, or socialize them is a policy choice. A choice future generations may make differently.

CHAPTER 2

Macrosoft

The original platform giant

Microsoft was the original tech monopolist of the software age. Rising on the strength of an association with analog high-tech colossus IBM, the network effects of the software industry cemented Microsoft's position, as its widely used operating system was the most appealing for third-party application writers. The company's monopoly position as an industry standard became almost inevitable—along with a position of extreme market power.

This success fed longtime CEO Bill Gates's abusive tendencies toward his subordinates, as well as his hostile posture toward competitors, which often manifested as an openly expressed desire to destroy all rivals. "'We're going to put Digital Research out of business,'" a company history recounts Gates saying, "slamming his fist into the palm of his other hand. He would issue a similar vow twice more during the next year . . . promising to put MicroPro and Lotus out of business, each time emphasizing his promise by smashing his fist into his hand." Corporate historians observe that "it was clearly not enough for Microsoft to beat the competition; Gates wanted to eliminate his opponents from the playing field."[1]

Today Microsoft is considered to have been late to the mobile revolution, and thus a less hip tech giant relative to the other four titans examined in this book. Gates, for many years the richest man in the world, is now eclipsed by Amazon CEO Jeff Bezos. However, the company has come back strong in recent years, with spiking profits and a robust private platform, and it periodically exchanges the title of world's biggest company with Apple and Amazon. But it remains the only one adjudicated by a US court as a monopolist before the law.[2]

Breaking Windows

Microsoft was a tiny software company in the US Southwest, writing programming languages for small makers of early personal computers (PCs) in the late seventies. Its break came when it was hired to write the operating system and other programs for IBM's new personal computer in 1980. For decades, computers were huge mainframes, the "heavy iron" run by IBM to crunch data and store information for large corporate and military customers. But miniaturization, and especially the advent of semiconducting processor chips, meant that individual-sized computers for personal workstations were becoming technically feasible.

IBM was relatively late to realize the threat this posed to its main business center of gigantic business computers, and so in its haste to get a PC to market, it used commercially available, "off the shelf" parts from various computer component manufacturers. IBM's long-established reputation as a reliable business partner, and its history of setting standards for computing that other firms followed, meant its PCs were extremely popular among corporate America.

However, the use of sourced parts for a large majority of the machine, along with licensing of components, meant the IBM PC was an "open architecture," meaning its components could be obtained piecemeal on the market, rather than being fully proprietary. Since this PC could be easily copied, companies like Dell,

Hewlett-Packard (HP), and Compaq brought the many IBM "clones" into existence. Industry historians hold that this variety of suppliers, along with IBM's existing reputation, is the key reason the PC became an "industry standard"—a hardware and software framework that creators of software would be attracted to.[3] And when these clone manufactures proved themselves happy to follow IBM's lead in buying Microsoft's operating system, that too became part of the industry standard. This meant the wide supply of clones helped to reinforce the IBM-compatible PC's dominant role.[4]

Perhaps significantly, Gates himself would later suggest it was his elite social connections that landed Microsoft this pivotal gig. William Gates III came from an aristocratic Seattle family, his father an attorney and president of the state bar for a time, and his mother later a regent of the University of Washington. Washington State's Republican governor was a family friend and frequent houseguest. His mother sat on the board of the United Way, the national charity, along with John Opel, then chairman of IBM, and she encouraged the hiring of her son's small software concern.[5]

Crucially, this did not "set a standard" in the conventional use of being the best product in a market that others are then judged against. As I discussed in chapter 1, in markets based on networks, a technical industry standard is necessary for participants to communicate and to create products or services that can be understood and used by others. Much as telephones need basically compatible technology to connect a call, so do computers and their programs. This was not lost on the young Microsoft, and "We set the standard" was its corporate motto since its early days as a tiny Albuquerque startup; it was "preached by Gates as gospel until it had been burned into his company's psyche," as a company history puts it.[6]

As late as 1981, the industry was still fragmented and lacked standards, which meant that the market for application software was limited, since new programs would only run on certain computers that they were written for. The PC was an immediate hit, thanks to IBM's name, the swarm of clones all carrying shared computer languages like BASIC (used for creating computer programs, including applications that run on an OS), and Microsoft's disk operating system, MS-DOS. Journalists James Wallace and Jim Erickson suggest that "arguably, MS-DOS became an industry standard as much from the momentum generated by the huge success of the PC as anything Microsoft's brash, competitive chairman did." And crucially, "as the IBM PC gained in popularity, more and more programmers wrote software for that machine and for the operating system Gates had acquired."[7]

This advantage—in which a dominant platform attracts programmers looking to secure the greatest possible audience for their work—is pivotal since it gives the already-dominant company an even stronger position: consumers and companies will be attracted to its product not only because it has become a standard, but also because it will come to have far more useful applications than other, less-dominant alternatives. In Microsoft's case, this meant that its monopoly operating system was further protected by a belt of applications that were built to run on DOS (and later its successor, the more user-friendly Windows). In other words, by setting a standard with its OS, Microsoft has over time magnetically drawn an "ecosystem" of software applications, which protect its operating system like a moat. The Office suite, including Word and Excel, was itself produced by Microsoft. And more useful or fun applications impose a cost on anyone wanting to switch—a good deal of PC software isn't available on other platforms, or would have be reinstalled and perhaps paid for again.

Many Microsoft corporate emails and memos were entered into the public domain in the course of the antitrust trials (discussed below), giving us an incredibly valuable window into the strategizing of the first great software monopolists. In an email to major Microsoft investor Warren Buffett, senior executive Jeff Raikes wrote: "If we own the key 'franchises' built on top of the operating systems, we dramatically widen the 'moat' that protects the operating system business. . . . We hope to make a lot of money off these franchises, but even more important is that they should protect our Windows royalty per PC."[8] Raikes is admitting that what critics call the "applications barrier to entry" is real and was part of the company's own strategizing. The conservative *Economist* agreed: "The applications barrier to entry gives Microsoft its enduring monopoly power."[9]

Under a 1982 deal, Apple Computer contracted Microsoft to write software programs for its Macintosh PC (see chapter 3) and provided the Seattle company with prototypes and program-writing tools. Gates copied most of the visual elements to create the interface for Windows, which was much more intuitive than DOS. Rather than the mathematical programming language prompts then used on PCs, Windows was a graphical user interface (GUI), with visual cues for things like files, programs, and simple actions like deleting by dragging a file to a trash icon using a mouse cursor. This was a major innovation at the time.

But Windows' similarity to the Mac OS was so great that Apple Computer threatened to sue Microsoft for copying its GUI fundamentals and thus undermining demand for Apple's more expensive Macintosh, which was released as Windows was rolled out in the early 1980s. Microsoft later acknowledged in the agreement's announcement that "the visual displays . . . are derivative works of the visual displays generated by Apple's Lisa and Macintosh graphic user interface programs."[10] Indeed, a company manager said the newer OS was named Windows because "we wanted to have our name basically define the generic"—in other words, the company's product would have the name of the windows-based graphics displays themselves.[11] But Gates showed that old-economy arm-twisting was still a rule of the road in the new economy of Big Tech, as he forced a settlement by threatening to stop development of both the Word software processing program for Mac and Excel, the spreadsheet program. This was hardball, since Apple had few software applications, and it ultimately backed down.

The nature of platform economics also played a role in Apple's failure to create an industry standard in PC software, instead becoming the "other" user interface in the industry until the advent of mobile technology and the release of the iPhone in 2007. Communications scholar Tim Wu finds Windows was "a partially open system," meaning it invited software writers to connect to its platform and create new programs.[12] In contrast, Apple CEO Steve Jobs kept control over software development and prevented free access for accessories (or "peripherals"). Wu suggests that

> [Jobs's] decision to close the Macintosh helped make Bill Gates the richest man on earth. . . . Even if Windows was never as advanced or well designed as Apple's operating system, it enjoyed one insuperable advantage: it worked on any computer, supported just about every type of software, and could interface with any printer, modem, or whatever other hardware one could design. Windows ran off with the market Apple had pioneered.[13]

Thus, Gates's better intuition of platform economics meant that Microsoft could attract a large body of third-party programs, helping to build a huge installed base of users and thus decisively beating Apple to setting a standard.

The significance of this episode in platform economics is confirmed by Albert-László Barabási, physicist and network studies pioneer. In his book *Linked*, he observes: "[A]s everyone knows, Windows prevailed despite the fact that Microsoft was not the first mover. When the first version of Windows came out, it looked like an ugly rip-off of Apple's revolutionary operating system. Apple, however, kept a rigid monopoly on its hardware, while the PC offered a free ride to all computer makers. Therefore the PC became the dominating platform in our computer-driven world."[14]

Apple's suit, however, speaks to a major theme in Microsoft's corporate history. Despite its claims to be a great economic innovator, Microsoft actually has a notorious record of nakedly stealing technology to strengthen its software monopolies, and to secure new ones. Even in the earliest days, the company owed its cash cow to the work and funding of others, as BASIC was originally developed by a pair of Dartmouth professors through a National Science Foundation grant to develop an easier means of teaching programming to students.[15] Public funding in fact has a long history of creating the basic technologies that the Silicon Valley tech giants later enjoy taking credit for. (I discuss this at greater length in chapter 8.)

Further, the original disk operating system Microsoft developed for IBM has a similarly dubious history. IBM's urgent need for an operating system meant there was insufficient time to develop a new OS, so Microsoft actually purchased one from a tiny company called Seattle Computer Products in 1981 for $75,000, renaming it MS-DOS.[16] Wallace and Erickson's popular book *Hard Drive* describes Microsoft's reputation in the industry as "notorious" for "predatory pilfering," mostly committed against far smaller companies, who can be picked on safely. The classic pattern is for Microsoft to approach a company and express guarded interest in its product, and to suggest a possible partnership. "After Microsoft is given a glimpse of how the software works, it suddenly loses interest in the deal—only to announce later that it has been working on surprisingly similar, but competing, software."[17]

Indeed, a company project manager relates that "frankly, that is Microsoft's forte: A competitor comes in and does something interesting, then we come in and basically clone it; do it marginally better and throw some clever marketing clout behind it, then relentlessly make it better over the years."[18] This history is ironic considering Gates once indignantly told a 1976 hacker gathering that he was "ripped off" by early software pirates making copies of MS-BASIC.[19]

This episode itself speaks to another major theme of Microsoft corporate history: tech CEOs are often gigantic assholes. Sadly, this will be a recurring theme in this book—the towering arrogance of awkward tech entrepreneurs who rise to positions of incredible power and gigantic wealth, and then abuse employees with a mode of bullying that is protected by their corporate hierarchy.

Anyone skeptical of the power of hierarchical business structures to create cultish conformity should contemplate business reporting like the following, on Gates's habit of rocking in his chair: "It has become part of the corporate culture at Microsoft among programmers trying to re-create themselves in the chairman's image. Gates often rocks himself in a chair, elbows on knees, to contain his intensity, especially when the talk is about computers; it's not unusual to walk into a room of Microsoft managers and find most of them rocking in sync with him during an important meeting."[20] Yikes. His corporate tenure was also marked by "childlike temper tantrums" in which he berated his employees on a fairly regular basis, and even walking out on a softball Connie Chung interview.[21]

By 1992, Gates was the richest man in the United States. As his charming, boyish nerd image faded and his reputation for ruthlessness and abusiveness spread, journalists began observing the similarities between Gates and other great capitalists of American history. Most notably, Gates himself saw his reflection in John D. Rockefeller, the definitive US monopoly capitalist with his nineteenth-century oil products empire. Gates spoke with admiration of *Titan*, Ron Chernow's enormous biography of Rockefeller.[22]

To protect its monopoly, Microsoft developed a clever policy for its original equipment manufacturers (OEMs)—the companies that produced the actual desktop and laptop PCs. The OEMs were essentially kept in Microsoft's orbit through an ingenious "per processor" licensing scheme. Microsoft offered the computer makers two options: either pay a simple license per copy of the DOS or Windows OS that the OEMs preinstalled on their machines for sale to consumers; or pay a royalty to Microsoft for every computer they sold, at a major two-thirds discount or higher. This discount option was of course extremely appealing to Dell, HP, and other manufacturers, but it also created a disincentive for them to offer any competing operating systems, since they would effectively be paying for two of them—the discount was only obtained if the per-processor royalty was applied to all PC units shipped by the OEMs, whether they had Windows or not. For other software makers, this was a craftily devised barrier to entry—one that ended up keeping Apple and other companies from licensing their own OSs.[23] When one OEM decided in 1992 to ship just 10 percent of its units with a competing OS, Microsoft doubled the price for DOS, and the OEM immediately backed down and shelved its plan.[24]

But all this was just the beginning of Microsoft's predatory leveraging of its OS monopoly. Crucially, Microsoft maintained certain policies on its application programming interfaces (APIs). These are codes in an operating system that allow it to efficiently respond to applications, like word processors, spreadsheets, or games. If the design of an app was not tailored toward a set of APIs, it could run poorly on that operating system, or not at all.

Microsoft decided not to reveal all the Windows APIs to outside developers, and as a result its native Word and Excel performed better on its now-universal platform. That's a big deal, since writing and number crunching are among the most used purposes of personal computers. Microsoft indignantly denied any suggestion it had any hidden APIs, until it was later forced to concede it had over a dozen of them for its Office programs.[25]

And since Microsoft created its own word processing and spreadsheet applications, it had a further potential advantage over third-party app makers in that its in-house software writers would have access to new versions of the OS before outside developers would. To fight criticism over this further unfair advantage, Microsoft began to suggest it maintained a "Chinese Wall" between its operating system business—which made software to run the processor and the basic computing environment—and its application business, which made programs that ran "on top of" the OS.

The problem was that there was no "wall," and the claims about it were apparently mostly fraudulent. While the company was willing to imply the wall's existence publicly to mollify competing app publishers, a senior company application programmer is quoted in Wallace and Erickson's book saying, "I remember Bill Gates saying many times, 'There is no Chinese Wall.' Somebody got this idea there was this wall between systems and applications so we wouldn't talk to each other. There's no such thing. We don't have any separation here, just one big company."[26]

The early 1990s software marketplace saw the "software wars," in which applications-writing firms like WordPerfect and Novell teamed up to fight Gates, and still perished. Microsoft prevailed in these fights not just with its hidden APIs and processor-licensing advantages, but with more classic monopolist tactics like underpricing. Microsoft wanted prices low to gain market share and solidify its application dominance, and unlike smaller competitors it could afford microscopic profit margins on its applications sales, since it held the steady revenue stream generated by its near monopoly of the OS market. Similarly, Microsoft refused to share the basic communications protocols used for computer servers providing database storage. Microsoft thus used what economists call asymmetrical information, in which one party knows more than another, to put competing server companies at a competitive disadvantage.

But notoriously, Gates failed to anticipate the advent of the Internet, with a Microsoft board member telling *BusinessWeek* that Gates was immediately dismissive: "His view was that the Internet was free," and "there was no money to be made."[27] Hence, no interest from a defining figure of modern capitalism. But as the Internet and its World Wide Web grew rapidly, early web browsers like Mosaic became popular. Soon redeveloped by the same engineers into Netscape Navigator, it went on to set an industry standard for web browsing. The actions the monopolist took to crush Netscape and wrench away that standard ended up leading to the first antitrust trial of a modern Big Tech corporation.

But despite the dawning of a new industry and its challenging technical details, the overall economic setting was unchanged since the early days of the market economy. During development of Microsoft's competing browser, Internet Explorer, one software writer suggested that it be made freely available online like Mosaic/Netscape. Gates called him a communist.[28]

Gates Litigates

In the words of one tech journalist, Gates wanted "Microsoft to set up toll booths on the information highway."[29] And in particular, the company now saw the threat that Windows OS could be replaced as the dominant information technology platform. The primary concern was the potential for the Internet, and in particular the potential of a browser enabling its use (such as Netscape), to perform the same functions as a computer operating system—store files, run important programs, and allow access to media, news, and entertainment. Crucially, this meant Internet browsers were potentially "middleware": software running on top of a basic OS but capable of largely replacing its functions. In particular, if a browser grew popular, third-party software developers would write applications to run on it—to play video, or manage large files, or run flashy games. This could end up attracting enough developers to create a new "applications barrier to entry," like the one that made Windows the industry standard. And once Microsoft finally realized that, it went to war.

This period is described in business and computing history as the "browser wars." Microsoft began by withholding its APIs from Netscape when the browser company requested a preview of them for the next version of Windows. Then it approached Netscape's management, and according to them offered to divide the browser market, with an executive offering a "special relationship."[30] Netscape rejected this because of the gigantic advantage that it would give Microsoft's new browser, since it would likely come packaged with the ubiquitous Windows OS updates.

Thanks to the ensuing legal challenges, we know a fair amount about Microsoft's browser war strategy. The discussions reveal fairly naked plans to use monopoly power to crush a startup competitor. Microsoft got a license from the rights holders to the original version of Mosaic, which it redeveloped it hastily into Internet Explorer. Gates and his minions had feared that Netscape had already reached a tipping point where, through network effects, it would be embraced as a new standard and would become "locked in." Thus a top Windows executive said in an email, "I don't understand how IE is going to win. . . . We must leverage Windows more"—meaning, for IE to beat Netscape, Windows would have to come packaged with updates for the whole OS.[31]

In another internal email from Gates himself, he suggested using the Office application monopolies to further weaken Netscape's position: "One thing we have got to change in our strategy—allowing Office documents to be rendered very well by other people's browsers is one of the most destructive things we could do to the company. We have to stop putting any effort into this and make sure that [rendering] Office documents very well depends on PROPRIETARY IE capabilities. Anything else is suicide for our platform."[32]

Several additional measures followed in which Microsoft used its monopoly to block Netscape from other platforms. They pressured Intuit, the home accounting software maker, to switch its default browser from Netscape to Explorer for "something like $1M," according to an email from Gates.[33] They did the same to Apple and to AOL, sending an email describing the CEO's offer to the online firm. "Gates delivered a characteristically blunt query: how much do we need to pay you to screw Netscape? ('This is your lucky day')," as an AOL internal email described the offer.[34]

Allegedly, Microsoft vice president Paul Maritz infamously stated their goal in making their own browser free on their OS: to "cut off Netscape's air supply."[35] By the time of the release of Windows 98, the company had gone further and barred OEMs from ever removing IE from their desktops, and in that update the software would at times override the consumer's browser choice and launch IE, which even Microsoft internally called "a jolting experience."[36]

The company was even more aggressive toward Sun Microsystems, a Silicon Valley computer company that was marketing an innovative new product, Java. Java is a software program that created an OS-neutral platform for applications, meaning programs written for Java standards could run on computers operating Windows as well as Apple's Macintosh computers and the few machines running UNIX—creating the potential for a new form of "middleware" that might weaken the Windows monopoly. Microsoft's reaction was to distribute with its OS updates a deliberately poorly functioning, or "polluted," version of Java, which kept applications from running well on Windows. An appeals court later released an internal Microsoft document stating the goal by name: "Kill cross-platform Java by growing the polluted Java market."[37]

Besides using its leverage with other companies and users to destroy the threat of middleware, the company needed to seize their markets too. For this, Microsoft employed a strategy that would play a crucial role in court—integration. Taking advantage of its existing monopolies, Windows updates would begin to include generic knockoff versions of middleware companies' products, which would instantly gain major market footholds because they would be included on any up-to-date PC, since they all ran Windows. Thus, Microsoft's Internet Explorer browser was "bundled" into Windows 95, and along with Netscape Navigator being thrown off the OEMs that Microsoft controlled, and dropped by AOL, the browser market share swung dramatically away from Netscape and toward Microsoft. Navigator was finally crushed when Microsoft used its leverage over Apple, including its $150 million investment in the company and its porting of the popular Office, to get Steve Jobs to remove Navigator from the Mac.[38]

Then Gates went even further—in the IE 3.0 update in 1996, the software was changed. Previously, the browser was a separate application, with software code distinct from the operating system. But the 1996 update began the process of including code for the operating system in the browser and vice versa, making it difficult to remove either. This "commingling" had helped Windows itself get widely adopted, as its early versions were similarly commingled with MS-DOS.[39]

But Microsoft's hardball tactics in the browser wars, and its endless parade of power plays, from chip design to media players, now began to catch up with it. It was attracting more critical attention from the media, and from government regulators. And there was indeed something for them to see, beyond all these technical details. Gates had become a modern monopoly CEO, and he knew it. In public he said: "Who decides what's in Windows? The customers who buy it." But at a dinner party with his then fiancée, Melinda French, the talk turned to politics and he bragged, "Of course, I have as much power as the president has."[40] And indeed, he golfed with President Clinton, had dinners with House Speaker Newt Gingrich, and had Vice President Al Gore visit Microsoft's Redmond corporate campus. Like all great capitalists, he enjoyed the company of powerful figures with abutting interests. But his company's flagrant monopoly, and in particular the aggressive attempts to extend it by leveraging its monopoly power, were forcing the government's hand.

The first national anti-monopoly action against Microsoft was brought by the Federal Trade Commission, over the per-processor license system. But the FTC ultimately deadlocked on the issue in 1993, after one commissioner recused himself. This led to a handoff of the case from the FTC to the Department of Justice, which suspected Microsoft of abusing its monopoly by tying its new products into its existing dominant OS to develop new monopolies in related industries, such as web browsing. Crucially, US antitrust law does *not* outlaw monopoly, especially if it is obtained through market processes—processes including the network effects of software compatibility (see chapter 1). What *is* illegal is actively leveraging one monopoly into another, and, as we've seen, Microsoft did a ton of that. However, on appeal the DOJ settled for a consent decree that required Microsoft to quit tying new products to its OS but, crucially, did allow the integration of new *features* into its operating system. This was a position the company strongly held, and so a draft decree allowed "integration which offers tech advantages." Seeing integration as a way to allow monopolization of adjacent markets, Gates insisted to his attorneys, "Remove those last four words!" This was eventually achieved.[41]

Unsurprisingly, Microsoft went on to claim that browser technology was not a separate product (although Netscape and IE had both been independent software for years) and that it was instead a feature of the OS. This didn't satisfy the DOJ, which accused Microsoft of violating the 1994 consent decree and thus went back to court in 1998, as the company readied its Windows 98 update with IE bundled in. The presiding judge took a critical stance toward Microsoft but, crucially, did not issue an injunction in the early stages of the case, which could have blocked the company from making IE mandatory on Windows PCs and given Netscape some breathing room. As a result, Microsoft was able to take major market share from Netscape throughout the legal process, such that by the time of Microsoft's loss in court the issue was nearly moot in the market.[42]

The trial itself is fascinating for several reasons, not the least of which is Gates's performance. He gave hours of videotaped testimony for the case, viewable today online.[43] Besides being a transparently evasive and condescending douchebag, Gates made a long list of explicit claims that would soon after be directly refuted in court when compared with his own emails. According to his private words and those of his management team, numerous company claims were shown to be naked lies, from the denial of the meeting with Netscape to divide the market, to the existence of a wall separating OS development from application software development. Soon, ace designers from Apple were testifying that their company had found no advantage to mixing browser and OS code.[44] Steve Ballmer, then a Microsoft executive, memorably declared at a company event, "To heck with Janet Reno," the US attorney general—which didn't make the company seem any more reasonable.[45]

But importantly, it was during this time that Gates discovered charitable giving. Launched in 2000, a time when Gates was looking like a heartless, lying corporate tyrant, the Gates Foundation has since become the largest and most widely recognized global charity, managing an endowment of $44 billion that is used to support economic development. Indeed, the philanthropy of the world's richest men and women serves as one of the main arguments of their defenders—sure, Gates and other billionaires make a lot of money, but then they use it to help us. So generous! But if we review the business press's own observations, we can gain a fuller picture: "Twenty years ago, people associated the name Gates with 'ruthless, predatory' monopolistic conduct," a wealth manager frankly stated to the *New York Times*. "His philanthropy has helped 'rebrand' his name." The dark side of charity is easily seen in Gates: "After taking a public relations beating during [the Microsoft antitrust] trial's early going in late 1998, the company started what was described at the time as a 'charm offensive' aimed at improving its image. . . . Mr. Gates contributed $20.3 billion, or 71 percent of his total contributions to the foundation . . . during the 18 months between the start of the trial and the verdict."[46]

After an attempt at arbitration under a business-oriented judge failed, the court formally ruled that Microsoft had a monopoly on Intel-based PC operating systems, and that it had used illegal monopolization tactics to crush middleware threats from Netscape, Sun, Apple, and others. These findings survived appeal, meaning Microsoft stands convicted today as a tech platform monopolist. The findings of law also concluded that Microsoft should be split—as with AT&T after its own antitrust conviction, Microsoft would be forced to divest large parts of its business.

The form of breakup the DOJ sought was called "ops-apps"—splitting the company into one unit selling the operating system, and another selling applications like the Office suite. While in this arrangement, both units would still be monopolies in their respective areas, they would be weakened since the apps company would likely sell to other companies and the ops firm might have reason to work with other application developers, thus ruining the application barrier to entry it had created. On the other hand, Microsoft and its allies argued that the efficiency of the Windows standard might be broken, since it wasn't certain that new firms would produce compatible products.[47] After weighing the arguments, the court formally ordered in June 2000 that Microsoft be broken up, along with other significant restraints on its behavior.

Microsoft, of course, appealed this verdict, but during the wait for appeal hearings, the US held its 2000 election, in which George W. Bush took office under highly disputed circumstances. Republican administrations have historically been more lenient to antitrust defendants, and the new DOJ announced in September 2001 that "the Department will not seek a break-up of the company into separate operating systems and applications businesses."[48]

The settlement gave Microsoft far more leeway in its API disclosure, and rather than bar Windows from including IE, the decision was to allow OEMs to hide the browser from the end user, hopefully encouraging the manufacturers to include independent browsers or other middleware. So users would see desktop icons on their PCs that might include other browsers and not necessarily IE, even though it was still present.

But other aspects of the settlement, including a lack of reduction in royalties owed to Microsoft if other middleware was installed, limited the importance of the change in browser status. The bar on the bundling of IE was only set to last for five years, although it could be extended. And amazingly, Microsoft could override any OEM-added desktop icons (for other browsers, for example) starting two weeks after activation, if the user approved a simple prompt.[49] Overall, Windows remained bundled, IE dominated the browser market, and Netscape remained defunct. As law professors Andrew Gavil and Harry First concluded in their book on the Microsoft litigation, "Courts cannot raise the dead."[50] The limited restraints on Microsoft's behavior expired several years later, with its desktop OS monopoly intact. The *New York Times* observed that the verdict "imposed few new restrictions that would slow Microsoft's aggressive push into new markets"; it was an "ineffective slap on the wrist."[51]

Clouds Gather

Having covered Microsoft's victories on appeal in the United States, which coincided with the European Union's imposition of similarly limited remedies, we can now review the evolution of the corporation's platform power into the era of mobile and cloud computing. There are some surprises, but Microsoft's market weight has remained heavy and its conduct only somewhat restrained. Even an incredibly uncritical blogger covering the company wrote in her book that "Microsoft learned some valuable lessons, thanks to the U.S. Department of Justice and the handful of states who sued. . . . Instead of being quite so blatant, Microsoft has taken a quieter back route to achieving the same ends."[52]

The first thing to consider is whether Microsoft is even in the top tier of tech giants anymore. Many articles and reviews of the largest tech corporations don't include it, or mention it in passing. However, Microsoft retains ownership of a number of pivotal platforms that make it enduringly powerful and important, and it remains among the five-largest world companies by market value—trading the number one spot back and forth with Amazon and Apple, and standing a bit above Google and Facebook.[53] Microsoft, today worth around a trillion dollars and with its own lasting platforms on mobile devices, stands among the Big Five tech giants that now tower over the rest of capitalism.

When Windows 10 was released in summer 2015, Microsoft made the dramatic change of not charging for the upgrade, which had been a cornerstone of its business model for years.[54] The change seems to be an effort to bring the giant closer to Google and Facebook, which make their software available for free,

and to Apple, which provides free updates to the programs running on its hardware. The reason for this shift lies in the industry's
structural evolution and the rise of mobile computing. Microsoft,
having missed the advent of the Internet, and bringing the US
Justice Department down upon itself in the effort to claw back
the lost opportunity, also missed the explosion of mobile devices.
And it has paid for these strategic missteps in lost revenue and
prestige—for a short time in March 2010 Apple surpassed Microsoft in market value, around the quarter-trillion-dollar mark,
while Facebook founder Mark Zuckerberg declined Microsoft's
offer to buy the social network for $24 billion in its early years.[55]

The key fact lies in a detail of CEO Satya Nadella's decision
to make Windows free—it applies only to devices with screens
smaller than nine inches. This includes phones and tablets but
not laptops or desktop PCs, suggesting the goal is to transition
Microsoft's application software monopolies to the rising mobile
platforms while still preserving Microsoft's full OS dominance
of the desktop, where Windows updates still come with a cost.
Microsoft has cut its per-processor license fee for lower-end
OEMs but kept the basic business model intact for anything
larger than an iPad.

The *Wall Street Journal* reports that Microsoft has not only
returned to growth after years of stagnation (albeit at a giant level
of profitability), but has become "the only pre-internet tech giant
to escape the decline of its legacy product," in this case the Windows operating system. Microsoft's persistence in the top ranks
owes to a number of strategies. One is a relentless campaign of
big acquisitions of valuable firms and startups that look to provide unique tools or software to help Gates's colossus survive in
the mobile world. Microsoft bought LinkedIn, the job search
hub, for a whopping $26.2 billion, and GitHub, the open-source
software development platform, for $7.5 billion; and these acqui-
sitions happened on top of the company's absorption of smaller
software developers using Microsoft's coding language to create
programs for mobile platforms. These led the *Wall Street Journal*

to pronounce in a 2016 headline, "Microsoft, Rebooted, Emerges as a Tech Leader."[56]

The company's bigger hardware efforts are evident in its Surface line of laptops and tablets, which are slick and run on strong processors—part of an effort to compete with Apple's famous style and power. Many of these models are built with the sophisticated and efficient ARM chips used in Apple machines (see chapter 3). With the desktop PC market now shrinking, Microsoft has no choice but to create a hardware habitat outside PCs, which may in the future be found primarily in the workplace.[57] And Microsoft is unwilling to leave mobile hardware platforms entirely in the hands of its rival Apple and the manufacturers of devices running Google's Android operating system, especially Samsung (see chapter 5).

But above all, Microsoft has held on to its place in the top rung of Big Tech thanks to its success in the transition to cloud computing. Cloud computing refers to the remote provision of computer services that were once delivered on-site by large networks of servers around the world. This allows for major efficiencies, as large corporate and government institutions can now lay off IT staff and sell equipment that were only sometimes needed, and services like computing power or database management can now be provided online. This is a major shift, as computing becomes closer to a paid utility like the power bill.

Microsoft's cloud computing program, called Azure, is a strong second-place contestant to market creator and leader Amazon, so the main discussion of cloud computing has been saved for chapter 4. For now, though, it's important to realize that besides Microsoft's enduring monopolies in PC operating systems and office productivity software across platforms, it's the growth of Azure that will keep the company relevant. The business world's judgment is that Microsoft is "the stiffest competition" to Amazon, and it has pulled away from Google Cloud, which now stands in a distant third place.[58] Microsoft now supplies 13.3 percent of the market's services, while Amazon supplies 51.8 percent and Google 6.0 percent, and the company is aided both by its long history supplying business with IT and by corporate wariness of being totally dependent on Amazon.[59] Still, Microsoft and Amazon do often work together, which is typical of oligopolies—markets, like the cloud computing industry, that are dominated by just a few enormous firms. Most recently this has taken the form of merging the "skills" of their creepily feminized digital assistants, Cortana and Alexa, respectively.[60]

In individual fiscal quarters, the company's cloud infrastructure revenue is growing at rates kissing double digits as the market grows rapidly, helping enormously to offset declines in PC license sales.[61] The company is investing massively in this new sector, spending a couple billion every quarter on enormous data centers. The scale of these "server farms," built around the country and world to provide quick data access, is enormous. "Three important economies of scale," to quote Microsoft's financial filings, have been the impetus for this new direction:

> Larger datacenters can deploy computational resources at significantly lower cost per unit than smaller ones; larger datacenters can coordinate and aggregate diverse customer, geographic, and application demand patterns, improving the utilization of computing, storage, and network resources; and multi-tenancy lowers application maintenance labor costs for large public clouds. As one of the largest providers of cloud computing at scale, we are well-positioned.[62]

Economies of scale, of course, have a long history in industry of encouraging aggressive growth in company size and market share, as firms invest to achieve high levels of mass production and the low costs that come with them. They apply to the demand side of this relationship too, as suggested by a memo released by Gates (but actually written by a software engineer): Clients "are increasingly considering what services-based economies of scale might do to help them reduce infrastructure costs or deploy solutions as-needed and on [a] subscription basis."[63] New cloud products include customer service "bots" for corporate clients looking to cut call center workers, as well as tools for clients looking to build their own. But again, the enduring capitalist motives shine through the bleeding-edge hi-tech. In the bland words of a corporate researcher speaking to the *Wall Street Journal*: "There's huge interest from enterprises in deploying bots for customer services. . . . The intent usually is to reduce cost by reducing head count."[64]

The rocketing growth of cloud computing has led to the one of the greatest internal reversals in the company's history: it downgraded the status of Windows, folding its pivotal platform for software makers into the fast-growing Azure unit, in a recognition that the mobile era is seeing stagnating desktop computer sales. Windows remains hugely prevalent, however—the business press reports that almost 700 million devices run Windows 10, and some version of Windows runs on over 1.5 billion devices globally.[65] But the main platform for developers is now the cloud.

The growth in Microsoft's cloud arm has also been particularly helpful for its Office suite of work software, since those apps have their own network effects. This manuscript was written on Word, because that's the document format publishers usually want, it's the one most often used by writers, and most editors are familiar with it. Likewise with Excel, a near-universal tool for basic spreadsheet work. And today, as mobile applications are replacing their desktop-bound predecessors, Office is most often provided through the cloud via an Office 365 subscription. The service today has 120 million monthly users, according to the company.[66]

Critics of Excel often point to its role in several high-visibility disasters like the enormous financial losses suffered in JPMorgan's infamous 2012 "London Whale" trade. Yet Microsoft's biggest disasters still seem to come from its deliberate decisions. One truly staggering case involves the 2017 epidemic computer virus WannaCry, a ransomware program—once installed on a computer, it encrypts files and deletes them unless the owner sends a payment to the hackers within a certain time limit. The *Financial Times* found that Microsoft withheld a free patch from users of older versions of Windows that would have blocked the virus's activity.[67] Freely distributed to users of newer versions of its OS, those on older ones were charged $1,000 per device for "custom" support such as the anti-virus patch, but with a $750,000 minimum payment that scared off many PC users. The company, along with chipmaker Intel and the later generation of online companies, has continued to announce patches that must urgently be made to its software, each time starting an arms race with criminal hackers to exploit the vulnerability.[68]

The insanely high fee meant that only large corporate customers could possibly afford this "custom" support, so clients like Britain's National Health Service had no choice but to go without it—leading it to become one of the most globally prominent victims of the ransomware, and disrupting the health needs of untold numbers of UK patients. The *Financial Times* suggested that this reflects a "quandary" for Microsoft, "as it tries to force customers to move to newer and more secure software, while at the same time earning a profit from the army of engineers it employs on security issues."[69]

Microsoft does not lack for profitability. The "quandary" is how much to twist vulnerable clients' arms for a security patch that was developed with revenue from several monopolies, costs almost nothing to distribute to at-risk users, and would have prevented millions of dollars in ransoms and disruption. Screwing over clients who made them rich makes Microsoft hard.

Networkforce

After charting this long record of corporate monopoly and legal maneuvering, we should contemplate the workers who actually produce the useful software that has put monopoly power in Microsoft's hands. While the white-collar workforce designing and integrating software at Microsoft is far from toiling in a coal mine, the company remains notorious for its work conditions and the helplessness that many of its workers feel.

We've already taken note of the abusively tyrannical tirades of the company's cofounder and longtime CEO, Gates. Even sympathetic biographers refer to his frequent "abrasive, childish rants" and "childlike temper tantrums."[70] Gates's number two and CEO successor, Steve Ballmer, maintained this tradition of management by yelling like an ape. These are the patterns of human behavior that are encouraged by the strict hierarchy found in the business world.

To complement this portrait of hierarchical workplace bullying, consider the demureness expected from some sections of the workforce. It was current CEO Satya Nadella who infamously suggested at a conference that female staff should not push for raises, but instead wait for management to notice their contributions. This immediately made Nadella the poster boy for the Clueless Tech Bro, and rightly so.[71] Nadella has since made conspicuous efforts to condemn Silicon Valley's tilt toward male engineers and managers, a conversion that convinced few people. The bigger point perhaps is that while management is free to scream in an employee's face and blame them for its own failures, the employee is not only barred from yelling back; for many, even asking for an increase in compensation is a little too cheeky.

Beyond the worker abuse and open sexism typical in capitalist systems, there are more particular examples of power mongering, like the opportunistic use of the H-1B visa program. The visa allows for the temporary (three- to six-year) hiring of foreign workers for specialized occupations, and it has been most heavily used by two sectors: outsourcing firms and Silicon Valley. Gates argued in a 2007 *Washington Post* editorial that further technological progress requires we "make it easier for foreign-born scientists and engineers to work for U.S. companies." The CEO wrote: "American competitiveness also requires immigration reforms that reflect the importance of highly skilled foreign-born employees. Demand for specialized technical skills has long exceeded the supply of native-born workers with advanced degrees," a shortfall that has reached "a crisis point."[72]

On the other hand, Senators Bernie Sanders and Chuck Grassley have been less gung ho about the visa program, arguing that companies should be restricted from using H-1B visas if they have had mass layoffs within the last year. The senators' goal, as a 2007 article on *Ars Technica* put it, was "to ensure that US companies are not exploiting the H-1B system by essentially replacing US workers with cheaper foreign talent."[73] Sanders observed that under legislation then under consideration (but not enacted), the number of additional visas would be approximately equal to the projected number of high-tech jobs created in the sector. Ultimately, the motive of Gates and the industry in their aggressive support of the visa program seems to have less to do with their professed cosmopolitanism than with their structural need to keep programmer salaries depressed.

But above all, the classic feature of labor exploitation in tech is a traditional one: overwork. As far back as the late eighties, the *Seattle Times* ran memorable articles describing the company's work environment as a "velvet sweatshop," an early view of the tech industry's culture of overwork, referred to in the industry as "crunch time" or, indeed, "death marches." In one notable example, it reported that "sixty-hour work weeks without overtime are common" in the company's "woodsy corporate headquarters" that evokes "the quiet intellectual industry of a college campus." However, "the word 'unions' make[s] the blood drain" from the faces of tech company executives.[74] The *Times* continued:

> Workers quick to extol the multiple charms of their employer prefaced all negative comments with a request for anonymity, and even ex-Microsoft employees expressed concern about repercussions, since many still have affiliations with Microsoft or the high-tech industry. Halfway through the research for this article, sources began calling back frantic, demanding to know which parts of their statements would be used—the result of a memo . . . requesting that any contacts with outside media be sanctioned first by corporate communications. In some cases sources were asked to check with the reporter

about what would be printed, and report back to the company their findings.[75]

The paper suggested that "this strategy had its Orwellian aspects." George Orwell, a socialist best remembered for his damning portraits of totalitarian thought control, would probably want to take down the bars on these Windows.

But the technology is evolving in the opposite direction, with the business papers today reporting that "Microsoft Corp. tallies data on the frequency of chats, emails and meetings between its staff and clients using its own Office 365 services to measure employee productivity, management efficacy and work-life balance. . . . Earlier this year, Microsoft sales team members received personalized dashboards that show how they spend their time, insights that managers cannot see." Cannot see *yet*. But "companies, which have wide legal latitude in the U.S. to monitor workers, don't always tell them what they are tracking. . . . Microsoft also sells that type of workplace analytics software to other companies."[76]

BusinessWeek has also reported on the company's work conditions. Reviewing legal actions in which Microsoft attempted to enforce non-compete agreements on workers defecting to Google or other companies, it observed that the 2005 hearings "painted a distinctly unflattering picture of the company's inner workings." The company's low morale is related in part to aggressive cost cutting:

> Microsoft sliced health benefits, introducing, for example, a $40 copayment on some brand-name prescription drugs. . . . Even the cuts that seem trivial have dampened morale. Just whisper the word "towels" to any Microsoft employee, and eyes roll. Last year, Microsoft stopped providing a towel service for workers who used company locker rooms after bike rides or workouts. Employees who helped the company build its huge cash stockpile were furious.[77]

More importantly, due to Microsoft's stock price stagnating for many years around the turn of the century, "more than half of Microsoft's employees have received virtually no benefit from their stock holdings. . . . Microsoft's compensation moves have created a haves-vs.-have-nots culture. Newbies work for comfortable but not overly generous wages, while veterans have a lucrative treasure chest full of stock options." Even within the more privileged white-collar workforce, corporate hierarchy and class distinctions still loom large.

Other classic white-collar policies at Microsoft have unfortunately become the standard among members of the Fortune 500, like the company's policy of peer review. Up until 2013, software developers were evaluated by their colleagues every six months, and the lowest-rated 5 percent were fired.[78] This "rank and yank" policy is a familiar tool in powerful hierarchies, in which labor exists as simple input tools to be thrown out if performing poorly in the short run. Gates said: "There are other jobs out there. . . . If they don't have what it takes to work at Microsoft, they can go to Boeing or back East." And eat cake. Gates again illustrates the unflattering personal ramifications of holding enormous power over other people, including enormous obliviousness, like the French aristocrats of old. Indeed, journalist James Wallace more than once refers to the industry term "Microserfs."[79]

But the serfs do rise up, as when the company's workers in 2018 questioned CEO Nadella and handed him a petition with three hundred thousand signatures, including those of five hundred Microsoft workers, demanding the company cease its data processing and AI contracts with Immigration and Customs Enforcement, criticizing its role in incarcerating immigrants and refugees, and separating children from their parents at the border. The *New York Times* noted the petition came at a delicate time, as the company had the truly hilarious hope of "positioning itself as a moral leader of the technology industry," making it ironic that the workers speaking to reporters "declined to be identified for fear of retaliation."[80]

Microsoft has also been the target of some of the limited labor litigation in the industry. This has mostly been in regard to another common feature of modern labor markets: precariousness and insecurity. The most prominent of these lawsuits was *Vizcaino v. Microsoft*, in which "permatemps" hired by Microsoft were found to have been under-compensated. However, only the blocked access to Microsoft's stock purchase plan (then allowing a 15 percent discount on share buys by employees) held up as an official violation. Further, the verdict only applied to those long-term "temporary" workers who actually worked for Microsoft, rather than independent contractors hired through a broker, so the case seems to have held little of value for today's tech workers.[81]

Microsoft ultimately settled for $97 million, a pittance by their standards. One analysis concludes that "the court's decision in favor of the contractors resulted in Microsoft implementing a policy to make the distinction between permanent employees and contract employees even more clear, rather than reducing the number of contractors."[82] This seems to conform to past experience, in which labor has rarely been significantly helped by simple court actions, owing not only to labor's inability to match its opposition in terms of affording legal expenses, but also to the unfavorable nature of US labor laws, largely written under the influence of corporate lobbyists.

And generally, over the last forty years Microsoft has played a major role in establishing the human standards of the tech sector. In 1991, at the height of Microsoft's monopoly over computing and before its legal troubles, the company threw its annual Christmas party in Seattle. The theme was New York City, with areas set up to resemble Greenwich Village and Little Italy. Paid actors attended dressed as street people.[83] Even in its off-time celebrations, the company includes the hierarchies of the capitalist landscape it rose from, even if there's no clear rationale at all.

It was Microsoft that showed the world that the "New Economy" of sophisticated, high-tech corporations was not fundamentally different from the Old Economy of capitalism in its core characteristics: monopoly and class conflict.

CHAPTER 3

The Apple Bitten

The long road to number one

In January 1984, Apple Computer aired a striking commercial during the Super Bowl, in which an image of a totalitarian ruler spouts propaganda at cowed workers until a sexy athlete with an Apple logo on her shirt runs in with a giant hammer, which she swings into the screen, destroying it. The ad became famous, both for its then-innovative art design and its tagline, "You'll see why 1984 won't be like *1984*."

The reference, of course, was to the famous satire *Nineteen Eighty-Four*, socialist George Orwell's critique of totalitarianism. The creative director at Apple's ad agency said the spot "explained Apple's philosophy and purpose—that people, not just government and big corporations, should run technology."[1] The beloved computing nerd icon and creator of the original Apple Computer, Steve Wozniak, captured this spirit when he said, "Our first computers were born not out of greed or ego but in the revolutionary spirit of helping common people rise above the most powerful institutions."[2]

To quote a former member of Apple's marketing staff, "*Revolutionize* may be the most used word in Apple marketing."[3]

Yet, Apple is now among the three biggest corporations in the world, and the very first to reach a trillion dollars in market value. Far from encouraging revolution and opposing totalitarianism, it uses exhaustively exploited labor at every turn, has a famously oppressive and hierarchical work climate, and is itself among the most powerful institutions in the world today.

Apple Tarts

Well before its modern era of flashy mobile devices, Apple was known for its sleek, user-friendly personal computers. These were groundbreaking because of their "graphical user interface," or GUI, which freed the user from having to learn computer code commands. Instead, a simple visual desktop metaphor allowed files to be opened and altered, different programs run, and media accessed.

While Apple has reliably taken credit for its technical and design innovations down the years, as with Microsoft (see chapter 2) much of the most innovative work occurred elsewhere, often by public institutions. Apple booster Steven Levy recognized in his book on Apple's early years that among its innovations, "the best ones were borrowed."[4] The original development of visual windows opening on a computer display, representing particular files or programs, was funded by the military's Defense Advanced Research Projects Agency (DARPA discussed at greater length in chapter 8).

In particular, a good deal of the GUI elements most associated with Apple's computers (and later Microsoft's Windows) were created at the Palo Alto Research Center (PARC) operated by Xerox, including the window display and the mouse. When DARPA's modest funding for research was cut back, several scientists went to PARC to continue their research on computer interfaces.

Years later, a young Steve Jobs and other Apple staff went to PARC, and in exchange for valuable Apple stock, were allowed to observe PARC's Altair computer, with its movable windows and pop-up menus, leading Jobs to jump up and exclaim: "Why aren't you doing anything with this? This is the greatest thing! This is revolutionary!"[5] In fact, when Jobs later accused Bill Gates and Microsoft of copying Apple's own GUI, Gates replied, "No, Steve, I think it's more like we both have this rich neighbor named Xerox, and you broke in to steal the TV set, found I'd been there first, and said, 'No fair, I wanted to steal the TV set!'"[6] Notably, these are founders of companies that are now well known for spending millions to take others to court for infringing on their intellectual property.

Apple was first founded in 1976 by Jobs and computer whiz Steve Wozniak (little-known cofounder Ronald Wayne sold his shares early). From the earliest days, the ambitious Jobs had a tendency to connive and use his friendship with Wozniak (or "Woz") to his advantage. When Jobs got an early break designing a game for video game giant Atari, he found the circuitry too difficult and got Wozniak to design it. Yet after delivering the game, Jobs dragged his feet on paying Wozniak and eventually gave him $350. Years later, when Wozniak discovered Jobs had received $5,000 for the program from Atari, he realized he had been betrayed by his friend. "I just cried," he remembered.[7]

Jobs and Wozniak went into business producing and selling computers, at first essentially glorified circuit boards, later adding keyboard interfaces and monitors. The 1977 Apple II was the first milestone, with an open setup and a licensed version of Microsoft's BASIC programming language, allowing software developers to write supporting applications like games. However, the Apple III, released in 1980, was a closed system, meaning independent developers couldn't write programs to it; and its lack of software and external slots for peripherals hindered its ability to become a platform by attracting software developers. So was the 1983 Lisa, meant to be the first computer to fully exploit PARC's GUI technologies. It bombed because it had wildly inadequate memory and a high price tag, especially damaging in the face of the exploding dominance of the IBM PC (running Microsoft's operating system) during the same period.

When the Lisa sold below expectations, Jobs said to the staff, "You guys really fucked up. I'm going to have to lay a lot of you off."[8] Indeed, on February 28, 1981, Apple laid off forty-one of the company's fifteen hundred employees, later known as "Black Wednesday." Levy called this "the loss of Apple's virginity" and "the end of innocence."[9] This would be just the first, and far from the worst, of Apple's sins against working people.

Much as with Bill Gates, Jobs became notorious for preserving the very worst of hierarchical capitalist tyranny into the information age. On the one hand, Jobs became the icon of the tech CEO, charismatic and brilliant, and a gigantic amount of glamorizing coverage has passed for analysis of the figure and company for years, serving as the clear basis for big-budget movie heroes and villains. However, in almost all firsthand accounts, Jobs was known for his abusive tirades against his official subordinates and for being a general heel. He mocked the idea of extending stock options to a former best friend working at the company who had been too naïve to ask for them early on, and he lied about having no control over the process. *Macworld* publisher David Bunnell recounts that Jobs parked his car in a handicap space at the Mac building, since his car would be keyed by disgruntled workers if he parked at the side of the building or behind it. Stanford business professor Robert Sutton wrote, "It sometimes seems as if his full name is, 'Steve Jobs, that asshole.'"[10] Truly, a classic capitalist.

But the wreckage of the Lisa led to the rise of the Macintosh, which would in time become Apple's signature product before the mobile era. Jobs, having been pushed away from the Lisa team over his inability to work with others, ended up taking over the Mac project from other managers, even though he had argued for killing the project in the early days. He later took credit for it in the press. As Wozniak has said, "With Steve you never know exactly where an idea comes from."[11]

Launched with the famous 1984 ad, the Mac fixed some of Lisa's problems, introducing more memory and more affordable pricing. Its interface was truly elegant and utterly intuitive, the consummation of the GUI. But its sales still struggled for years (after a brief surge of buying among Apple enthusiasts), again owing partially to premium prices—Apple's "standard markup" was in the neighborhood of 300 percent. And even this was exceeded when the Mac, $500 to manufacture, was priced at nearly $2,500.[12] Sales were also dampened by performance issues, including the manufacturer's failure to include an internal cooling fan, which Jobs refused to approve on the grounds that it was inelegant.

But in the end, as we saw in chapter 2, Apple's computers were swamped by the huge success of the IBM PCs running Microsoft software, which were revolutionizing computing at the time. The obvious question in this period of the industry's history is why Apple's fine, if expensive, products were definitively beaten out for market share by computers running Microsoft's operating systems, MS-DOS and then Windows.

The reasons were the network effects and platform economics discussed in chapter 1. For something important happened between the Apple II and all the company's computers that followed—Jobs closed the system. While the Apple II had many peripheral slots to attach drives, printers, and other software enablers, the III had no slots, nor did the Lisa or Mac. Further, Apple would not license its operating system to other manufacturers like Dell, as Microsoft had. This meant corporate purchasers were leery of widespread investment in Apple machines, since if anything went wrong they had only one company to turn to, unlike the variety of PC-making OEMs. And those low adoption rates in turn led to the Mac having significantly less third-party software than Windows.

These combined factors meant that the Mac OS could not become an industry standard, while the more-open Windows OS could, and did. Journalists and business analysts covering Apple recognized its goal was to set "an industry standard alongside DOS, the inferior but widely accepted IBM and Microsoft system," but

Apple wanted more control and feared repeating IBM's experience. Its use of third-party parts, and an operating system from Microsoft, meant that the PC "clones" from Dell and other OEMs ate into the sales of IBM's own machines. So out of fears of "cannibalizing" its own hardware sales (and their premium prices), Apple never licensed its OS and therefore missed its chance to gain major market share, as Microsoft had done.

Apple's niche market role was further assured by the strong tendency of corporate buyers to use what Levy calls "an unwritten code: one would never, ever go wrong by sticking to whatever IBM called a standard."[13] This was so because, in addition to having a wider market for supplies, IBM PCs were becoming widely used by other Fortune 500 firms, limiting incompatibility issues—a standard network effect. Despite these continual missteps by Apple, which have drawn enormous criticism from business historians and were indeed later repeated in the mobile era, Jobs did recognize that setting a standard was the goal. But he mistakenly believed Apple could create "a second industry standard," rather than being part of the one already started by the IBM PCs.[14] This plan shows a real failure to understand platform economics.

Even in the markets for application software, Apple's moves hurt its chances of becoming an industry standard. It broke with tradition by not including a programming language with its computers, thus limiting users' ability to modify programs. Also in this period, the company actively discouraged the "porting" of applications—altering programs so they could run on a different operating system.[15] The purpose of this move was to encourage the creation of entirely new apps for Apple's machines, but it also undermined the application barrier that the more open Apple II had cultivated, further weakening Apple's ability to set standards.

However, the major exception to this policy was Microsoft—besides BASIC, it ported the predecessors of the crucial Word and Excel productivity programs to Apple's OS. Business histories record that at times, Microsoft had as many workers developing Apple software as Apple had employees in total.[16]

As with past network monopolists, they soon turned to struggle against each another, with enormous consequences for our digital economy. Microsoft's work on Apple applications, using secretive Mac prototypes, allowed Gates to use the knowledge gained to develop similar GUI-based applications for the IBM PCs for which Microsoft created operating software.[17] Failing to stop Gates, Jobs himself attempted to double-cross him by developing Apple's own programming language, MacBASIC, but gave that up when Apple's existing BASIC license lapsed and needed to be renewed—the company couldn't risk being without a programming language. And when Windows 1.01 was about to be released, to forestall an expected lawsuit from Apple, Gates threatened to cease work on porting its business apps as well.

But most stunning of all is a memo from Gates himself to Apple's CEO a John Sculley, essentially imploring Apple to learn from Microsoft's standard-setting, competition-destroying example and desist its stubborn refusal to license its OS. Gates's memo is an open explanation of the network effects and platform economics that gave him his own monopoly, including the crucial role of network standards and the lock-in experience of users of applications. As such, it deserves to be quoted at length:

> Apple must make Macintosh a standard. But no personal computer company, not even IBM, can create a standard without independent support. Even though Apple realized this, they have not been able to gain the independent support required to be perceived as a standard. The significant investment . . . in a "standard personal computer" results in an incredible momentum for its architecture. . . . The industry has reached the point where it is now impossible for Apple to create a standard out of their innovative technology without support from, and the resulting credibility of other personal computer manufacturers.[18]

Gates added that the lack of "Mac-compatible" manufacturers meant that "corporations consider it risky to be locked into the

Mac, for reasons of price AND choice." Therefore, Apple should license the Mac to three to five OEMs, and "Microsoft is very willing to help Apple implement this strategy." A second letter from Gates to Apple repeated the offer to help, concluding, "Please give me a call."[19] In 1997 Gates invested $150 million in Apple, along with extensive patent sharing, in order to keep it alive as the Department of Justice investigated Microsoft for monopoly.[20]

Wozniak, far from a scheming strategist, himself wrote that "the computer was never the problem. The company's strategy was. Apple saw itself as a hardware company; in order to protect our hardware, we didn't license our operating system."[21] For this reason, analyst Owen Linzmayer wrote that "Apple itself is really to blame for the success of Windows."[22]

Because of all these factors, as Wozniak implied at the time, the company's real platform power would not come from its software, as it did for Microsoft. Instead it would come from the hardware itself, and it was its hardware that would soon open up an entirely new form of computer use that has reshaped our society, becoming the gateway through which the Internet itself is accessed and therefore the means for the other Big Tech giants to interact with us. It was the iPhone that created Apple's platform power on the new terrain of mobile hardware.

But before the advent of Apple's mobile devices, the company saw its darkest days, with years of declining sales and various explorations of selling the company, especially around its brush with bankruptcy in 1997. This period saw the dramatic events that are the stuff of corporate biography—Jobs chafed under the leadership of CEO Sculley, causing problems to the point that Sculley had the board strip Jobs of his formal title and roles in the company. Jobs in fact attempted a failed boardroom coup while Sculley was overseas, and he returned later as interim CEO, at the time that Apple was finding more success with its strikingly designed iMac desktops, styled by Apple's rising design star Jonathan Ive.

Jobs's return was shortly followed by the beginning of Apple's stunning rise in handheld products, when the pioneering iPod was released in 2001. Clunky and limited by today's standards, it was a major innovation at the time, mainly due to its large storage capacity for music previously transported through large quantities of CDs. But crucially, here platform economics again played an important role—much like the original Mac and other expensive Apple products, sales fell after an initial boom, once enthusiasts had done their buying.

It was only with the introduction of the iTunes music-buying and -playing software in 2002, including a negotiated deal with the major record labels to offer their music through the service, that iPod sales shot up. The presence of a sturdy seed of listeners attracted the music labels, in turn attracting more non-Mac users who valued the richer selection available to them as more music listening migrated online with the rise of Napster, and the rising quality of broadband made downloading media feasible. Soon iTunes was so dominant Jobs called it the "Microsoft" of music streaming.[23] And above all it was the porting of iTunes to Windows in 2003 that led to the real takeoff of iPod and iTunes sales, as the dominant OS platform now put that software before millions of new users. Notably, Jobs initially resisted the iTunes idea.[24]

The early success of the iPod showed what was possible with new mobile technologies—the source of Apple's great platform power, profit, and capitalist growth. But despite the huge effect of smartphones on our society, the apple doesn't roll far from the early corporate tree.

ImperiOS

The smartphone revolution has reshaped society. It has made instant gratification available for anyone who can afford a phone and data plan, and added a new, enormous obstacle to social exchange as our eyes lock onto screens instead of other people. Adam Greenfield observes in his book *Radical Technologies* that "refugees recently arriving from warzones have been known to ask for a smartphone before anything else, food and water not excluded."[25] The *Wall Street Journal* has published estimates that each iPhone customer is worth about $1,000 in profit every two to three years, while tech journalist Brian Merchant called the iPhone "the pinnacle product of all capitalism to this point."[26] And Apple has rushed to take credit for this potential, but as with much of their earlier tech, most of it had already been developed, often by the public sector.

This subject is dissected in chapter 8, but for now it's perhaps most crucial to observe an interesting fact—mobile multi-touch displays, the basis for modern smartphone interaction, were first developed by publicly funded scientists working in the same giant physics research facility where the World Wide Web was created. British scientist Tim Berners-Lee is credited with the creation of the data protocols that allowed the sharing of online documents and websites using a uniform set of rules. He worked at the European Organization for Nuclear Research (known by its French acronym CERN), a major European physics lab located below the Swiss-French border whose facilities include the Super Proton Synchrotron, an enormous subterranean supercollider. The facility was so big that manually adjusting the system's controls along the 1.3-mile-wide collider wasn't practical, so mobile handsets were developed to allow scientists to efficiently operate the system. This ended up including the capacitive touch screen, which executes different commands based on the strength and nature of the user's touch, allowing the whole system's controls to be accessible in just a few clicks or taps.[27]

The phone's components also have wide roots, including the special display glass (from Corning), its touch sensor chip (from Broadcom), and even the central processor chip (from Samsung).[28] The pioneering multi-touch screen technology had been refined by the work of a victim of hand injuries who built a touch-sensitive interface to allow him to type better, which resulted in the development of a product named the iGesture NumPad. Apple later bought the small company and acquired its patents.[29] And although Apple design head Jonathan Ive said Jobs was initially "very, very dismissive" when the original iPhone prototypes were shown to him, at the product's debut in the famous 2007 launch, Jobs said: "We have invented a new technology called multitouch, which is phenomenal. . . . And, boy, have we patented it."[30]

Even the standardized cellular network protocols and the Wi-Fi technology used by smartphones to connect to data networks were developed by public workers, at the European Commission and the University of Hawaii, respectively.[31] So the frequently repeated claim that Apple and other Silicon Valley giants deserve their huge profits and power because they invented today's fancy tech crashes like an overloaded Apple III.

As fancy as it is, the iPhone relies for its production on very familiar patterns in capitalist markets. The labor to produce and sell it, from mines in Bolivia and the Congo to manufacturers in China to retail clerks in Apple stores worldwide, is insultingly undercompensated and aggressively kept from having any influence over the process. (The labor forces required to make Apple work are reviewed later in this chapter.) Environmentally, it's a similarly traditional story, with colossal volumes of upturned earth in China's rare earth element mines needed to build the phone, and huge amounts of aluminum that is incredibly energy-intensive to refine. A single iPhone 6 requires seventy-five pounds of ores for the metals, along with one hundred liters of water and twenty grams of cyanide for separating the tiny amount of gold, creating giant amounts of poisonous by-product.[32]

Greenfield writes that "the polluted streams, stillborn children and diagnoses of cancer, too, become part of the way in which the smartphone has transformed everyday life, at least for some of us."[33] But Apple's toys are the ultimate sleek modern products, and the dirty, cruel realities of their production are kept far from the minds of its purchasers; despite significant press coverage of the production chain, Apple's brand identity is one of the world's strongest, and consumers' reliance on them itself discourages looking under the hood.

This brings up the truly incredible marketing apparatus used by Apple to move phones. Apple has been called a leader in "creating want, fostering demand, and broadcasting technologic cool."[34] This has been crucial for the firm's growth into the world's largest corporation, and indeed Apple's own corporate filings state that the company uses "frequent product introductions and transitions" in order to "stimulate customer demand."[35] And after the flashy launches, Apple's brand awareness hinges on the spending of large amounts of cash so that the company's commercial messages are repeated over and again in every medium.

More broadly, the company's mystique is managed as aggressively as any other giant agglomeration of capital. Commenting on the company's famously tight-lipped PR discipline, Adam Lashinsky writes, "Apple's public relations department operates not so much on a need-to-know basis as a you-will-not-know basis."[36] Amazingly, Apple says it has never paid for product placement, despite being featured in countless TV scenes and movies. Apple's cachet among creatives and college campuses seems to have made its Old Testament logo a new testament to the power of capital and its ability to get Apple's brand identity into people's minds—a task made easier if you monopolize publicly developed technology that meets legitimate needs. Also helpful is Apple's practice of "escalation"—code for product requests by celebrities, who get special VIP customer service, like replacement displays in under an hour.

Apple may not need to invest heavily in favorable coverage anyway, as even its own investors have come to feel that the mobile phones unleashed by the company have borderline addictive effects. User surveys indicate that over a third of US teenagers wake up during the night to check their devices, and about a quarter of parents do so.[37] Almost half of users also say they feel addicted to their phones, which is among the reasons that large Apple shareholders JANA Partners and the California teachers' pension fund asked the company to address the "unintentional negative side effects" of such obsessive phone use among young people. Unusually for large investors, they made this move publicly, and they included the release of data showing half of US teenagers look at screens for over four hours a day, and a quarter for eight hours a day.[38] Notably, these typically short-term, profit-obsessed funds want Apple to address the problem with better parental control software, rather than rethinking private capitalist ownership of one of our main windows to the world.

But however marketed, Apple's nature as a maker of "closed" systems has remained remarkably consistent into the mobile era. When Jobs unveiled the new phone, he openly disdained allowing third-party applications—software made to run on the iPhone by a developer other than Apple. This made the phone a "walled garden" in industry parlance, meaning it was under the total control of its owner. Even the constant demand from developers for access, and hackers breaking the phone so independent apps could be installed, didn't move Jobs. What did move him was falling sales. Once again, Jobs had failed to understand platform economics and network effects, and much as with the original iPod/iTunes system, it was opening the platform up that ultimately attracted a community of users and developers, making the platform a success.

Granted, the early iPhone did have some software that was inherently open—mainly its web browser (in the form of Apple's own browser, Safari), which allowed access to the Internet. But there was not enough useful software to make the phone a hit, which struggled much like the iPod did before iTunes was released for Windows. So among the earliest phone updates was addition of the App Store, an iPhone feature that allows users to buy software applications written by third-party developers.

While far from the ocean of apps available on Windows-based PC systems or Android, the App Store has grown vigorously, broadening the range of software for an otherwise-closed platform and making the devices a lot more fun and useful. Crucially though, even this nominally open setting is tightly curated by Apple, which lists dozens of reasons it may choose to reject a third-party app, and refers to some that are secret. Perhaps this is why, despite its lucrative proceeds, the app environment is relatively limited thematically—by far the most popular apps are games, making up over 80 percent of sales.[39] These are followed by streaming apps like Netflix, Hulu, and YouTube, which along with Tinder make up almost all the total sales.

Nonetheless, today Apple would be a Fortune 100 company just on the revenue from its App Store, with billions in annual sales, which are a gold mine for the company since it takes a 30 percent cut simply for making the platform available to app developers. Indeed, Apple's own SEC filings recognize this essential role of independent software in making the hardware appealing, reporting that "competitive factors . . . include . . . a strong third-party software and accessories ecosystem." In other words, the presence of games and apps made by outside companies is essential for the iPhone to remain relevant to its relatively elite market segment. Further, Apple's "future performance depends in part on support from third-party software developers," and in turn "developers' perception and analysis" of the popularity of Apple's products "compared to Windows-based products."[40]

And much like Microsoft's "moat" from its "applications barrier to entry," the use of these downloaded software applications makes it harder, more expensive, or simply more of a nuisance to switch to any other smartphone. Getting another phone and loading it with your favorite apps typically means buying them again, along with the time required to download and configure them. Worse, the reality is that some apps simply won't transfer to other phones, for proprietary or compatibility reasons, as the *New York Times* and other sources have reported.[41] Since applications are used far more than traditional voice calling, this creates a barrier to switching that benefits Apple (and other phone makers). Reviews also note that iPhone messaging has significantly limited functionality when texting an Android user, with no message receipt acknowledgments and sometimes lost messages, and this makes switching from Apple to Android very challenging if your friends or family use it. One reviewer puts it: "Apple has erected some high walls around its iPhone users."[42]

But, especially in the iPhone's early days, before the App Store and during its initial development, its closed nature meant that useful software would be especially important, after the early sales to Apple superfans gave way to limited public interest, just as with the Mac twenty years earlier. And it was here that a new firm—Google—made a crucial contribution, with a full suite of highly useful and popular applications. The later platform struggles between Apple and this upstart shape the mobile hardware markets to this day.

Cores

To achieve its sales targets for iPhone, Apple needed software, which was limited for the new kind of mobile product and especially due to Apple's long-standing closed structures. But Google offered a lucrative set of apps, which were not only popular but also partially opened up the system—Google Search, Gmail, Google Maps, and YouTube, the video hub. These, along with the Safari browser, gave the phone far more appeal and are considered to have greatly helped the iPhone's gigantic popularity.

The giant corporations needed each other, as Google was desperate for mobile search traffic to help build its algorithms and gain resulting network effects (its own rise will be discussed in chapter 5). Thus they worked closely together at first, in particular against what tech journalist Fred Vogelstein called their "common enemy: Microsoft."[43] Microsoft's enduring PC monopoly was not replicated in the mobile market, but, on the other hand, the Microsoft antitrust settlement specifically did not apply to cell phones. This meant Google was anxious to get market share on mobile search, especially after Microsoft released its own competing search engine, which went through various names before the company settled on Bing. Google's CEO, Eric Schmidt, sat on Apple's board of directors and, in a disgusting display of their corporate aspirations, Google's founders looked up to Jobs.

This alliance was born out of Apple's particular form of platform economics. While Microsoft's platform is composed of PC OS software that decides how your workplace computer functions, along with productivity applications that, as a result of network effects, are widely used in the workplace, Apple's is hardware based—but no less crucial. Smartphones are now the main way that users interact with not only the Internet, but also the other corporations in the Big Five—giving Apple (and in time, Google) the ability to decide what you see on your phone. This means that the other tech giants, including Facebook, Amazon, and Microsoft, all have to go through the smartphone makers to reach us. And that is platform power indeed. The *Wall Street Journal* reports that Apple's phones have been "a catalyst for the growing dominance of tech-industry titans," and have "made it easier for big companies to connect with customers."[44] For better or worse!

This was well recognized at the time—Eric Schmidt thought Apple would end up with a smartphone platform monopoly, rather than the duopoly with Google that would shortly emerge. "It was not obvious to us . . . that it would be a two-horse race between Apple and Google. . . . These are network platforms, and it is traditional that you end up with a couple as opposed to ten." Indeed, a Google engineer suggested that "Apple might be even worse than Microsoft—the way they curated out everything they didn't like from their app store and all that."[45] And Apple was far from moving away from a closed hardware platform—in fact, by this time it had begun using "pentalobe screws" to physically enclose the iPhone, meaning that specialized equipment was required to even open the device.

Meanwhile, Google's own network effects in desktop search, along with its purchase of YouTube—itself a platform monopoly, had in time made it one of the most powerful companies on the web. And watching Jobs repeat his mistake of running his hardware as a walled garden over which the company had total control, Google's execs saw an opportunity to better exploit network effects and create a rival open phone operating system that would encourage far more third-party support and thus reach a potentially bigger market. Google had bought Android, a small handset designer, in 2005, and in the years after the iPhone's success (partly due to Google's own software), it gradually developed the Android OS and made the decision that it wouldn't make the phone—the actual handsets would be made by different original equipment manufacturers (OEMs). Google would just make the operating system and many applications, a software-based strategy much like what Microsoft did to gain its monopoly on IBM-compatible PCs twenty years before.

By 2008, Google's founders were ready to provide their OS to OEM phones, despite their lucrative relationship with Apple. When Jobs saw the first Android-running phone, an HTC "Dream," he was incensed. A meeting between Jobs and Google founders Larry Page and Sergey Brin involved nasty threats of legal action, as Jobs called it "a fucking rip-off" and demanded a crippling removal of anything resembling the iPhone's multi-touch GUI.[46] Page and Brin bowed to this at first, wrecking the very first version of the phone's chances, but Google soon pushed forward on new phones. By this time, "the Apple-Google partnership to protect the world from Microsoft was unraveling . . . they were a lot more angry at and scared of each other than either of them were of Microsoft."[47]

Despite the charming picture of may-the-best-man-win competition promoted by economics textbooks and libertarian politicians, the reality was that Jobs was berserk with rage at any competition in the smartphone market. At an employee meeting, he unloaded: "Apple did not enter the search business. So why did Google enter the phone business? Google wants to kill the iPhone. We won't let them. Their Don't Be Evil mantra? It's *bull-shit*."[48] Even more memorably, Jobs said in his authorized biography: "I will spend my last dying breath if I need to, and I will spend every penny of Apple's $40 billion in the bank, to right this wrong. . . . I'm willing to go thermonuclear war on this." There are few offenses to a monopoly capitalist greater than competition, which they are supposed to welcome. We may be reminded of Bill Gates's demands to "crush" his competitors, slamming his fist into his hand.[49]

Jobs kicked Google's apps off the default iPhone setup (they could still be downloaded from the store), including Google Maps, which was replaced by Apple Maps, software so utterly inept it remained a major black eye for Apple's reputation for some time. Meanwhile, sales of both versions of smartphone exploded, as Android phones of various makes and styles were soon selling forty million units a quarter, and iPhone sales doubled with each new product update. Meanwhile PC sales began to decline, and, in a turn with added symbolism, in 2010 Apple passed Microsoft as the biggest tech company by stock valuation, a position they trade back and forth with Amazon to this day. The App Store and the premium prices on the phones themselves both contributed massively to this achievement.

But Jobs's wrath was bottomless, leading to litigation. Since Google would be difficult to sue, as it made no competing hardware and gave its own software products away for free, Apple resorted to suing Google's handset-making proxies. The main event was a major suit Apple filed against the giant South Korean conglomerate Samsung, the largest Android phone maker, despite the fact that Apple is also Samsung's biggest customer, doing several billion dollars in mobile chips and other annual business. *BusinessWeek* described the litigation cases as "Apple's Jihad" against Google, which "reflects life in the tech big leagues: Apple sharply reminding a formidable rival who's boss. . . . The combatants barely notice the millions of dollars in legal expenses," as Apple fought "mere proxies for another foe—Android."[50] But the suit, which actually went to a rare Silicon Valley trial and resulted in a victory for Apple, led to a wave of countersuits by the Android OEMs. Thus was inaugurated the grand tradition in Big Tech of using patent litigation as another weapon, like ad campaigns and corporate alliances, often ending in large omnibus patent cross-licensing agreements where the firms agree to share tech to end the wars of legal attrition. Largely in response to these moves, Google bought phone maker Motorola in 2011, mainly to protect itself with the addition of the company's large, seventeen-thousand-strong patent portfolio.

Since Android was a more or less open platform, it quickly built an application developer community and caught up with the early lead held by Apple and its iPhone-iTunes hardware-content platform. Much as Microsoft beat Apple in the eighties by more widely distributing its software and thus attracting more applications with network effects, so the various Android-running phones were able to magnetically attract a fast-growing crowd of third-party developers. But Apple's three-year lead meant it too had an ecosystem of software partners, managed through the App Store. The app lock-in, estimated to often cost around fifty to one hundred dollars to replace apps at this time, discouraged much switching of platforms once most customers had one or the other.[51] And so, as millions of cell phone users globally switched to a smartphone running Android because of the lower costs and wider array of software, the world market settled into a smartphone OS duopoly—one that avoids the usual monopoly outcome, but just barely, being tilted heavily toward Android.

Crucially, "the more successful Apple became, the more Google and Android hewed toward Apple's 'we control everything' approach," as Vogelstein puts it.[52] Ultimately, Android came to global dominance, with the *Wall Street Journal* reporting in 2017 that iPhone's US market share had declined to 32.5 percent, with 25.7 percent belonging to Samsung, and a total share of all Android-running companies' phones now claimed over 50 percent.[53] Globally, Android's share is several times the size of Apple's, with more affordable phones running Google's software, along with premium models like Samsung's Galaxy series and now Google's own Pixel line. But crucially, while Android made applesauce out of Apple's monopoly, and Apple ships only one-sixth of phones worldwide, it makes a staggering 91 percent of the smartphone industry's profits.[54]

But whether you run your life through an Android or iPhone handset, you're part of the modern world's data-hoarding, location-tracking corporate panopticon. Journalist Yasha Levine writes:

> Where we go, what we do, what we talk about, who we talk to, and who we see—everything is recorded and, at some point, leveraged for value. Google, Apple, and Facebook know when a woman visits an abortion clinic, even if she tells no one else: the GPS coordinates on the phone don't lie. One-night stands and extramarital affairs are a cinch to figure out: two smart-phones that never met before suddenly cross paths in a bar and then make their way to an apartment across town, stay together overnight, and part in the morning. They know us intimately, even the things that we hide from those closest to us.[55]

We'll come back to today's relentless tracking technology in chapters 5 and 6, but the most amazing thing to consider from this perspective is that Apple has strived to make it itself into a champion of privacy, largely on the grounds of collecting less of our data than have Google and Facebook, which scoop up this kind of location-based data and much, much more. The press reports Apple has "weaponized privacy," despite hoarding a good deal of location and app data on its users even as it criticizes Facebook and Google. Google's CEO, referring to the more affordable prices for many Android-running models, shot back with a dig at Apple's premium prices: "Privacy cannot be a luxury good."[56]

Apple's limited market share is partially compensated for by its depth. Most of its users own other Apple devices, including watches, speakers, TV modules, and above all the iPad. Fascinatingly, Apple's tablet was designed specifically to increase Apple's revenue per user. Vogelstein memorably writes: "If Google was going to try to win the mobile-platform war on breadth, Jobs wanted the world to know he was going to win it on depth. . . . The people who owned iPhones would also own iPads, iPod Touches, and a slew of other Apple products that all ran the same software."[57] In this way, despite having only minority market share, Apple maintains major network platform power through its linked devices' premium prices, and it is well on its way in its transition to selling services like music and apps, which make tens of billions annually as the smartphone market matures and comes to resemble the car market, where the products are seen to have a relatively consistent level of quality, and buyers want to get several years of use out of them rather than constantly update. The transition was symbolized in 2019 by the departure, after a long estrangement, of Ive, Apple's famous hardware design head, and the second most powerful figure at the company, according to Jobs's own assessment years before.[58]

Indeed, Apple has doubled down on its extortionate price points, most conspicuously with its iPhone X and its thousand-dollar price tag. To make sense of it, the conservative *Wall Street Journal* was forced to take the loathed step of citing the economic theory of an anti-capitalist figure—Thorstein Veblen, the American economist who coined the phrase "conspicuous consumption." The idea is that people buy certain costly products partially because "the expense broadcasts status, taste, and wealth," as with the flashy sports cars bought by young business executives.[59] The *Journal* insisted such goods "violate the economic laws of gravity," but class signaling is real enough for Apple to maintain its enormous iPhone revenues.

Another stale economic "law" that Apple violated involved its battery scandal, in which Apple acknowledged (after a blog broke the news) that its software updates slow the processor of older phones in order to keep the aging batteries from overloading and abruptly shutting off the phone. This has been called "programmed obsolescence," after the idea that a company holding market power may deliberately shorten the lifespan of its products in order to encourage replacement sales.[60] To deal with the bad publicity, Apple generously offered a discount for battery replacements, charging twenty-nine dollars rather than seventy-nine dollars in yet another tone-deaf response that failed to deter the individual lawsuits, many of which seek class-action status.

Other moves suggest Apple, while having risen through its power-mongering history to become for a time the very largest corporation in the world by market value, has reached a certain plateau. For years, Apple did not pay a dividend to stockholders—a regular payment of a piece of the company's profits to its owners. Failing to pay a dividend is common among growth-hungry Silicon Valley tech giants, which plow most revenues into investments for continued expansion. However, in March 2012 new CEO Tim Cook finally did just that, partially due to the company's gigantic foreign cash pile, which reached a peak of a quarter trillion dollars in 2017. (Some of this cash was built up under an arrangement with Ireland that allowed Apple to avoid almost all tax on its foreign earnings, which the EU has since declared illegal.) Apple openly said it wouldn't bring that cash home until US tax law changed—which, thanks to the 2017 tax bill that President Trump signed into law, it did. The vast majority of the foreign cash was returned under the low onetime 15.5 percent rate on foreign earnings, allowing the company to engage in a $100 billion stock buyback plan for its wealthy stockholders rather than make job-creating investments.[61]

In another sign of industrial maturity, Apple has built an insanely fancy new headquarters in Cupertino, California, a gigantic ring-shaped hive that cost $5 billion to construct. The *Journal*'s business section put it perfectly in a headline: "At Apple, One Ring to Bind Them All: Booming technology titans build glitzy architectural marvels to project power."[62] When its cutting-edge theater for product launches was opened, company cofounder Wozniak remarked, "Wow, this is not normal."[63]

Spoiling the Others

But as with all corporations, it's the workers who actually design the specs, build the device, and flog the products. And the labor policies of the world's biggest corporation are emblematic of the early twenty-first century—temporary work, long hours under extreme duress, low pay relative to the company's towering profits, and conformity to corporate hierarchy. That came into clear view when a longtime *Wired* journalist and prominent Apple ass-kisser wrote of Jobs's "acid humiliation" of workers "even on occasions when Jobs himself was unqualified to judge the quality of the work in question." He recounts an episode in which Jobs aggressively belittled an employee, "complaining about a preexisting problem that the employee hadn't even addressed yet. Defending yourself was out of the question."[64] As "revolutionary" as Apple pitches itself to be, its workplace hierarchy is based on the same thing as every other business: capitalist class power.

Jobs was long on taking credit for his workers' labors, but he was not an engineer himself, to the point that his staff sometimes committed "silent mutinies" over his dictates, like adding more memory to the famously wimpy original Mac.[65] But those workers were exploited to the limits that were acceptable in the professional classes of the developed world; some wore T-shirts reading "90 HRS/WK AND LOVING IT." Likewise, programmers for big product launches referred to the weeks- or months-long grinds without seeing their families as "death marches," much like what employees have reported at Microsoft.[66] A Silicon Valley businessman comments, "No other company has that level of fear," although as this book shows, that's a competitive distinction.[67]

Indeed, even things that would be utterly conventional at less secretive corporations, like a company organizational chart, are hoarded by management and deliberately made unavailable to the workforce. When business magazine *Fortune* designed its own Apple organizational chart in 2011, outsiders visiting the campus said workers were eager to avoid being seen looking at it.[68] Nondisclosure agreements, in which a party legally swears not to publicly disclose embarrassing information, are commonly used in corporate settings to gag employees from blowing the whistle on their dirty dealings. But at Apple, some new hires have to sign a "preliminary NDA first, agreeing that they would never discuss the existence of the next NDA they were about to sign, in case they didn't want to sign that one."[69]

But the software these white-collar employees write for the phones would be useless, of course, if not for the physical electronics themselves. And Apple's toys are brought into being, on the most physical level, the same way other home electronics are—with highly exploited third-world labor. Child miners in Bolivia's globally infamous Potosí mine bring out the silver content; brutalized Congolese miners produce the cobalt and tantalum. The rare earth metals come from China's Inner Mongolia Province, the tin from Indonesia in a mine marked by small pay and high worker mortality. As ephemeral and increasingly services-based as Apple's business is, its hardware comes from hard labor.

But Apple's most notorious labor issues involve its principal contractor, the giant Taiwanese manufacturer Foxconn (formally known as Hon Hai Precision Industry), which makes electronic parts and assembling final units for many global electronics firms. A gigantic corporation itself, it employs a staggering 1.3 million people—twice the raw head count of all five top tech giants put together.[70] It became infamous in 2010 after reports of a series of suicides in its gigantic manufacturing complexes.

Conditions on the factory floor include psychotic production speeds of smartphones and video game consoles, in twelve-hour shifts. Workers who do not meet the borderline-impossible production quotas have their workstation sign turn red, and are afterward subject to extended public humiliation by line supervisors. (Notably, some Apple engineers have commented on "eerie parallels with this and the public humiliation" Jobs subjected his own white-collar teams to.)[71] Workers are expected to be silent on the line, and they report being rebuked for requesting restroom breaks. Turnover is extremely high, for those who can afford to quit. Such exploitation is how Apple is able to maintain its gigantic profit margins on its products, and still turn over its entire corporate inventory every five days.

In protest and despair of this exploitation, more than a dozen workers in 2010 alone threw themselves from the enormous factory dorm buildings, with similar numbers talked down by management. The corporate reaction was to install suicide nets on the rims of the buildings. In true dark comedy, management also ordered workers to sign oaths not to commit suicide.[72] Also hilariously, Jobs claimed "Foxconn is not a sweatshop," while his heir Tim Cook toured the United States with a company PR team calling for corporate "moral responsibility."[73]

While these abuses were widely reported—something human rights workers have said is helpful in putting pressure on the company—the more interesting part of the story is what happened next. Journalist Brian Merchant relates: "In 2012, a hundred and fifty workers gathered on a rooftop and threatened to jump. They were promised improvements and talked down by management; they had, essentially, wielded the threat of suicide as a bargaining tool. In 2016, a smaller group did it again."[74] This astonishing turn is a rare instance of a suicide strike, demonstrating that worker inventiveness and solidarity can still wring concessions out of capital, even possibly at life's last instant.

But even in far better work conditions thousands of miles away, Apple's US operations still exploit labor to the greatest degree possible. Apple's stores are certainly a sensation by retail standards, as its mall outlets have stupendous revenue-per-square-foot numbers, even as the overall sector declines in competition with online commerce, above all with Amazon's platform. But service work, including retail, remains based on today's "neoliberal" approach of offering limited pay and little to no benefits and hoping that the worker moves on after a few years. Apple has kept tightly to this approach—while each Apple retail employee handles over $480,000 in sales a year, they earn no commission and wages run in the neighborhood of nine to fifteen dollars per hour.[75]

Speaking to the *New York Times*, a sales staff member said workers are so enamored of Apple's brand that they're willing to work for less: "When you're working for Apple you feel like you're working for this greater good. That's why they don't want a revolution on their hands." On top of receiving low pay, the "Genius Bar" technicians who troubleshoot devices were ordered to limit customer appointments to ten minutes as the stores' popularity took off, which could lead to large pileups of customers stuffed around the help area if complaints took longer to cope with. Many techs ended up missing their state law–required breaks and then were required to affirm when clocking out that they had taken them, even when they hadn't.[76]

San Francisco workers found that "some systemic problems" were too challenging to cope with, like management giving part-time workers full-time hours without changing them to benefits-eligible status. And so, using social media and then a dedicated website to reach other stores' employees, but refraining from using the word "union," workers began organizing the flagship store. Management quickly distributed "union training materials" to scare workers off, but ultimately it had to resort to offering early pay hikes and even extending benefits packages to part-timers. That reaction again shows that organizing retains its strength even in the Big Tech era. However, as often happens when management shows some flexibility and spreads around some relatively petty wealth, the organizing drive lost momentum.

But the ultimate story of labor at Apple is probably the wage-fixing conspiracy. From 2005 to 2010, the market for software engineers became rather tight as fast-growing giants Google and then Facebook aggressively hired to build out their platforms (discussed at greater length in chapters 5 and 6). Typically, tight wages lead to higher pay when workers are scarce, and that probably would have been the result, had a legally adjudicated corporate conspiracy in Silicon Valley not acted to keep salaries in line. And Steve Jobs's Apple was at the center of it.

The plan was based on a set of no-poaching agreements, in which Big Tech companies secretly agreed not to cold-call experienced engineers at other companies. The rationale behind the agreements is that because experienced software designers are rare, they are unlikely to respond to simpler hiring techniques like job listings or employment fairs, while direct cold-calling yields somewhat better results. Once again, thanks to the subsequent court cases filed over the agreements, we have internal documents and emails from the great tech powers, and they're even juicier than the Microsoft antitrust memos.

Among the evidence were emails from ringleader Jobs, who, for example, wrote to Google CEO Eric Schmidt in response to its efforts to recruit Apple engineers, "If you hire a single one of these people, that means war." Given the mutual reliance of those firms reviewed above, the threat was not empty. Google's human resources hiring documents indicated that Google had "special agreements" with certain companies and were thus on "Restricted Hiring" lists, and also a "Do Not Cold Call" list that included Apple, Microsoft, Intel, and other tech and telecom firms like IBM and Comcast.[77]

Apple reciprocated, with an internal email reading: "Please add Google to your 'hands-off' list. We recently agreed not to recruit from one another so if you hear of any recruiting they are doing against us, please be sure to let me know." Emails from Schmidt on the subject started with "DO NOT FORWARD," and indeed in later emails that referred to bringing eBay into the circle, he wrote that he would "prefer" that the communication be done "verbally since I don't want to create a paper trail over which we can be sued later?" His HR head replied, "Makes sense to do orally. i agree."

At one point a Google recruiter, apparently ignoring the illegal agreements still in effect, attempted a cold call to hire an Apple employee working on web browsers. Jobs complained peevishly to a chastened Schmidt, who shortly wrote back to Jobs with an email saying the offending recruiter would be "fired within the hour." Jobs responded with a smiley face.[78]

Later, when word of the wage-fixing deals got out, the companies faced a Justice Department lawsuit and then a large civil suit by sixty-four thousand employees. The DOJ action was settled with an agreement that the firms wouldn't collude again to restrict attempted recruiting, even though, of course, the behavior was already illegal. But the class action suit was the bigger affair, and it resulted in the presiding judge making the unusual move of rejecting an early settlement.[79] That original $324 million settlement was later raised in 2015 to $435 million, to be paid by the various corporations involved, coming to several grand awarded per class member.

The point of the episode was summarized by liberal economist Dean Baker, who observed that the scandal proved Silicon Valley libertarians

> really don't think about the market the way [they] claim to think about the market. The classic libertarian view of the market is that we have a huge number of people in the market actively competing. . . . There is so much competition that no individual or company can really hope to have much impact on market outcomes. . . . However, the Silicon Valley non-compete agreements show that this is not how the tech billionaires believe the market really works. This is just a story they peddle to children and gullible reporters. . . . They believed that they had enough weight on the buy-side of the market for software engineers that if they agreed not to compete for workers, they could keep their wages down.[80]

As we saw in the opening of this chapter, Apple began with a real revolutionary spirit, and carried it into a corporate golden age with an anti-establishment marketing slant. However, the rules of capitalism and platform economics meant that the company became a great anti-worker institution, married to the most conservative institutions of our time and incredibly aggressive in defending and expanding its strictly controlled territory, from driving workers to suicide to wrecking the environment to conspiring illegally against their engineers.

The early days may have been marked with a revolutionary spirit and commercials quoting socialists like Orwell, but monopoly capitalism has its effects. An Apple software manager on the original iPhone team put it well: "It's interesting to see how people perceive the company now versus then, how that has changed. It's not that kind of Rebel Alliance vibe—we're Big Brother now."[81]

CHAPTER 4

Amazon's Smile

Snowballing scale in online retail

Amazon's founder and CEO Jeff Bezos became the world's richest man in the summer of 2017, edging out former Microsoft CEO Bill Gates, who held the title for a decade—although that's after Gates put billions into his foundation while he was looking bad in the press during the trial for his PC operating system monopoly. Bezos retained the crown even after his 2019 divorce, the world's most expensive, and also retained control of company voting rights.[1] Bezos's $108 billion fortune arose from his enormous company, which in recent years has traded the title of number one largest company globally with Microsoft and tech colossus Apple.

Amazon says its huge growth and success owes to being "obsessed with the consumer." In fact, the record shows the company's rise has been fueled by the growth-boosting momentum of economic network effects, horrifying levels of labor exploitation at both the white- and blue-collar levels, and a boost from a fortunate sales tax exemption.

But most interestingly, in the very early startup days of the company, Bezos explained to a colleague why the company was so hell-bent on fast growth: "When you are small, someone else that is bigger can always come along and take away what you have. . . . We have to level the playing field in terms of purchasing power with the established booksellers."[2] But once Amazon itself reached great stature, it did not encourage a level playing field; rather, it used its own increased leverage and bargaining power to drive whole market sectors into surrendering their profitability to Amazon's growth. As a former content writer for the company's front page wrote, "As the public saw it, we had morphed from David to Goliath."[3]

Formerly "Relentless"

Bezos founded the company after several successful years at a Wall Street hedge fund. From the very beginning, the plan was to "exploit" the Internet, as Bezos's biographers describe the business model.[4] The Internet itself was developed by public research entities including the Pentagon's research arm, DARPA (where Amazon's first tech officer previously worked), and European physics research agencies. The strategic value of running a retail business online was that it had almost no "transaction costs"—the term economists use to describe the costs of doing a deal. In-person retail requires significant transaction costs, like driving to a store, paying for gas or transit, conforming to retail hours, and the nuisance of being presentable enough to appear in public. Shopping via the then brand-new World Wide Web potentially offered major convenience, as it does to this day. These lower transaction costs have been a major part of online retail's expansion at the expense of brick-and-mortar stores.

Bezos actually chose books to begin building his empire for purely utilitarian reasons—they shipped relatively well, didn't spoil, and were available from wholesalers. The company soon became the standard for rapid growth—the original company motto was "Get big fast." Sales grew quickly in the mid-1990s, with the company expanding into new merchandise categories like DVDs and music, and then toys and electronics. The goal of unceasing growth was fundamental in those far-smaller days—among possible early names for the company was Relentless.com—type it in your web browser and it still takes you to Amazon.[5]

The company's growth was stupendous, with its top-line revenue shooting up by over 50 percent during some quarters, before gradually lowering into 20 percent growth per quarter as the laws of large numbers kicked in. These numbers were still huge, however. This famously fast growth owed to many factors. Beyond the low transaction costs of the business model, there was also the fact that years of previous consolidation in the bookselling industry had left large stretches of the United States with few or no bookstores, creating a near-captive market for Amazon.

But the crucial factor was the network effects. In markets run through networks, services get more valuable as more people use them, like the telephone network. Over time Amazon has had a number of features fitting this pattern, including in the very early days, when the book review feature was added. Business journalist Brad Stone explains that "Bezos believed that if Amazon.com had more user-generated book reviews than any other site, it would give the company a huge advantage; customers would be less inclined to go to other online bookstores."[6]

Author Nicholas Carr, too, observes that "much of Amazon.com's early appeal came from the book reviews donated by customers."[7] This constitutes a mild net effect, as the number of customers writing reviews made the site more attractive to others. Bezos himself recognized the dynamic at play, and according to Stone, once said that "the company that got the lead now would likely keep it"—a recognition of a key feature of the network industries we've already observed.[8]

But the real net effects arose as Amazon gradually groped toward becoming not just a sprawling online retailer, but a platform—a network based on allowing other users to bring their own goods to sell at the company's central network location. For Microsoft and Apple, this meant software applications running on their PC operating systems or mobile phones, whereas for merchandise-mover Amazon it meant creating an essential venue for other retailers. Indeed, Amazon execs saw Microsoft as the archetype for this business model.[9]

The platform was built over several fits and starts, beginning in 1997 when the company opened Amazon Auctions, then zShops, both of them attempts to get smaller retailers to set up virtual storefronts on Amazon's larger site. These sites saw little business, but Bezos kept them open, suggesting his understanding of platform economics, as he told execs he hoped for third-party sales via these sites to grow as fast as the company's own sales. Indeed, former Amazon front-page writer James Marcus claims Bezos openly said at the time that "if necessary, we should decimate the books division to make [the] auctions [division] work."[10] This may have been an overreaction to the rise of auction site eBay, but it also speaks to Bezos's clear vision of network effects. When sales from zShops stagnated, Bezos realized they could be juiced by linking to those third-party items from Amazon's own product pages. As Stone puts it, that move "was the central insight that not only turned Amazon into a thriving platform for small online merchants but powers a good deal of its success today."[11]

That's because higher sales of all types meant higher volumes with lower costs, allowing Amazon to lower its prices, a short-term boon to the consumer but also a move bringing more business to the company, allowing it to further cut costs and, of course, to attract more third-party sellers to its platform. It was thus a self-reinforcing virtuous cycle the company called its "flywheel," better known as "platform economics." The conservative *Economist* magazine found Amazon enjoyed not only "increasing returns," including the capitalist hallmark of "economies of scale," but also network effects: "More shoppers on the Amazon site make it more alluring to third-party sellers, which increases the range of goods it can offer, which attracts more shoppers."[12]

The company's huge growth became caught up in the feverish mania of the 1990s tech stock bubble, and only a luckily timed issue of bonds just before the 2000 crash kept the company from declaring bankruptcy, unlike many of its ignominious tech-bubble colleagues. By 2002, third-party sales had reached a third of cash flow.[13] Also in that year, Amazon, no longer enjoying the protection of the tech bubble, was forced to turn its first modest profit to appease investors. But the company kept its foot on the gas to build its platform power.

That push forward included the creation of Prime, Amazon's loyalty program that offers fast shipping (and now streaming media) for an annual fee. The program lost money for several years, but, as a company exec said, "it was really about changing people's mentality so they wouldn't shop anywhere else." This again helped drive up volumes and push down costs, and allowed more aggressive negotiations with suppliers. But above all the drive to retain and expand the platform, connecting buyers and other sellers, was the biggest goal—the company's later invention of Prime Day, a national Amazon-themed shopping holiday, was "another way to tighten its grip on shoppers," as the conservative *Wall Street Journal* put it.[14]

The platform push continued, and by 2012 Amazon's third-party sellers sold nearly 40 percent of the items shipped, with over two million retailers on the rechristened Amazon Marketplace.[15] By 2019, 58 percent of all sales came from Marketplace, with almost 1 percent of all Americans selling goods on Amazon.[16] Taking a flat commission off each sale in the neighborhood of 10 percent, the platform was profitable and above all became a magnet for thousands of small and midsize companies wanting to sell on Amazon's incredibly visible website, without having to create their own web presence. The *Journal* reported that "those sales are nearly pure profit margin because Amazon doesn't have to buy and hold the product itself. It also gets paid for items that sellers ship in for Amazon to fulfill."[17]

But as owner of the platform, Amazon takes advantage beyond the commission. When particular items sell unusually well, the company takes note and starts selling them itself, meaning the small sellers are in part product scouts for Amazon. The company claims not to do this, with an exec asserting, "We do not allow anyone inside Amazon to have access to individual sellers' data in order to build a private-label product."[18] But product data are what would help a company most in picking a category to invade, and this disavowal of sharing precious data between different arms of one company sounds a lot like the "Chinese Wall" that some execs alleged to exist between Microsoft's operating system and application arms. Bill Gates and others later mocked the silly idea, making it at least plausible that Amazon is happy to look at independent seller data to develop its own brands. And indeed, in time Amazon began its "Accelerator" program for third-party merchants, giving them more prominent placement on the crowded site, and waived fees and other perks, in exchange for which Amazon gains the right to buy the brand outright for a mere $10,000, crumbs to the world's richest man.[19] This strongly suggests Amazon is interested in profiling indie merchants for profitable categories.

Further, because small sellers are competing among one another and Amazon proper, the Marketplace platform creates a "race to zero," as one entrepreneur calls it, with sellers aggressively fighting to offer the very lowest price point since doing so puts their offering in the website's "buy box," Amazon's default selling slot for the product.[20] But because of Amazon's hundreds of millions of customers and the site's visibility, even those companies that get fed up with this setup tend ultimately to return, their arms twisted by platform economics.

To this day, Amazon prioritizes the health and growth of the platform. Its financial filings describe its "A2Z Guarantee," which will "reimburse buyers [of independent sellers' products] for payments up to certain limits" if the product isn't received or doesn't match the descriptions, although "as our marketplace seller sales grow, the cost of this program will increase and could negatively affect our operating results."[21] The company has essentially put itself on the hook for making petty fraud victims whole in order to preserve its platform.

Maintaining the platform's growth has come at various costs. One is difficult relations with big brand-name companies and luxury goods sellers, who fear that the price cutting common in the Marketplace is undermining their brand prestige and pricing power, along with advancing a brisk trade in knockoffs. Apple famously refuses to provide iPhones to Amazon for resale, and brands like Nike and Louis Vuitton fear the loss of "a sense of exclusivity," as the *Journal* put it.[22]

More impressively, to protect and expand the platform, Amazon actually began lowering the prices charged by the independent sellers and paying the difference itself. This "Discount provided by Amazon" measure would make no damn sense at all, unless we realize the importance the company puts on its platform power.[23] And as Amazon and the other tech platforms expand globally, Amazon has resorted to actively "recruiting" small merchants to sell on its site, to build out its platform power in other major economies like India. The business press reports Amazon has gone to the extent of lending small firms the money for inventory in order to get it available on Amazon.in, thereby gravitationally attracting more business.[24] The company even faced a legal challenge in 2018 from eBay, which filed a lawsuit accusing Amazon of poaching its higher-value sellers by infiltrating its internal member message system.

As Amazon grew, it continued to lose money overall—an enduring feature of most of the company's history and often held up to showcase the "boldness" of Bezos and his venture capitalist (VC) backers, bravely withstanding heavy losses in the name of growth. But obviously, most businesspeople can't get away with such a strategy—if your company keeps losing money, your VC backers on the board are going to throw you out and get a new CEO who makes them money. So how could Bezos keep his investors from getting spooked? Business reporting has regularly concluded that it's Amazon's gigantic, platform-fueled growth rate that's kept them quiet.[25] This growth into ever more industries means insane future profits and enormous market power, and investors have by and large been willing to accept this. But this all means Amazon's bold acceptance of near-term losses or tiny profits, along with Bezos's famous claim that "your margin is my opportunity," can all be attributed to one thing—network effects.

In addition to this long history of platform building, Amazon's "Relentless" expansion also relied on its exemption from collecting state sales tax (save in its home state of Washington), as national law for decades spared online retailers from collecting it in states where it had no substantial physical presence. Amazon went to great lengths to protect this advantage over brick-and-mortar stores—as it grew and built giant sorting centers for its widening selection of merchandise, it cutely classified them as "wholly owned subsidiaries" earning no revenue.[26] Indeed, before opening these giant centers it would often negotiate with each state in order to secure gentle tax treatment in exchange for hiring local workers. When cash-strapped states started declaring Amazon's affiliate sites (websites carrying its ads) to be storefronts qualifying for state taxes, Bezos cut off the affiliates rather than confront a tax bill.

Most amazingly, Bezos justified these tightfisted moves by claiming the company got no benefit from public services and thus should be exempt from the taxes that paid for them: "We're not actually benefiting from any services that those states provide locally, so it's not fair that we should be obligated to be their tax collection agent since we're not getting any of the services."[27] This is arguably the most degenerately stupid statement made by the tech CEOs in this book—Amazon is a huge devourer of public services—it intensively uses public roads with its fleets of owned and hired delivery trucks; it leans heavily on intellectual property laws to protect its numerous patents; and it demanded in its search for a second US headquarters that the local workforce be highly educated. Compared with a typical human family, Amazon is a giant public services hog, and Bezos's pitiful claim otherwise is a hideous farce.

Indeed, the company's 10-K filing for fiscal year 2016 states, "We regard our trademarks, service marks, copyrights, patents . . .

and similar intellectual property as critical to our success, and we rely on trademark, copyright, and patent law . . . to protect our proprietary rights."[28] For example, Bezos patented the site's "1-Click" ordering functionality, forcing Apple to pay a lucrative license fee to use it for iTunes. But despite its dependence on the government to protect its intellectual property, Amazon devours most of its public services at the state and local level, as its trucks and hired delivery partners drive a surging river of products to homes nationwide, putting wear on those expensive infrastructures. So Bezos's opportunistic, self-serving claim of Amazon not benefiting from public services doesn't pass the laugh test.

And even when Amazon finally yielded to increasing numbers of states forcing it to collect sales taxes to remit to state treasuries (and beginning to call for a single national standard), it usually worked out deals to delay the start date by a few years. And far more importantly, Amazon *exempted* the sales of its third-party sellers when adding the tax, leaving it to them to collect it, and thus remained rare. The US Supreme Court ruled in 2018 that e-commerce operators like Amazon must collect sales taxes, but the ruling only applied to those crucial third-party sales in the fifteen states that have enacted legislation putting tax collection responsibility on "market facilitators" like Amazon.[29] This shows again that Amazon holds its platform above anything else, maintaining after all these years the significant edge of not collecting taxes on indie sales in most states, even as Marketplace sales make up over half Amazon's total.

And the picture looks unlikely to change, since Amazon's SEC filings indicate they hold over $600 million in federal tax credits, to be used to offset future taxes. Amazon received these credits mainly under the US research and development tax credit program.[30] And the *Seattle Post-Intelligencer* reported that Amazon's own regulatory filings indicate the gigantic organization paid nothing in federal income taxes in 2017.[31]

As of this writing, Amazon is now the second-biggest company in the world by market value (behind Microsoft and ahead of Apple, Google, and Facebook), with $177 billion in yearly revenue and a few billion in actual yearly profit, thanks mainly to its remote-computing cloud services unit. This gigantic firm has developed a major internal hierarchy, despite Bezos having claimed that "a hierarchy isn't responsive enough to change," and early on delegating decision making to various business units. Stone notes: "Microsoft took a top-down management approach with layers of middle managers, a system that ended up slowing decisions and stifling innovation. Looking at the muffled and unhappy hierarchy of the software giant across Lake Washington" turned Bezos away from a corporate ladder, we're told. This led to the famous "two-pizza teams," small numbers of workers (able to be fed by two pizzas) working autonomously toward management-set goals.[32]

Yet despite this feel-good decentralization rhetoric and day-to-day autonomy, the reality of capitalist workplace hierarchy is very present at the company. It adopted from Microsoft a system of numerically ranking workers and then firing the low-rated ones.[33] When complaints or customer-related problems reach Bezos, he's known to forward the email to a unit manager with a mere "?" at the top, which to employees "has the effect of a ticking time bomb" indicating they have hours to fix the problem. Their fix "will be reviewed by a succession of managers before the answer is presented to Bezos himself."[34] These question mark–tagged emails are called "escalations" within the company, an interesting terminological parallel to Apple, whose "escalations" refer to requests for quick repairs and upgrades from celebrities or VIPs.

Stone reports that "Amazon styles itself as highly decentralized and promises that new employees can make decisions independently. But Bezos is capable of stopping any process dead in its tracks," and employees can find themselves "in the hottest possible spot at Amazon: under the withering eye of the founder himself."[35]

And that's not so good, since even Amazon's most sycophantic yes-men in the field of business journalism describe Bezos as a particularly notorious corporate tyrant. Much like the other executive-founders profiled in this book, the picture conforms toward the same temper tantrum–throwing corporate bullying seen across the tech sector and indeed capitalism in general. Bezos is so prone to over-the-top chewing-out of his subordinates that they began referring to his "nutters," and actually compiled a list of the worst episodes. Highlights listed in corporate histories include "Are you lazy or just incompetent?," "If I hear that idea again, I'm gonna have to kill myself," and "Do I need to go down and get the certificate that says I'm CEO of the company to get you to stop challenging me on this?"[36] Clearly no corporate hierarchy here! Bezos later hired a management coach, surely fixing the issue completely. Or not. Describing a company pep rally where Bezos "chewed out" a logistics exec onstage with "a very public, very petulant scolding," one observer noted that the outburst led to no one wanting to sit with Bezos and his wife at the post-speech dinner.[37]

Unsurprisingly, Bezos is politically inclined toward libertarianism, a preference picked up from his prosperous oil-engineer father who fled the expropriations of the Cuban Revolution. But again, nothing about Bezos's personality or political proclivities would be important or interesting except that thanks to the centralized power wielded by huge corporations under capitalism, he has enormous power over people.

Leaders of this type, including Bill Gates and Steve Jobs, are well known to be idolized and imitated by their corporate subordinates, as illustrated by Gates's rooms full of rocking men and Jobs's campus of turtlenecked jackasses. Likewise, Bezos has cultivated his own inner circle of dickish subordinates that, as Stone reports, even within the company have the "playfully derisive" nickname "Jeff Bots."[38] Like the other power-mongering capitalist lieutenants of the tech giants in this book, these MBAs praise their boss frequently and recite his management ideas like cult members.

Luckily, the Jeff Bots don't act at their full discretion—actual robots are involved, too. Amazon is among the leaders of the "optimization" of business processes, using metrics to evaluate every decision and then building the preferences into the algorithms that run a large part of the day-to-day activity on the platform. In the past, Amazon had book-category and genre pages that attracted significant online readership, and the website's front page was carefully curated by writers as well as corporate sales staff. Long ago those staff were laid off or reassigned as these functions could be conducted automatically. In his memoir *Amazonia*, former company writer James Marcus describes being replaced by the "Culture of Metrics," which "had an Orwellian ring to it."[39] This automation is perhaps a sign of encouraging gains in productivity in the abstract, but today Amazon relies on these systems to regularly "scrape" pricing data from competitors' sites and then automatically match or slightly underprice them, in order to leverage its platform power into more market share.[40] As we'll explore in the discussion of technology in chapter 8, algorithms are typically written by managers and other representatives of corporate power.

As the richest man on God's earth, Bezos's $108 billion has allowed him the usual bouquet of lush properties—the ten-acre mansion complex in the same posh Seattle suburb as Gates, four adjoining luxury apartments in Manhattan, three hundred thousand acres in Texas, and a pair of neighboring houses in Beverly Hills. The neighbors say that "Mr. Bezos doesn't seem to be home very often," reflecting the busy lifestyle of the man the *Wall Street Journal* calls "the Amazon czar."[41] More impressive are Bezos's new twin mansions in Washington, DC, the former site of the Textile Museum. More public than the Amazon CEO's other properties, the mansion is expected to be Bezos's launchpad for extensive DC lobbying and influence mongering, much as the LA properties are in part intended to anchor Amazon's big push into movies and TV.

The gigantic firm finally reached a scale where it could manage a dividend in 2015, and the next year it even began buying back stock to more directly enrich its wealthy shareholders. But the gigantic twisted giant that is Amazon has proven itself to be a true bully of the markets, with a long history of using its huge market weight to undo client after competitor after customer. It's a fascinating story, in which the company again and again justifies its ever-growing power in the laws of the jungle whose name it takes.

Let Us Prey

Amazon's explosive growth soon proved Bezos correct that "when you are small, someone else that is bigger can always come along and take away what you have." But now it was Amazon that was bigger, and it would do the taking. Surviving the dot-com crash thanks to its well-timed bond sale, Amazon pushed past additional growing pains, including a lawsuit from Walmart after several of its execs defected from the offline tyrant to the online one. It also faced down a scandal when the *New York Times* reported many of Amazon's recommended products were chosen as a result of the seller making "co-op" payments—what is often called "payola" in other industries, a term referring to any undisclosed payment by a company for favorable promotion of its good or service.[42] But Amazon's growth continued and led it to gain increasing credibility with manufacturers and suppliers, which in turn led to getting direct shipments from them.

Amazon's enormous power is now relatively well recognized in the mainstream, including what economists call "monopsony" power—the ability to exert power as a huge buyer, which is distinct from the selling power of a monopoly.[43] This became relevant fairly early in Amazon's record of torrid growth and in its negotiations with UPS, the major US commercial shipping company. Amazon had contracted with them for much of its shipping, but as its stature rose, Amazon approached Federal Express (today known as FedEx) and began quietly integrating their data systems while increasing shipments.

When UPS declined to negotiate rates, Amazon virtually cut it off as a shipping vendor, such that UPS went from receiving millions of Amazon parcels daily to only a handful. Its cultivation of FedEx, combined with Amazon's ability to rely on the US Postal

Service to deliver a large number of boxes—allowing it to continue smooth service for buyers—meant UPS caved after seventy-two hours and offered Bezos lower rates. Stone observes that the experience taught "the company an enduring lesson about the power of scale and the reality of Darwinian survival in the world of big business."[44] This natural selection framework is frequently used to justify the business world, but it's a pretty phony use of the idea because while successful biological organisms must start over each generation—as new individuals may inherit their parents' successful traits but must fend and grow for themselves—corporations absorb their rivals, and grow and grow.

The case of Amazon and baby products shows how monopolization works in real-world markets: through predatory business strategy. As Amazon expanded into more and more product categories, certain holdouts came to its attention. One was Diapers.com, a startup selling baby products, run by entrepreneurs who idolized Bezos. The delivery service was a godsend to some exhausted parents, and the small outfit attracted millions in venture capital investments, bringing them to the attention of Bezos's executive team.

Spotting potential prey, Bezos's team told the Diapers.com founders that Amazon was readying a large launch into the category, and therefore it would be in everyone's best interest to negotiate a buyout immediately. When this "offer" was declined, Amazon cut prices for baby products by up to 30 percent, although Amazon later said its pricing had nothing to do with this upstart company. But hilariously, the small businesspeople noticed that when they tweaked their posted online prices, the Amazon website's algorithms changed its own prices accordingly.[45] The gigantic company's web-crawling software was automatically tracking the prices of its small competitor.

While the startup flirted with selling itself to Walmart, Amazon ratcheted up the existential pressure by announcing a new loyalty program offering a whopping additional 30 percent off diapers in return for joining a subscription program, Amazon Mom. Diapers.com staff estimated the program was losing $100 million a quarter, and once Diapers caved and sold, Amazon closed its money-losing program to new members, although it later had to hastily reopen it after the Federal Trade Commission started sniffing around.[46] These moves show that Amazon wasn't trying in good faith to compete, as sunny libertarian pictures of markets assume. Rather than being "obsessed with the customer" and seeing who could best satisfy the market demand for the lowest sustainable price, Amazon purposefully ran the category at a giant loss in order to drive its smaller, cash-poorer rival out of the market, and then monopolized it. It's a predator—a gigantic, immortal economic predator gaining strength with each meal. Capitalism keeps its stripes!

But books were Amazon's original market category, and in the end they were the site of its cruelest predations.

By 2004, Amazon was selling a large portion of the books purchased in the United States. So it began to display its now-famous aggression with publishers, and here I quote at length a recounting by Stone, revealing, among other things, the frank, analytical approach of corporate reporting:

> Amazon approached large publishers aggressively. It demanded accommodations like steeper discounts on bulk purchases, longer periods to pay its bills, and shipping arrangements that leveraged Amazon's discounts with UPS. To publishers that didn't comply, Amazon threatened to pull their books out of its automated personalization and recommendation systems, meaning that they would no longer be suggested to consumers. . . . Amazon had an easy way to demonstrate its market power. When a publisher did not capitulate and the company shut off the recommendation algorithms for its books, the publisher's sales usually fell by as much as 40 percent. "Typically it was about thirty days before they'd come back and say, Ouch, how do we make this work?" says Christopher Smith, a senior book buyer at the time.
>
> Bezos kept pushing for more. He asked [then–head of Amazon publisher relations Lyn] Blake to exact better terms

from the smaller publishers, who would go out of business if it weren't for the steady sales of their back catalogs on Amazon. Within the books group, the resulting program was dubbed the Gazelle Project because Bezos suggested to Blake in a meeting Amazon should approach these small publishers the way a cheetah would pursue a sickly gazelle.

As part of the Gazelle Project, Blake's group categorized publishers in terms of their dependency on Amazon and then opened negotiations with the most vulnerable companies.[47]

Yes, Bezos sees himself as a predator, even though his sharp teeth arise not from his own prowess but from the large size of his corporation, which itself owes mainly to network effects underwriting its fast growth. Stone adds that "soon after the Gazelle Project began, Amazon's lawyers heard about the name and insisted it be changed to the less incendiary Small Publisher Negotiation Program."[48]

Stone notes that these lower wholesale book prices allowed Amazon to lower its retail prices, which attracted more consumers and put more pressure on physical bookstores. The record is full of episodes where executives openly acted as predators to remove competition. "By his own admission," one executive (named Randy Miller) charged with squeezing publishing houses

> took an almost sadistic delight in pressuring book publishers to give Amazon more favorable terms. He ranked all of the European publishers by their sales and . . . persuaded the lagging members to alter their deals . . . once again with the threat of decreased promotion on the site. Miller says he and his colleagues called the program Pay to Play. Once again, Amazon's lawyers caught wind of this and renamed the program Vendor Realignment.

When negotiating with European publishers,

> "I did everything I could to screw with their performance," he says. He took selections of their catalog to full price and yanked their books from Amazon's recommendation engine;

with some titles, like travel books, he promoted comparable books from competitors. . . . These tactics were not unique to Amazon. The company had finally learned the tricks of the century-old trade that is modern retail. . . . Walmart in particular had mastered this perpetual coercion of suppliers, and it did it with missionary zeal and the belief that it led to the low prices [the company promoted].[49]

Against this background of naked power plays, by the mid-2000s Amazon had finally reached a scale where it could match Walmart's price cuts, and for some years it even won contracts to run the online commerce sites of Target and Borders books, as they had fumbled the development of their own web presences.

The giant brick-and-mortar booksellers Borders and Barnes & Noble never launched online operations that could compete, leading in large part to the latter's constant retrenchment and the former's bankruptcy filing in 2011. This was an especially grotesque development, as Borders and B&N had pursued their own aggressive corporate expansion strategies, often siting their gigantic stores, with correspondingly huge selections, directly next to mom-and-pop independent bookstores. The small shops' inevitable closures in the face of the big-box giants meant that when they were in turn steamrolled by Amazon, millions of Americans were left without any local bookstore and thus no recourse but Amazon itself.

As the company turned the screws on the publishers, in 2004 it began to prepare the Kindle. Amazon had an early flirtation with online music, but Bezos realized that Steve Jobs beat him to the punch with the 2001 iTunes release, and he "ultimately concluded that if Amazon was to continue to thrive as a bookseller in a new digital age, it must own the e-book business in the same way that Apple controlled the music business."[50] This led the company to develop hardware for reading electronic versions of books, a risky strategy given Amazon's lack of manufacturing experience. Its eventual e-reader tablet, the Kindle, was far less versatile than a smartphone but had longer battery life and a better display for reading.

To make the new book format and device a success, Bezos apparently pulled the e-book price of $9.99 out of thin air, which, as a result of his power, had serious consequences for the publishing world. Amazon knew publishers would be horrified at this price point, which would be money-losing for the publishers, but it needed them to commit scarce resources to digitizing their large libraries in order to establish the platform power of the new device. So the executive staff decided not to give advance notice of this money-losing price point, lest the publishers balk, and so the publishing houses' first knowledge of it came when Bezos announced the product publicly in 2007.

Importantly, Amazon sustained its model of operating as a tech company as well as retailer and, like later Big Tech rivals Google and Facebook, never forgot to record a single thing a customer did, as Yasha Levine recounts: "Amazon deployed a system for monitoring and profiling. It recorded people's shopping habits, their movie preferences, the books they were interested in, how fast they read books on their Kindles, and the highlights and margin notes they made."[51]

The Kindle 2, released in 2009, was the breakout version, and in the years until Apple's release of the iPad in 2010 and Barnes & Noble's Nook e-reader in 2011, Amazon held a staggering 90 percent of the e-reader market. To the publishers, "Amazon's dawning monopoly in e-books was terrifying."[52] The enforced low prices "tilted the field" further against physical bookstores, and gave "Amazon even more market power. The publishers had seen over many years what Amazon did with this kind of additional leverage. It extracted more concessions and passed the savings on to customers in the form of lower prices and shipping discounts, which helped it amass even greater market shares—and more negotiating leverage."[53]

Amazon's rising demands and especially its under-ten-bucks prices drove European publishers to dig in their heels as the company apparently sought to "control every square on the publishing industry chessboard."[54] George Packer broke the story about payola's continuing role in Amazon's book recommendations, revealing in a 2014 piece for the *New Yorker* how "co-op" fees, extracted from the publishing houses to pay for said recommendations, grew along with Amazon's influence. Even large houses had effectively given Amazon a discount of over 50 percent, and for smaller houses it had reached 60 percent off, perilous numbers for an industry with notoriously thin profit margins.[55]

This led US publishing houses to take their famous "agency" action in 2010, which, with their joint 60 percent share of books sold on Amazon, demonstrated they were a collective threat with some countervailing bargaining power. By transitioning to an agency model, the book publishers would become their own retailers and could thus set their own retail prices. This plan did require another means to sell in the new and growing e-book market, but luckily by 2009 they had the option of another physical platform with Apple's iPad—although it was one that itself took a generous 30 percent commission.

Bezos lost his mind when word reached him of the industry's attempt to defy him, and Amazon removed the "Buy" buttons completely from Macmillan books after the publisher informed Kindle execs in person of the change. The company stripped the Kindle editions from its website for days as well. US monopoly scholar Barry Lynn writes, "The reasoning was obvious: the sudden loss of sales, which could amount to a sizable fraction of Macmillan's total revenue, would soon bring the publisher to heel."[56] Amazon even posted a public message on a company forum: "We have expressed our strong disagreement and the seriousness of our disagreement by temporarily ceasing the sale of Macmillan titles." The price increase actually made the Kindle more money for some time as Amazon's dominance of e-books only slowly eroded, while the book publishers were able to stay solvent through their ability to charge prices that better covered their digital and production costs.

Ironically, Bezos was able to get his revenge for this partially successful act of defiance. First, he contained the revolt by going to midsize publishers and bluntly telling them they didn't have the bargaining power to try the agency model as the larger firms had, and that Amazon would deliver a potentially fatal blow to their thinner margins if they tried. Then, staying true to his tendency to use the public services for which he doesn't feel obligated to pay taxes, he filed a complaint with the Federal Trade Commission, the US anti-monopoly regulator, and suggested that the publishers and Apple were conspiring to raise e-book prices.

The fact that Amazon held a near monopoly in these e-books didn't taint the move, because, as with Microsoft, Amazon had acquired its monopoly power without raising prices or merging with an oligopoly competitor. The FTC complaint gained steam after several imbecilically casual remarks from Steve Jobs about working with the publishing houses to raise book prices via the agency model, and ultimately the staggering book publishers were formally accused by the Justice Department of conspiracy, paying heavily to settle with the regulators. Apple contested the verdict, and the case spent years winding through court, while Bezos's Kindle grew fat with sales.

So Amazon, similar to other great monopoly capitalists like Rockefeller, has a long record of stopping at nothing to clear the market of competition, which stands in stark contrast to the conservative economists' rosy picture of healthy market efficiency. The lengths Bezos was willing to go to crush even small competitors are rough to read about. He forced the online shoe retailer Zappos to sell itself to Amazon after he spent $30 million building a separate website, Endless.com—which offered different styles and sizes of shoes with free overnight shipping—demonstrating Amazon's usual strategy of losing money to pull market share away from vulnerable competitors. This bite apparently wasn't enough to break the company, so Bezos, unbelievably, added a five-dollar bonus to its overnight shipping rates, meaning customers were paid five bucks to buy shoes. Faced with this plus several pressures arising from the Great Recession after 2007, including lower consumer spending and freezing credit lines, Zappos's investors sold out to Bezos, after which the shipping bonus was discontinued. He claimed, "When given the choice of obsessing over competitors or obsessing over customers, we always obsess over customers."[57] Obsessed with giving them five dollars until the market is consolidated, I guess.

The company's broader retail platform has grown through all this corporate arm wrestling, with Amazon being willing to antagonize higher-end companies by allowing the independent sellers to continue aggressive discounting. Companies like Sony and Black & Decker have gone back and forth with Amazon on allowing regular sales of their products on Marketplace at rock-bottom prices, but they usually come crawling back because of Amazon's unique market strength.

Amazon's pissing contests extend, of course, to the public sector. Amazon's self-serving views about not being obliged to pay for the public services it vacuums up reached a new level with the company's new headquarters search, which the *New York Times* described as "the most dramatic sweepstakes of modern capitalism."[58] After grandly announcing, in 2017, its need for a new "HQ2" to complement its enormous footprint in costly Seattle, the company received an ocean of applications from 238 North American cities and regions. By design, the process was a media frenzy, with endless free publicity for the company while America fell over itself trying to offer free things to the world's richest man.

The results were a truly pitiful display of local officials groveling. Cities filmed video after video overflowing with the empty language of marketing and conservative government, with flimsy attempts at charm. But, of course, Amazon's real interests were more material. The *Wall Street Journal* reported that the company's "in-house economic-development team shows how vital tax-incentive deals have become to its business model and gives a window into why the company pitted cities against each other to win the biggest subsidy package possible."[59] Amazon claims its "emphasis on taking advantage of incentives is part of its culture of frugality." A research report found the company had already raked in $1.1 billion from some form of public subsidy on its facilities and operations since 2000.[60]

Many of the bidders were among the poorest in North America, offering money and subsidies from budgets already bleeding and cutting back public services. Detroit offered the company thirty years tax-free. New Jersey and the city of Newark put together a staggering combined package of $7 billion in tax cuts and subsidies, and Governor Chris Christie openly dared other states to top it. Charmingly, the *Journal* noted that the company "has advised HQ2 candidates to keep this phase private."[61] And of course, why should we taxpayers intrude on this process, as the company decides where to move on the basis of how much of our tax money is thrown at it?

Worse, the very public nature of Amazon's search has led to "unintended demands" from other giant corporations now demanding the same sweeping concessions Amazon wrung out of the states, including the "hefty tax breaks."[62] The *Wall Street Journal* opined that "[this] is a pitfall that often accompanies large tax incentive packages used to lure employers to a state"—interesting from a paper that continuously supports granting more of those packages to our glorious job-creating companies. And, of course, Amazon ultimately made fools out of most North American cities by ultimately splitting the investments in New York and the Washington, DC, area—the two greatest existing centers of commercial and political influence and power in America.

The company now earns half of every dollar spent online, and it continues its relentless expansion: into food with its acquisition of pricey premium grocer Whole Foods, which it's integrating into its Prime discount and delivery service; into online advertising to compete with Google and Facebook; and into shipping by land, sea, and air, with its creation of a sea-freight forwarding service, plans for an air cargo hub, and the beginning of a "last-mile" delivery business.[63] And Bezos himself bought the journalism institution the *Washington Post* for half a billion dollars. But it's Amazon's growth in utterly new industries that is now getting the most attention.

The Cloud of War

Cloud computing refers to the development of technology allowing information-processing needs, like storage, database management, or processing power, to be provided online instead of through a company's own hardware. The data is stored and processed in computing centers built by tech companies—huge, windowless warehouse-like buildings filled with tall rows of computer servers, managing data or doing calculations for clients around the world. A quickly growing portion of today's computing requirements are done through cloud computing, and Amazon is the market originator and leader (with Microsoft a strong second).

As industry analyst Nicholas Carr observes in his book on the new field, *The Big Switch*, Amazon was technically providing basic utility services to clients back in the 1990s, when "companies and individuals could become 'Amazon affiliates,' giving them the right to market Amazon's products through their own sites (in return for a small cut of any resulting sales)." The cloud technology let the affiliates connect to Amazon's databases to display product information and images on the affiliate site.[64]

The project grew out of the company's ambitions to be seen as a tech company like Google, rather than a mere retailer like Walmart. The company sat on a giant pool of data on customers' buying and rating behavior, the currency of the tech age, and early on it made some available to publishers, later creating APIs (application programming interfaces) that let software developers collect price and product data. Other APIs let clients use Amazon's shopping cart and payment system. Meanwhile the fast-growing company had internally made computing resources available to its many divisions, devoted to functional operations (called "primitives") like basic processing and data storage. These projects were later grouped together as Amazon Web Services (AWS), which today includes these functions as well the Simple Storage Service (S3) and the Elastic Compute Cloud (EC2) for data-crunching needs.

These à la carte, online-enabled services at first attracted small businesses that had a hard time paying for all their own IT hardware and staff, but soon large firms took notice. The service grew quickly, in part, again, due to low prices that Amazon's investors tolerated in exchange for breakneck growth. Also, Bezos had learned another cautionary lesson from other tech titans, and "he didn't want to repeat 'Steve Jobs's mistake' of pricing the iPhone in a way that was so fantastically profitable that the smartphone market became a magnet for competition," as Stone puts it.[65]

The efficiency of cloud computing is that it reduces the need for expensive in-house hardware and software, which traditionally allow for high data processing speeds and handling heavy data traffic, but are often only needed in the busiest conditions and are otherwise unnecessary. Amazon's own systems were built to manage the traffic flood the week after Thanksgiving, and the rest of the year much of it sat idle. "Most of the system's capacity went unused most of the time," Carr observes, and Bezos said in 2006 that "there are times when we're using less than 10 percent of capacity." Now computing power can be bought as a utility, like the power bill, and business observers hope it will end up benefiting smaller firms and startups, which would otherwise struggle to afford the big IT assets of large corporations. Cloud computing could thus "level the playing field," as Carr suggests.[66]

Amazon utterly dominated the cloud computing market for some time and is now the largest player, at about 51 percent market share, followed by Microsoft's Azure cloud service at 13 percent and Google at 6 percent.[67] The highly widespread use of Amazon's remote servers has made them at times a chess piece in Amazon's larger rise, as when Walmart pointedly told its tech contractors in 2017 to keep their applications off Amazon's cloud if they wanted its business. And unlike the rest of Amazon's famous cash-burning business model, AWS is profitable—highly profitable. Indeed, only when AWS blew up did the company begin to take a few billion in profit a year (rather than reinvesting the full torrent), and even embark on share buybacks; cloud computing is responsible for half of Amazon's profits to this day. In the *Economist*'s analysis, AWS "operates with economies of scale that are practically impossible to reach."[68]

And crucially, big corporations are not the only ones seeing the value in Amazon's services—other big institutions, like the Pentagon, are noticing as well. Since 2013, Amazon has hosted data for the Department of Defense, the CIA, and other security agencies. Gaining clout with the security establishment by helping to manage the transition from on-site mainframes to the cloud, Amazon has been able to "lock in an advantage over the competition . . . the U.S. Transportation Command, which manages transportation for the Pentagon, said it was prepared to award AWS a contract without a competitive bid."[69] And the market is thin for alternatives anyway—few have Amazon's security-state seal of approval.

Amazon's dominance of the security cloud is thus unlikely to wane soon. The *Wall Street Journal* reported that the three-biggest cloud providers together invested over $30 billion in 2016 alone in their gigantic data centers, filled with cold-stored banks of computer servers, to run their corporate services. The business paper found "the massive investment is creating a barrier for would-be rivals that would need to spend tens of billions of dollars to match the computing capacity Amazon, Microsoft and Google already have," and quoted an investment banker: "They've created a powerful moat." High barriers to entry are a classic feature of long-lived monopolies and oligopolies.[70]

Amazon's central role is likely to grow, as the DOD has been taking offers for a gigantic multibillion-dollar contract for years' worth of cloud business, code-named JEDI, which is an outrage unto itself. But crucially, the Pentagon has insisted that all the business will go to a single company, giving Amazon the inside track on the basis of its experience providing computing to public institutions from the CIA to the Smithsonian. And as the *Wall Street Journal* notes, the Pentagon also insists "that bidders provide a cloud that can handle unclassified, secret and top-secret data. Only Amazon so far has received government approvals to house its most highly classified data in the cloud."[71]

For all this (somewhat menacing) potential, the cloud has very real downsides. Amazon's military work has led it to drive off other entities frowned on by the military, above all the state-secret-releasing site WikiLeaks, which it kicked off its servers, causing famous Pentagon Papers leaker Daniel Ellsberg to cancel his Prime membership on principle and to call for a boycott.[72] Further, the fact that companies allow Amazon, Microsoft, Google, or Oracle to be custodians of their data, stored many miles from the company's actual operations, imposes new risks. As with any utility, service can be disrupted, like when a snowstorm pulls down power lines and you have to sit in the cold until service is restored. But now the stakes are higher. With information essential to core business processes being managed in the computing centers of the "cloud," the scope of potential disruption is significantly widened, and is only partially compensated for by redundancy in the network.

In 2012 a large electrical storm, or "derecho," on the Atlantic Seaboard caused heavy rains, flooding, and downed trees, leading to the failure of local power grids. Nicholas Carr relates that as computing access for millions of people hung in the balance,

> the data centers in the Amazon complex immediately began switching over to their backup diesel generators. But there was a glitch in the system. The switchover failed at one of the centers, and its servers went dark. Compounding the failure was a bug in the load-balancing software Amazon uses to route traffic around problem spots in its network. As if that weren't enough, another software bug prevented some backup data stores from kicking in. Amazon's technicians acted quickly. . . . But though the outage was brief, the recovery proceeded haltingly. It took the company many hours to reboot its servers, reconstruct its databases and its virtual machines, and get all its systems working again.[73]

The problem wasn't a onetime event, as another outage in 2017 affected its S3 system and froze or slowed apps that require Internet storage from AWS. This outage, which lasted about four hours, began after an Amazon worker entered incorrect commands and disabled a large block of Virginia servers. It affected numerous US businesses, but this time Amazon's built-out network allowed some clients to move their work to other centers that stayed online.[74] The *New York Times* called it "a rare fumble for Amazon in cloud computing" and observed that large corporate customers were trying to diversify their cloud service by using different providers for different functions. This was in response to a "fear among businesses" that "Amazon's dominance could lead to a new form of 'lock-in,' giving it huge leverage over customers because of the costs of switching providers. In the 1980s and 1990s, those costs helped Microsoft gain a seemingly unshakable grip on personal computing."[75] Now Microsoft itself is Amazon's main credible competitor.

Amazon and the other cloud oligopolists are investing heavily in their centers and systems to avoid these kinds of disruption in the future, but it illustrates that when a few firms run an industry, the stakes are raised if anything goes wrong. And given the new scope of the cloud in running virtually every data-based service we rely on, those stakes are high indeed. But for business journalists, there's no problem that can't be dealt with through effective PR, as Stone blandly suggests: "Outages had widespread repercussions, and chronically secretive Amazon found it had to get better at explaining itself and speaking to the public."[76]

Those stakes increasingly extend not just into big corporate databases but into the home, too, since it's the power of the cloud that's allowing a new wave of small hardware products that use specialized cloud connections to punch above their weight, including "smart speakers." These small computers and stereos deployed around the house allow "voice computing," in which simple verbal commands or queries activate the speaker to run a function like playing music or searching online. The cloud enables these devices, therefore extending its presence right to your bedside.

As with the cloud itself, Amazon has been the leader in the smart speaker market with its various Echo models, followed by the Google Home, the Microsoft Invoke, the Facebook Portal, and the Apple HomePod. Market analysts find Amazon leads the market in part by offering characteristically rock-bottom prices, because Amazon sees the speakers as "an entry point for e-commerce."[77] Thus, having its speaker rather than another company's in a home means regular chances to push its own retail products, to entice more households into Prime, to collect more data, and to charge monthly streaming music fees.

These always-listening devices have already led to a number of innovatively creepy episodes, like the one involving a Seattle woman whose Echo mistook parts of a conversation as commands, recording the conversation and then sending it to a person on the user's contact list without the user's consent.[78] Google, for its part, conceded that its own smart speaker picks up some conversations, even when the speaker hasn't been addressed by its activation phrase. Some of these "audio snippets" are listened to by live language experts to improve its voice-recognition AI—issues that might seem minor, except that the press reports over fifty-three million smart speakers were sold or issued globally in 2018 alone.[79]

And when a coalition of child- and privacy-advocacy groups tested the Echo Dot Kids Edition service, they found that the information it recorded about children's requests and searches couldn't be deleted by employing parental controls but required contacting customer support. This could become a major issue later as federal law increasingly protects minors' online privacy, especially since apparently 85 percent of apps in the Alexa store have no privacy policy at all.[80]

Gradually the tech majors are eroding the walls of how deeply we let them hook into our lives, and the speaker market is a bleeding-edge example of that. Users now allow the speakers' algorithms to help decide if one outfit looks better than another on them, and with Amazon's purchase of a company making smartphone-connected, camera-equipped doorbells—and its new service of delivering products inside your home when you're not there, or even inside your car—the company integrates itself ever deeper into customers' lives.[81] Amazon now deploys "personalized pricing" on many goods categories, showing different users different price points for the same product, depending on their past behavior, and allowing Amazon to experiment with users' shopping decisions. Its giant pool of extremely low-wage freelancers through its "Mechanical Turk" program, which allows people to participate in social science research surveys for pennies, have given researchers a highly convenient but also statistically skewed survey research pool, as the *Technoskeptic* relates.[82]

But all these cutting-edge, creepy cloud-based toys rely on human labor to be produced and to operate. And Amazon's labor history is less than Prime.

Picking Fights

Amazon grew up in Seattle in Microsoft's shadow, and this chapter has reviewed the numerous ways the company took inspiration from its forbear, from rank-and-yanking employees to cultivating platform users. Sadly, this also extends to labor conditions. James Marcus cites paperwork he signed while joining the company as a writer in its early days, headlined "Job-Related Stress":

> The Employee . . . recognizes that his position may involve a high degree of job-related stress. As a condition of employment, the Employee agrees that he will not bring an action against the Company for . . . damages alleged to have resulted from such job-related stress, and will indemnify the Company.[83]

The clause was well founded, especially in the company's early days, when coders and warehouse workers alike were consumed in "Death Marches"—as other tech giants playfully call them—where major software reconfigurations or warehousing clearance pushes were completed over many days, with sleep brief and on-site. In general, workers often didn't take even weekends off, giving up a precious legacy of the labor movement.[84] Stone relates that Bezos "was imagining a different culture for Amazon, one where employees worked tirelessly for the sake of building a lasting company and increasing the value of their own ownership stakes." Yeah, so different. But during hiring interviews, "if the potential employees made the mistake of talking about wanting a harmonious balance between work and home life, Bezos rejected them."[85]

But of course, the ramification of this work policy is that women, who society still widely expects to take the primary caregiver role for a family's children, will be disproportionately discouraged from working or advancing in such an environment. Silicon Valley's well-documented problem of drastic underrepresentation of women is in significant part due to its embrace of a fanatical worth ethic that leads to sneering at any work-life balance, meaning Bezos's rejection amounts to form of institutionalized sexism.

The white-collar staff was subjected to nightmarish conditions similar to those at other tech giants, including long double shifts in the warehouse when the company was shorthanded during the holiday season—orgies of work whimsically called "Operation Save Santa." Bezos refused to subsidize bus passes for years, to prevent against a situation where some workers leave to catch a bus earlier instead of working late and driving home.[86] Writing in *Jacobin*, Joe Allen documents how "emails arrive past midnight, followed by text messages asking why they were not answered." Unsurprisingly, management is given a prepared set of "leadership principles" that are a heinous caricature of libertarian authoritarianism. A standouts: "Leaders are right a lot. They have strong judgement and good instincts."[87]

And as the company grew, "Bezos drove employees even harder, calling meetings over the weekends, starting an executive book club that gathered on Saturday mornings. . . . As a result, the company was not friendly toward families, and some executives left when they wanted to have children." When a female staff member asked when policies supporting work-life balance might be put in place, Bezos responded that "we are here . . . to get stuff done, that is the top priority. . . . If you can't excel and put everything into it, this might not be the place for you."[88] Amazon is very much part of the gender imbalance in the broader market economy, where women's reproductive decisions can eject them from the workforce.

Yet despite the staff's extensive sacrifices, like delaying the start of a family or never seeing their existing one, the picture is different for the CEO. Although Bezos terrorized the workforce and consumed their waking hours, before their separation his wife MacKenzie (formerly his subordinate during their time on Wall Street) became pregnant, and the couple moved into a giant mansion in Medina near Bill Gates's estate. According to Stone, MacKenzie would drop off Bezos daily in a minivan after taking the kids to school, then retire to her separate apartment to write.[89] When their first son was born, Bezos took time off. As he should. As everyone should! But at Amazon, simply having a basic family-work balance requires major privilege.

Of course, many of the white-collar staff are privileged themselves in their relatively high salary levels, and most famously in the stock options that are commonly part of compensation packages, especially for early employees and senior staff. Marcus memorably describes himself and his fellow "vested" colleagues as "the arbitrarily rich."[90] However, as with Apple and other tech giants we've reviewed, options are restricted to certain white-collar workers who are already relatively well compensated. Further, Amazon backloads these options, so that larger payouts come after having worked more years with the company, which is unusual.[91] And there are some burdens that are carried beyond the grave of an individual's tenure at Amazon: the company has a record of enforcing non-compete clauses, threatening to sue workers who quit and get hired by competing companies.[92]

But the company is more notorious for its history with its blue-collar workforce. The warehouse "pickers" who hasten from shelf to shelf with carts gathering items, and then back to the central belts that send the combinations off for sorting and packaging, are the sweating workforce behind the delightful convenience of shopping online. From its earliest days, when knives sold in the new kitchen goods category came sliding down the conveyor system with no packaging, Amazon has worked its blue-collar workforce to the bone. Endless hours for limited pay is the norm, as are escalating performance targets that have workers continuously running from wing to wing of the warehouses.

Pickers carry handheld scanners to confirm the merch and direct them to the next shelf, which also allows the company to track them on a productivity-per-second basis. Managers frequently chew out the workforce for not meeting goals and threaten them with firing, sometimes on a daily basis. The demands rise and rise, suggesting a purposeful strategy of running workers to exhaustion and then replacing them. One picker wrote that the harried workers still show each other desperate support, like trying to cover for a coworker who's running late, but with little wiggle room for solidarity.[93]

The most nationally infamous episodes involve the Allentown, Pennsylvania, fulfillment center's issues with heat. Amazon balked at providing AC for its Midwestern and mid-Atlantic facilities, perhaps not realizing the feverishly hot and humid summers in the region. When temperatures reached triple digits in the warehouses in the summer, rather than spring for climate control the company decided to add a few minutes to breaks and hand out water or Gatorade to the workers running from shelf to shelf in the stifling heat.

But in Allentown the spiraling heat index and ludicrous productivity demands meant workers worked through pain and heat stress, to the point that some became faint or passed out on the work floor. This situation reached such a cartoonish extreme that Amazon hired paramedics to sit in an ambulance on-site, ready to treat heat-stressed and dehydrated employees. Some were taken to local hospitals and replaced by unsuspecting new hires.

This nightmare persisted until an ER doctor called government regulators after admitting temp worker after temp worker for heat strain, a complaint followed up by other witnesses, including one from "a security guard who reported seeing pregnant employees suffering in the heat," according to the Allentown *Morning Call*, whose bold reporting on a major local employer earned national prominence.[94] Subsequent OSHA inspections found fifteen workers fainted from heat on one hot June day, leading to the installation of more fans and cooling bandanas. Workers taking time off to recover incurred disciplinary points against them, which could add up to firing. Some took to chanting, "End slavery at Amazon."

Stone suggests the bad PR around this and other episodes led to Amazon's installation of AC in more fulfillment centers. Thanks to government disclosure rules requiring publicly traded firms to report their median worker salaries, we know Amazon pays an average fulfillment center worker $28,446 a year, or $13.68 an hour, typical of the US warehouse industry but not reflective of Amazon's incredible revenues and market stature.[95]

On the other hand, Amazon's federal filings say, "We consider employee relations to be good."[96] So that's reassuring, too.

On the warehouse floor, the corporate propaganda against theft is aggressive. Amazon cites concerns about stealing in its refusal to open large garage doors in shipping bays, which would significantly help ameliorate the heat. While waiting in line at the large security gates before they can leave (time for which the US Supreme Court has ruled they need not be compensated), workers get to look at large screens showing employees who have been fired for stealing, shown in silhouette with "terminated" stamped across them, next to a list of the products taken.[97] "Orwellian" is the word usually used for this kind of thing, but perhaps we rush to judgment. After all, Jeff Wilke, the powerful head of Amazon's logistics unit, wears flannel shirts during the holiday season "as a gesture of solidarity with his blue-collar comrades," Stone notes ironically.[98]

Wilke was the first to install time clocks in Amazon's fulfillment centers to introduce "discipline," also known as "Taylorism." Another important innovation of his was designed to help cope with Amazon's regimented, exhausting work, as execs deal with the holiday season stress. His solution: primal screams. And no, I'm not making this up.[99] These screams may fade over time because Amazon bought Kiva, the manufacturer of mobile robotics, for the better part of a billion bucks, likely with an eye toward making human workers less essential. The *Wall Street Journal* reports that so far, deployed robots work with humans to get orders located and packed more quickly, but picking itself, which involves retrieving merchandise of many different sizes and shapes, is harder to automate, "though developers are getting close."[100]

These kinds of practices help explain the enduring interest in unionization. But like the rest of Silicon Valley, the company has resisted unions for the workers, and while Stone notes that the Teamsters and the United Food and Commercial Workers have "tried to organize associates" in the fulfillment centers,

> Amazon's logistics executives quickly met these campaigns by engaging with employees and listening to complaints while making it clear that unionizing efforts would not be tolerated. The sheer size of Amazon's workforce and the fact that turnover is so high in the fulfillment centers make it extremely difficult for anyone to organize workers. . . . The unions themselves say there's another hurdle involved—employees' fear of retribution.[101]

This is understandable, after episodes like Amazon's closure of a call center in 2001, which the company claimed was unrelated to labor organizing there. Joe Allen wrote perceptively in *Jacobin* that "Walmart consciously built its distribution centers in remote, conservative regions of the country to avoid the threat of unionization," a pattern followed by manufacturers and other great retailers like Amazon. Operating globally does mean some traditions of worker solidarity will be unavoidable, as when thousands of European workers went on strike in late 2018, some chanting, "We are not robots."[102] In Spain, Amazon was even reported to have requested that police intervene in a strike and enforce worker productivity levels, which the baffled police declined to do.

In the United States, reports uncovered that Amazon even had its warehouse staff sign non-competes in their hiring contracts, barring them from work in any field competing with Amazon in any way—an almost-impossible standard to clear.[103] After a public backlash, Amazon announced it would stop requiring it, but only of its hourly temp workers. All the bad press must have gotten to the fulfillment arm, however, because the company deputized a number of warehouse workers to defend the fulfillment center conditions by taking to Twitter as "Amazon FC Ambassadors." The upbeat tweets defended the company's work conditions, and Bezos, with polite emojis and capital letters. (They were likely penned by HR or other on-site employees given new duties.)[104]

Amazon looks set to be a brutal frontier for labor organizing for years to come, as dramatically shown in the protests coinciding with the 2019 Prime Day, the grotesque sham holiday Amazon created to have another big-purchase day in the summer, to complement the Christmas buying season. By July 2019, more than half of US households were Prime subscribers, bringing real stakes to the Prime Day strikes waged by thousands of Amazon's workers across Western Europe, united by the rallying cry "No more discount on our incomes."[105]

Amazon's clear abuses of the legal rights and simple dignity of labor make it even more obnoxious that the company continues to hold so much power over publishing. By 2019 Amazon sold well over half of US books of all types—today it utterly dominates most publishers, letting us now explore, as the *New York Times* put it, "What Happens after Amazon's Domination Is Complete?" It turns out that towering over a market, partly on the strength of the sheer number of existing platform users, has detrimental effects.

Much like Google and Facebook are now accused of, Amazon makes pitifully little effort to police its platform or ensure product authenticity or quality. The inevitable result is an explosion of fakes, including counterfeit books, such as sensitive medical manuals that are shoddily scanned and sold online by independent sellers, sometimes commingled with Amazon's own stock so that the buyer has no way of knowing their book is counterfeit.[106] Until, of course, the print is illegible or the author's name is misspelled on the cover. And as with the other platform operators in this book, it's next to impossible to get the company to care or take action; and then reactions are reactive, not proactive—removing specific fraudulent seller accounts rather than committing resources to policing the platform for any quality standard. As the *Times* reported, "The company has such a grip on books that counterfeits do not seem to harm it. They might even increase its business," since, after all, Amazon still gets a sales commission. And worse, in order to get real books listed ahead of their cheap knockoffs, some sellers and publishers resort to paying Amazon for ad space or to place its items at the top of search listings—essentially rewarding Amazon for its lawless platform policy, often to the tune of thousands a month.

Many earnest book lovers now often turn to their Kindle for much of their casual reading, downloading books and reading them on the go. However, few read the tablet's fine print, which gives the company control over access to Kindle-formatted e-books, even after they're downloaded onto users' physical machines. And so there was a surprise in 2009 when Amazon deleted some editions of certain books, the rights to which hadn't been properly cleared—from users' Kindles themselves.[107]

Amazon controls the wireless network that allows downloading and synchronizing e-books, including the ability to delete them without user action or permission. Among the books remotely deleted were editions of *Nineteen Eighty-Four* by socialist writer George Orwell. Orwell would probably nominate Bezos, the twitchy-eyed corporate tyrant, as Big Brother's capitalist twin.

CHAPTER 5

Being Evil

The company that governs the Internet

Google is one of the modern world's most important institutions, playing a central role in how the entire Internet functions and providing access to the world's most relied-upon online platforms. Famous for its useful services provided for free, and its reputation for housing cutting-edge new technologies, Google has one of the most revered reputations of any corporation in the world, including being known for generous employee benefits. The company's lightning-fast search results and video loads are possible thanks to its gigantic global infrastructure of enormous data centers filled with servers, fully owned fiber-optic cables, and leading-edge software algorithms. Google's data centers are in nearly every country, including the arctic settlements of Greenland, war-wrecked Yemen, and besieged Gaza.[1]

Google is also known for pursuing inspiring ideals, represented in the company's famous motto, "Don't be evil." Industry magazine *Wired* happily quoted company cofounder Sergey Brin's comment that "the societal goal is our primary goal."[2] Even the sharp-minded communications scholar Tim Wu, coiner of "net neutrality," is willing to suggest that Google is a break from past cycles of monopoly, and "really is a different kind of firm."[3]

And yet, as it has grown to become one of the world's biggest corporations, it has begun to use its near monopoly in online search to build a towering empire of data that covers most of our online and offline lives. It has used its search power to "surface" results it favors and "downrank" those it doesn't, and made similar power plays on its other major platforms for smartphones and YouTube. In time this has led to software developers despairing at their dependence on the once-idealistic company, comparing it to Microsoft, and even describing it as an "evil empire."[4] And users have become wary, too, perhaps realizing the truth of what Google executive Andy Rubin said—"We don't monetize the thing we create. We monetize the people that use it."[5]

Synonymous

Begun in 1996 as a research program at Stanford University by young grad students Larry Page and Sergey Brin, the search engine that became Google was meant to satisfy a real need. The World Wide Web, the most popular Internet application, was still new to the public in the 1990s and growing explosively quickly. As users created an ocean of websites, attracting other interested users to those sites became fairly difficult, and at the same time people were becoming unsatisfied with the tame "walled gardens" of curated content run by the major "web portals" of that time like AOL and MSN. Web browsers like Netscape had made the web explorable, if you already knew the web address you wanted to get to. But finding sites related to an interest, whether cooking or cat pictures or celebrity nudity, was another story.

Search engines at that time were relatively primitive—AltaVista, the most popular, ran web searches using a simple process of matching keywords on sites, but this was a blunt approach that meant many irrelevant search results. Worse, as the web grew and search became more important, site owners began "gaming" engines by stuffing the bottoms of their pages with popular keywords, so results often included large volumes of useless spam-like sites.

Page and Brin's new search engine avoided this through the clever adaptation of a tool of scholarship—citation measures. The importance of academic papers is sometimes gauged (crudely) by determining how many other papers cite it—papers that are considered to be valuable or important by other figures in the field tend to be referred to and cited more frequently. Page developed an automated software process, or algorithm, that ranked websites by how many links they had from other sites, thus suggesting their relative importance to other web developers. The mathematical guts of the process were developed by Brin, and the algorithm, named PageRank, formed the early core of Google's search process. The two gradually added many other "signals," like the repetition or position of the keywords.[6] At the time, they named their search engine "BackRub" since it tracked backlinks from other pages to estimate relevance.

Notably, this algorithm was developed in an academic setting, where ample public funding supported the cutting-edge research. Brin had received a scholarship from the National Science Foundation to attend the school, and Page's mentor was awarded an NSF grant to study online information.[7] Further, the entire Internet and web themselves were made possible by funding from the NSF and the Defense Advanced Research Projects Agency (DARPA)—the Pentagon's research arm. Indeed, the clearest sign of Google's academic roots was that during its development, its original web address was google.stanford.edu.

Use of the search engine grew extremely quickly, in part because of its technical superiority, but also because of network effects. Net effects are important in search, as Silicon Valley historian Arun Rao describes:

> Search was a classic network effect service. The more people that used a search engine and clicked on results, the better a search engine could be at optimizing results and so have more relevant

results, attracting more users. As a result of a positive network effect, with current search algorithms only one firm should dominate.... On the technology side, it was impossible for most companies to enter search. Because most search algorithms optimized based on past users' searches, network effects prevent new engines from being as powerful as the dominant few. By collecting terabytes of data on past searches . . . the dominant core engines had erected an enormous barrier to entry.[8]

Rao adds that net effects and economies of scale in search were so great as to make online search "a natural monopoly" like a local utility company, where duplication is unneeded and wasteful.

Frequent Google ally Lawrence Lessig, at the time a Stanford law professor, also observed that Google "produced this amazing machine for building data, and that data has its own 'network effect.' . . . Every time you search, you give Google some value because you pick a certain result. . . . So each time you do a search, you're adding value to Google's data base," creating a major advantage and encouraging a market with one or only a few big companies.[9]

As with many technological breakthroughs, other researchers had developed similar software tools. The pattern is common, as with Bill Gates and Paul Allen buying a DOS system that they modified into MS-DOS, or with Mark Zuckerberg's many contemporaries working on almost-identical social media sites. In this case, an IBM researcher created a similar system that ranked sites by links, but the aging computer giant sat on it. And a Chinese engineer also developed a hypertext link–based search system, which his employer, the business-media holding company Dow Jones, also did nothing with.[10]

But as the engine's superiority became clear and user searches shot up, online portals became interested, and in fall 1998 the renamed Google engine was incorporated as an independent company. Soon it made deals to provide search services for major portals like AOL and Yahoo, along with the major browser Netscape, bringing huge volumes of user traffic that the company desperately struggled to accommodate by buying cut-rate servers it could reprogram for cheap, using cash raised from early "angel" investors, including Amazon's Jeff Bezos. The company's rocketing growth also required more mature corporate leadership, and the company's early board favored Eric Schmidt, a tech industry veteran formerly of Sun Microsystems and other firms.

The hundreds of thousands of daily searches all yielded data—data about what made search more effective, what made users search more, and what links they clicked on without returning for a second try—the "long click" that indicated relevant search results. This data attracted to its staff the young, freethinking engineers for which the company is famous, many of whom see themselves as part of the "anti-Microsoft," since that company had openly used its PC operating system monopoly to take over the web browser market. Ironically, the engine was created in a Stanford department housed in the Gates Computer Science Building, endowed by the adjudicated monopolist himself.[11]

Every time you conduct a Google search, literally hundreds of computers in Google's data centers or "server farms" fire up and extremely quickly look for matches to your search terms on the company's copy of the entire web, with each server searching one piece, or "shard," of the index. This parallel computing dramatically speeds up the process and lowers "latency"—how long you have to wait after typing for your search results. Some industry watchers estimate a full quarter of North American Internet traffic, from search to maps to online video, runs through Google's servers.[12]

The infrastructure required to bring millions of daily search results to billions of users globally is enormous, with dozens of gigantic data centers around the world connected by high-band-width fiber-optic cable. After renting center space in the early days, Google now builds its own centers and connects them with its own cables and networking equipment. These enormous centers are filled with racks of servers, made to be replaced as they fail, all of which devour electricity and are cooled by an elaborate evaporative cooling system. Today Google makes these servers itself, produced in such stupendous numbers that the company has claimed to be the world's biggest computer manufacturer, larger than Dell and other OEMs of PCs and laptops.[13]

A classic instance of the scale of Google's data centers is The Dalles, Oregon, a town on the Columbia River struggling with the decline of the aluminum industry. The small town had already invested in a high-bandwidth fiber-optic cable network at its own expense, and nearby hydroelectric dams meant cheap electricity. Google sited a server farm there, but only after scouting it in secret because "if people in a given locality knew it was Google they were dealing with, they might be less generous in giving tax breaks," as Steven Levy puts it. The town had already obtained a designation as an "enterprise zone," meaning many tax abatements and other incentives were in place, but Google wanted more concessions. For an estimated fifty to one hundred long-term jobs, the local congressional representative negotiated a deal for the company to site a server farm in the town in exchange for fifteen years of tax "relief." The company also demanded the entire town be sworn to secrecy before revealing itself as the buyer; local officials were made to sign NDAs, and even after the town's newspaper broke the story, Google insisted townspeople not refer to it.[14] To be fair, the company did make some goodwill gestures in exchange for the extremely favorable deal it received, including a donation to build a local Lewis and Clark Museum and a few grand in advertising credits for local nonprofit entities. These are the kind of one-sided practices used by Big Tech to put its footprint down in a community.

Soon the company's search business grew to become so dominant as to be literally synonymous with web search—most of us now refer to "Googling" something we want to know. In an effort to expand its free-access, advertising-funded, data-hoarding business model, it began a long-running spree of corporate acquisitions. The company has come to be derided in business circles as a "one-trick pony" since, other than search, every one of its major services was brought into the company as a purchase, from Maps to YouTube and even to its own Android smartphone operating system.[15]

The company's search model has clear value, in its reliability and strong relevance-ranking processes. But real flaws have been identified by critics, like University of Virginia media studies professor Siva Vaidhyanathan. His book *The Googlization of Everything* is an excellent exercise in critical thinking about the company, on a subject where original thought is rare. He observes that because PageRank was developed on the premise that pages with the most links to them are most relevant, the effect is to promote the dominance of those sites. In other words, "Web search is inherently conservative."[16]

People's use of Google tends toward wildly excessive trust in a corporation that uses opaque algorithms to rank the Internet. This means the stakes are high when the company creates new, increasingly authoritative-seeming but utterly uncurated search results; my favorite is the "Knowledge Panels." These are boxes appearing at the top of many searches, offering concise information about a common question or a biography of a person. Originally confined to famous people, many people now have them. But exactly how they're granted isn't clear, because, as the *Journal* reports, "no human being is in charge of making such selections."[17]

Google's algorithms make the call, and the common mistakes that often appear in people's panels as a result have taken months of user requests for Google to resolve. The company now encourages people with panels to get "verified" through a process the company runs, allowing faster changes. Hilariously, former company CEO Schmidt's own panel incorrectly claimed for some time that he wrote the book *Pharmacy Technician Exam Certification and Review*. Another mis-profiled person said of Google, "They have more authority over my life story than I do." Although users often are happy to accept the Knowledge Panels as fact, sadly these are often grossly wrong, with sources sometimes included and sometimes not.[18]

In a major transition, in 2009 Google rolled out "Personalized Search for everyone," in which results are tailored to the individual users, rather than the link-based consensus process that preceded it.[19] Even users logged in on computer labs at a public library have some personalization, based on location and other signals. This process is enabled because of the bottomless ocean of data Google has collected on us from its various services over the years, and, as *The Filter Bubble* author Eli Pariser concludes, this personalization means there is no standard Google search result for any subject, so the engine increases the chance of its users living in "bubbles" where the results they see and views they hear match what they already believe.[20] Even the number of search results for a single term now varies from one user to another, and for hot-button subjects like climate change you'll see utterly different results depending on Google's inferences of your political views.

Today Google's market share in online search is 78 percent on PCs, and a staggering 95 percent on mobile search, largely because of its Android smartphone operating system.[21] Google originally bought this open-source mobile OS as a "refuge" platform for its mobile apps to avoid depending entirely on Apple's iPhone. Android now runs the giant majority of smartphones globally, produced by many OEM handset makers. However, there are real blocks to Google's search ubiquity that are often legacies of the company's past battles. For example, an iPhone user wanting to search by voice must ask Siri, Apple's virtual assistant, to specifically "Google Search" for something; otherwise it will default to Microsoft's Bing.[22] And the company has struggled to absorb markets without a Latin character set, making Russia, Japan, Korea, and China its lowest-penetration markets (little data is available on search in Arabic).

Submerging Subversives

Many observers are reluctant to declare Google a monopolist; Tim Wu brings himself to call Google "technically" a search monopolist, while the great web inventor Tim Berners-Lee referred to the "near-monopoly status" of Google and Facebook.[23] More important than the label are the market share numbers above, and the question of whether the company has any meaningful competition or an insurmountable lead. Business journalists, including respected *Wired* journalist and author Steven Levy, have something to say about it in their reporting for investors and executives. In his 2011 book *In the Plex*, Levy recounts how Google's team sought to develop "innovation after innovation that would broaden Google's lead over its competitors and establish it as synonymous with search." Or, when acquiring cutting-edge ad-placement companies, how "Google felt that they had a window to be the only game in town."[24] Or how the company's combination of "engineering talent, fiber-optic cables, and data centers" created "a nearly insurmountable advantage over their competitors." Yet Levy also earnestly describes the company upholding its "Don't be evil" mantra: "An idea would come up in a meeting with a whiff of anticompetitiveness to it, and someone would remark that it sounded . . . *evil*."[25] So go figure.

To call a company a monopoly implies a lack of serious alternatives, so in tech markets a common question is the extent of "lock-in"—how much does a device, platform, or service lock consumers into sticking with it when they might prefer to leave, with Apple and Microsoft being good examples. Google has long claimed it has no real lock-in, with its attorneys reliably repeating that "competition is just a click away," meaning Bing is available for search and thus no monopolization is possible in the market. Company executives reliably cite a crucial episode to defend the company from antitrust action: in 2009, as a result of a rare Google service outage, the engine was unavailable for a period of hours. In that time, millions of users turned to Yahoo for their searches, a scenario in contrast to that of Microsoft's locked-in OS monopoly and its very clear and purposeful efforts to keep users or developers from any alternatives.[26]

But Vaidhyanathan observes the flaw in this argument, finding that it

> could be valid if boycotting or migrating from Google did not incur significant downgrades in service by losing the advantages

of integration with other Google services. Google's argument also ignores the "network effect" in communication markets: a service increases in value as more people use it. . . . Network effects tend toward standardization and thus potential monopoly. . . . If only a few people used Google for Web searching, Google would not have the data it needs to improve the search experience. Google is better because it's bigger, and it's bigger because it's better. . . . Opting out or switching away from Google services degrades one's ability to use the Web.[27]

He adds, "To search for something on the Web using Google is not unlike confessing your desires to a mysterious power."[28]

In other words, Google has a special status, one Wu described as the web's "master switch"—the most reliable means of navigating the great expanse of the Internet.[29] Switching away from it means using tools that benefit from significantly less data and thus give clumsier search results. And Google has played the main role in arranging for dangerous sites to be stripped from search results, like those with computer-infecting malware or ones repeatedly used for fraud, thus cleaning up the web. Further, Google's other services are all integrated (and the company aggressively encourages this), meaning that giving up one Google service weakens the strengths of the other applications a user may stick with. Giving them all up is a great sacrifice indeed for a person today, where everything from job applications to dating sites to most of the world's commercial services can be arranged online.

And since Google is the main way we navigate the entire Internet, it has enormous power in what it chooses to present (or not present) to us, and the agenda-setting influence of this role is hard to overestimate. However, the main way the company's power is exercised is not so visible. Google's simple ability to rank its search results (via backlinks, personalization, or other signals) puts incredible power in its hands as the world's dominant search engine. Of course, the company's whole pitch for PageRank is that crafty software automatically ranks the results, creating a neutral, technocratic means of sorting information. But Vaidhyanathan observes that in May 2007, Google removed the word "automatically" from its "Explanation of Our Search Results" page, a major difference.[30] The explanation also indicates the search results are absolutely under Google's control, and it has used this control to surface results it favors and to submerge those it doesn't.

Meanwhile, the extensive nature of the user settings means that there's great import to how the settings are initially set—the "default settings." The large majority of users of these platforms are barely aware these controls exist, and few use them, but to no one's surprise, the default settings are reliably those giving Google the most access to our data and the most leeway to use it for many purposes, including targeting ads to us. A former Googler and "design ethicist" comments, "If you control the menu, you control the choices."[31]

Other cases of the company's staggering influence are simple, as when Google withholds access to its popular apps from Android phone developers who alter the system too much for Google's liking. While the Android system is open source, and thus able to be altered or augmented by phone handset makers, Google draws red lines—above all, its search engine must be the default. Google's power is such that if a phone maker produces even one phone that doesn't meet Google's requirements, it withholds its crucial apps from all that manufacturer's phones, including those that do meet the requirements.[32] This is one among numerous practices that have gotten Google in trouble with the European Union's more assertive antitrust enforcers.

Likewise, when the Trump administration's immigration bans were first issued, Google engineers debated in an internal email thread the possibility of adding more search results that suggest benefits from migration.[33] While not enacted, the discussion itself indicates the potential influence at Google's discretion. A more expansive instance has been Google's treatment of online shopping sites. Google has been eager to augment its share of online shopping searches, which are often especially profitable but require more complex "vertical" search processes, where rather than searching for simple terms like "heart disease" or "local restaurants," the user types a far more complex question with multiple factors to consider, like "What's the best credit card for air miles?" Toward the goal of keeping shopping market share, Google has actively downranked competing shopping comparison sites, like Idealo or Foundem; the latter debuted in 2006 and appeared high in Google's search results at first, but after forty-eight hours was suddenly dozens of pages down. Meanwhile other engines like Yahoo kept them ranked high—suspicious.[34]

Thanks to a resulting European court case that found Google guilty of anti-competitive practices and fined it $2.7 billion in 2017, we now know that executives decided that Google's comparison-shopping results would appear at the top of price-comparing searches, regardless of the natural results of the search algorithm. One exec wrote, "Larry thought product should get more exposure." The technical means of this are complex, but the point is that Google holds the power to push a business out of public view by tweaking its algorithm to kick it down its results a few pages, which for most searches is enough to kill it. But Google may not deliver on the European requirement that the company allow other shopping services to bid on the top slots: the business press reported later the same year that "ads for products sold by Google and its sister companies appeared in the most prominent spot in 91% of 25,000 [post-settlement] searches related to such items. In 43% of the searches, the top two ads both were for Google-related products."[35] Tech industry magazine *Wired* was so skeptical that the title of its Facebook post linking its coverage of the settlement read "Monopolies gonna monopoly."

Other once-popular services, like the dining review site Yelp or travel planner TripAdvisor, rejected buyout offers from Google only to find that Google began pulling their content directly onto its search results, meaning most users never visited their sites. Today Google responds to commerce-related searches by putting prominent links at the top from companies that pay, or promotes its own results by putting Google Maps at the top. Google was also ordered by the European Union's competition regulators to allow companies to opt out of this practice of "scraping" content off other websites, which Google appealed.

But if Google can downrank into obscurity vertical-search websites in commercial categories where it wants "more exposure," it can do that same thing to political news and views. Google now plays a central role in how people keep up with the world, providing major news outlets with large proportions of their total online traffic through referrals and clicks from search results; about 40 percent of clicks on the company's trending topics are for news, and a recent study found Google makes almost $5 billion a year from their middleman role between consumers and news.[36] This is almost as much as the entire news industry made from ads that year, meaning Google is absorbing about half the industry's income without hiring a journalist.

Beyond starving a news industry that the public needs as never before, this significant dominance of online news means giant stakes come with any changes the company makes to its search rankings and content hosting. Figures on the political right have declared Google and Silicon Valley in general to be their enemies, partially owing to the predominantly liberal leanings of their workforces. But as usual, although conservatives angrily insist on their nationwide TV and radio shows that they are being silenced, it is in fact the political left that has been suppressed.

After the revelations in the wake of the 2016 election regarding Russian online ad purchases, Google found that about 0.25 percent of its regular traffic led to information it considered to be deliberately misleading or fraudulent, and so it adjusted its search algorithm toward more "authoritative" content. But, as the press reported, the change appeared to have a particular asymmetric nature. According to the *New York Times*, "The change drew complaints that it prompted a steep drop-off in traffic. But the organization that complained and all the sites whose traffic it cited leaned to the left."[37]

Indeed, the leftist media watchdog group Fairness and Accuracy in Reporting (FAIR) found that after Google's drive for more reliable content, the sites reporting drops-off in traffic are uniformly on the left, and often among the best left-leaning sites. They included the popular left news site *Democracy Now!*, whose traffic fell by 36 percent; *Truthout*, by 25 percent; *CounterPunch*, by 21 percent, and the liberal *AlterNet*, by a crushing 63 percent.[38] *AlterNet*'s graph of its site traffic shows the catastrophic impact of this move by the Internet's "master switch," with its visitor numbers gradually rising over several years to well over six hundred thousand and then plunging steeply after the new algorithm was introduced. *AlterNet*'s executive editor wrote, "It appears that Google has pushed popular, high-traffic progressive websites to the margins and embraced corporate media." For all the hype about right-wing figures like Alex Jones being "de-platformed" by YouTube sanctions, it is the left that has been stripped of its standing in the algorithms of Google Search.

Beyond the power-mongering chicanery specific to Search, Google has a long record of shady influence-spreading that is similar to those of other giant corporations. One example was uncovered by a *Wall Street Journal* investigation, which found Google was financing large numbers of academic research papers that reached conclusions supporting its views on regulation, data collection, and taxes, paying university professors fees from $5,000 to $400,000. Crucially, many of these papers did not include notice that the research was funded by a private entity with a material interest in the issues the papers discussed. Incredibly, *Journal* reporters uncovered that "in some years, Google officials in Washington compiled wish lists of academic papers that included working titles, abstracts and budgets for each proposed paper—then they searched for willing authors."[39]

On the other hand, scholars with a critical perspective are less favored. After the EU shopping service fine was imposed on Google, Barry Lynn, the US monopoly scholar and critic, posted a statement praising the fine on the website of the New America Foundation (NAF) think tank where he worked. CEO Schmidt made an angry call to the institution's head, and soon

Lynn received emails from his boss accusing him of "imperiling the institution as a whole"—Google was a major funder, and in fact the foundation's main conference room is the "Eric Schmidt Ideas Lab." Apparently some ideas aren't welcome in this "lab." In an email to Lynn in which she referred discouragingly to his earlier description of Google that included the M-word, she wrote "We are in the process of trying to expand our relationship with Google on some absolutely key points . . . just THINK about how you are imperiling funding for others."[40] Lynn's role at NAF was terminated shortly thereafter.

But the sneakiest way Google has come to exercise its market power is related to conditions where one party knows more than the other party—a situation economists call "asymmetric information." Painfully, while Google's staff pride themselves on their "anti-Microsoft" nature, the company is using informational asymmetry in ways very similar to Microsoft in its 1990s monopolist heyday. The *New York Times* has reported that "Google unfairly hinders the ability of search competitors—and Microsoft's Bing is almost the only one left—from examining and indexing information that Google controls, like its big video service YouTube. . . . Microsoft's Bing search service cannot examine and index up to half the videos on YouTube."[41] And much like Microsoft, Google hides this apparent use of its platform status to curb a competitor by claiming the services are "incompatible" technically—but by withholding certain technical standards, it can perpetuate that condition.

Indeed, former high-level Google exec Marissa Mayer remarked: "It's very, very complicated technology, but behind a very simple interface. . . . Our users don't need to understand how complicated the technology and the development work that happens behind this is. What they do need to understand is that they can just go to a box, type what they want, and get answers."[42] Mayer is openly celebrating a strategy of deliberate asymmetric information, one of the practices for which Microsoft was very nearly cleaved in two.

And the two firms have an ongoing antagonism—in an episode showing what a plaything US antitrust law has become to today's tech behemoths, Google and Microsoft got into an "antitrust complaint-off" in 2008. With Google taking over search, Microsoft made a hostile bid to take over Yahoo, leading Google to refer the antitrust implications to regulators, which *Wired* journalist Steven Levy noted was "a rather odd stance considering Google's previous insistence that the search marketplace had no lock-in and thus wasn't a valid candidate for antitrust action."[43] But in the meantime Google made a deal with Yahoo to set up an arrangement in which some Yahoo users would see Google's ads, and the adjudicated monopolist Microsoft then referred *that* to regulators. Google dropped the deal when the DOJ said it would sue, but then Yahoo announced it would sell its search business to Microsoft for a billion dollars; that business was combined with Microsoft's own data to create Google's main extant search rival, Bing.[44] Not much of a rival though: its traffic sources are cell carriers eager to annoy Google, and of course it's the default option on Windows PCs and Microsoft's web browser, Internet Explorer—suggesting people aren't turning to Bing because they see it as a real alternative to Google, but are using it when it's a default option presented on another platform. Its worldwide search market share is in the neighborhood of 5 percent, which means it trails not only Google but also the Chinese search engine Baidu.

Speaking to author Ken Auletta, Schmidt said he and the founders ask themselves, "How can you grow big without doing evil?"[45] One still wonders.

Ad Nauseam

An interesting research paper by a pair of Stanford grad students in 1998 had some intriguing findings:

> Currently, the predominant business model for commercial search engines is advertising. The goals of the advertising

business model do not always correspond to providing quality search to users. . . . We expect that advertising funded search engines will be inherently biased towards the advertisers and away from the needs of the consumers. Since it is very difficult even for experts to evaluate search engines, search engine bias is particularly insidious.[46]

The authors were, of course, Brin and Page, the Google cofounders who within ten years would be responsible for covering the entirety of the web with ugly, slow-loading, brain-eroding eyesore advertisements. The story is a classic case of capitalism molding thought around itself, even the thinking of clever Stanford grad students.

In the late 1990s, numerous search engines openly accepted advertiser money for their sites to be included at the top of search results, most notably GoTo.com. Brin and Page were disgusted, since whatever integrity the search algorithm had would be tainted by the crass commercial question of how much money changed hands. But, of course, as Google's traffic went vertical on the strengths of its superior technology and network effects, large amounts of cash were urgently needed to continuously add more servers and networking equipment that kept results coming and latencies low. And since Google was becoming a main channel for "intentional traffic"—consumers who know what they want and are looking for it—there was a natural opportunity to pay for all those servers and employees to operate them.

Taking advantage of this market opening began with the launch of new software called AdWords. This code placed text-only ads alongside of (not above) the "organic" results generated by the search engine itself whenever a user executed a search for commercial goods.[47] Importantly, Google created "quality scores" for the advertisements based on how often they were clicked— the guiding principle was that clicked ads were the ones actually interesting to consumers. The old cliché of advertisers not being sure which half of their ad money is wasted would no longer apply online—Google's analytics software would allow them to know precisely how many clicks resulted from a given ad. AdWords was self-service and easy to use, and for many search terms a relatively affordable and valuable option, especially for smaller businesses. Also, it was operated through a "Vickrey" auction, where the winner pays only a penny more than the second-place bid, which stabilizes bidding and reassures winners that they didn't wildly overpay. As AdWords became a major success commercially (and brought in large amounts of additional consumer data), Levy wrote, "From that point on, Brin and Page saw nothing but glory in the bottom line."[48] Google's 10-K SEC filing for fiscal year 2017 states that the company makes "substantially all of our revenues from advertising."[49]

Page's new view of ad-funded search was that Google maintains "a church/state wall" between search and ads, likening it to newspapers keeping reporting separate from advertiser influence—an idea mocked by the great satirist of propaganda George Orwell, who wrote: "Unpopular ideas can be silenced, and inconvenient facts kept dark, without the need for any official ban. . . . So far as the daily newspapers go, this is easy to understand. The British press is extremely centralized, and most of it is owned by wealthy men who have every motive to be dishonest on certain important topics."[50] So the influence of great capitalists over information through advertising-dependent business models is not new—but the technology and its reach are. In time, the AdWords spots were moved from the side of the organic search results to above them, and separated by a decreasingly visible blue line, after which they were marked by a small "i" or "sponsored," and today, "Ad" or "sponsored." Not for nothing did a mere 38 percent of Americans say they were even aware of the difference between the sponsored links and the organic search results.[51] Yikes.

Yet ad buyers have their own hierarchy in Google's eyes. Eli Pariser recounts an episode when an environmental group was running a campaign targeting the Royal Caribbean cruise line, demanding it quit its practice of dumping raw sewage into the ocean, for which they bought Google ads. Days later, Google pulled the spots, for "language advocating against the cruise line industry." But the ad text had only said, "Help us protect the world's oceans. Join the fight!"[52] Church-state separation indeed.

But it was AdSense that began the real transformation of the entire web. Drawing on technology acquired from the purchase of Applied Semantics, Inc. (ASI), the software pioneered an ad keyword–matching approach that could be applied to ads all over the Internet. Once implemented, a webmaster or blog owner could let Google sell ads to appear on their site that matched concepts, not just keywords, using ASI's "semantic analysis." This meant that ads for skis could be placed on mountaineering sites, ads for kitchen appliances on cooking blogs, and so on across the entirety of the World Wide Web. The technology meant "the whole Web can become a platform for Google and Facebook," as Pariser put it.[53] And indeed, as AdWords and then AdSense became extremely successful, Google purchased Blogger, the world's most popular blogging site. According to the consensus of business journalists and analysts, it did so for one reason: to expand its ads inventory. Now Google was the custodian of thousands of blog pages, previously bereft of ads—creating more ad surfaces that could be sold to meet the enormous demand from advertisers. This is especially painful in light of an opinion poll conducted at the dawn of the Internet era in 1995, in which two-thirds of US respondents said they didn't want any form of online advertising![54]

And similar to early efforts by other tech giants like Amazon to grow their platform at any cost, when it introduced the program, Google sacrificed significant near-term profit by approaching the publishers of blogs and websites to buy the ad space itself, and not even charging the AdWords advertisers for the click—as Levy put it, "Essentially, Google was paying all the costs from both sides, just to launch AdSense."[55] An ASI hire explained, "Google felt they had a window to be the only game in town," and the *Financial Times* reported on "the economies of scale and network effects that come from being the biggest

player in the market."[56] Once again, Google hoarded information from its business partners, refusing to reveal the split of
AdSense revenue between Google and the publisher hosting
the ads, until finally caving in 2010 to reveal a 32–68 percent
split, respectively.[57] Importantly, this wide reliance on Google
for modest income from blogs and websites created a significant
online constituency, willing to defend Google against charges of
power mongering and other sneaky tactics.

Soon after Google announced the purchase of ASI in 2003,
Microsoft and AT&T (both of which had been previously designated full monopolists and ordered broken up by federal judges)
publicly demanded regulators block the merger, as Google held 70
percent of the global search ad market and would now have 80 percent of non-search ads on third-party sites.[58] The two companies
were quite the Laurel and Hardy of monopolization here. Unbe-
lievably, the FTC allowed Google to further cement its online
ad dominance with its 2009 purchase of AdMob, which placed
ads on websites designed for mobile viewing on smartphones, the
main growth area in the online ad market. Google's dominance
(challenged only by Amazon's marketplace ads for indie sellers and
Facebook's own data hoard for ad targeting) is indicated by the way
it continually raises the minimum bids for more popular search
keywords, which disproportionately hurts smaller advertisers.[59]

Further, thanks to Google's extensive acquisitions, online
advertisers must deal with the company at nearly every stage, well
beyond search ads. To place ads on all those third-party web-
pages, companies use the leading tool for buying ad space, Display & Video 360, a Google-owned entity. Bids placed with that
tool or other ones go to online ad marketplaces for bidding on
space, with Google also owning the gigantic AdX, claiming half
the world market share of ad bids. Webpage operators sell the
space using AdMob for mobile apps or Google's DoubleClick Bid
Manager (discussed below).[60] This extensive presence throughout market segments is how Google, as the business press puts it,
"dominates" the online ad industry.

The company's 10-K filings also regularly indicate its fear of increasingly popular ad blockers, which constitute a real threat to Google's entire revenue model. But ingeniously, the company is itself promoting a new ad blocker on its own popular web browser, Chrome—but one that only filters out ads not placed by Google. The ad blocker is designed to prevent the loading of ads that don't meet certain standards, set by the Coalition for Better Ads. But the business press indicated that the coalition was not "a true joint effort but a Google-dominated one that, while reducing ads widely considered annoying, also could ultimately help Google's bottom line. . . . Google's leading role in the standard-setting process troubled some of the coalition's members, who observed that the black-listed ad formats generally don't apply to Google's own business."[61] The purpose of the Chrome filter is to block pop-up ads, auto-playing ads with sound, and ads that appear before website content can be accessed. The *Journal* noted: "The move could be a defensive one. . . . Some 26% of U.S. web users now employ the software on their desktop devices."[62] It was definitely a business-driven process—Facebook got exemptions for its ads featuring autoplay video with sound, for example.

But reminders of the web's early potential as an ad-free space still echo through the system. On Wednesday, November 12, 2014, two-thirds of Americans got their wish as a rare Double-Click outage globally freed the Internet from ads, for about an hour. Blank spaces remained where the ads were supposed to appear.[63] Sometimes capitalism's loss is our gain.

HugeTube

Ah, the YouTube. Easily one of the most important sites on the Internet, it has become the dominant online video hub and has reached truly preposterous proportions—YouTube users reportedly view over a billion hours of video, and upload the equivalent of sixty-five years (i.e., about 560,000 hours) worth of playtime *every day*.[64] The incredible prominence of the platform means that

its algorithm for recommending videos is one of the most important factors shaping human thought on the planet, meaning our
great social struggles may be canceled out or hugely boosted by
the unknowable whimsy of a giant company's intellectual property, and so far its record has ranged from abject neglect to actively
promoting some of the most heinous ideas possible.

UCLA professor George Geis wrote in his book on Google's acquisitions history that "YouTube's popularity enabled it to
achieve strong network effects resulting from coupling content
generating 'suppliers' with content consumers."[65] With the site's
rocketing potential, one might ask why the founders sold to Google in the first place. YouTube cofounder Chad Hurley said the
site lacked the resources to cope with explosive network effect–
fueled growth: "We thought we'd burn up our bandwidth. We
worried our servers would go down. . . . We needed resources to
scale the company. We only had a staff of sixty people dealing
with the weight of the world." Hurley knew that raising cash for
more servers would be a headache and time-consuming, and said
that Google "wanted to give us the freedom not to have to maxi-
mize revenues right away."[66] Soon YouTube was the second most
popular search engine in the world—after Google.

Entertainment industry veteran Jonathan Taplin makes a
fair case that YouTube's intense growth, besides the obvious network effects, owes to the site's early and explicit policy of allowing piracy of copyrighted content. The site's cofounder wrote in
an email: "So, a way to avoid the copyright bastards might be to
remove the 'No copyrighted or obscene material' line and let the
users moderate the videos themselves."[67] Plus, the platform benefited from brilliant startup tactics like taking out a Craigslist ad
offering one hundred dollars to "hot" women for every ten sexy
videos they posted (yes, really).[68]

Crucially, Google maintained this relaxed copyright posture
after it bought YouTube in 2006, with internal emails suggesting to
the company's leaders that Google should "pressure premium content providers to change their model towards free" and "set up 'play

first, deal later' around 'hot content.'"[69] The 1998 Digital Millennium Copyright Act (DMCA) largely indemnifies online sites from copyright violation, provided they obey "takedown orders" from copyright holders demanding that stolen content be removed. To give an example of what resulted from YouTube's copyright piracy strategy, in 2015 alone the site received five hundred sixty million takedown notices.[70] A suit by entertainment giant Viacom was dismissed under the DMCA's "safe harbor" provisions, which exempt many online venues from liability for hosting copyright-violating media.

YouTube's explosive growth also owes to its ad-free status for much of its early years, as once again the incentive to build a network platform exceeded the immediate need for short-term profitability. With the platform's dominance now fully cemented since the Google acquisition, multiple pre-roll ads are now typical for most clips, and longer videos have algorithmically inserted "mid-roll" ads that break in awkwardly during play. Notably, YouTube allowed Google to enter new advertising territory. In search ads, Google had focused on "directed demand" among consumers who had already decided they wanted or needed a product, but YouTube now allowed for more "soft sell" advertising aimed at building up corporate brands—the kind of ads on TV or Facebook. This allowed it to "present opportunities to ad agencies that related to general branding," as Geis put it.[71]

But crucially, YouTube operates toward the opposite algorithmic goal of Google Search. Search was designed to move users on to their web destinations quickly, with the goal of the "long click," where a user does not return to try other results. But with YouTube, Google has a stake in keeping viewers on the site to view more videos and more ads—prioritizing since 2012 the site's "stickiness." And Google's success in moving searchers on quickly has been matched in its engineering for keeping them around for online video.

Unfortunately, the platform has concluded that the best way to do this is to promote more extreme views in its "Recommended" or "Up Next" algorithm. This recommendation algorithm drives over 70 percent of YouTube viewing, according to the company. The *Wall Street Journal* conducted an extensive investigation of the platform's algorithm by hiring a former YouTube recommendations engineer to study the site, finding that it reliably promotes clips that draw strong traffic and keeps users clicking on more videos. When it comes to news-related subjects, these results tend to be those with more extreme views, especially conspiracy theories from the political right.[72]

Indeed, a search on Google for current political events will tend to surface mainstream news sources, while the same search on YouTube presents hyper-partisan, frequently conspiracy-mongering hysteria with no supporting evidence. The *New York Times* found the platform's recommendations have a "tendency to push everyday users toward politically extreme content—and, often, to keep them there." Videos that get emotional reactions or trigger curiosity through ridiculous claims in their titles are consistently favored in the algorithm, and with subjects like immigration that draw strong right-wing responses, users beginning with a relatively neutral news video can get deep into alt-right territory in only two clicks. Another former Google engineer cleverly examined the platform using the example of videos promoting the flat-Earth theory, "because it's apolitical." Videos promoting this ludicrous ancient dogma are still consistently promoted on YouTube astronomy clips, because they attract more clicks and get more watch time—public understanding be damned.[73]

This conspiracy theory–mongering tendency of YouTube has attracted more attention, and in 2018 executives announced their intention to "surface" more content from "an ever-changing list of authoritative news sources" selected with the staff of the Google News service.[74] As with Facebook, the platform is countering the toxic conspiracies its own algorithms promote by pairing it with material from the mainstream commercial press, but with all the limits Orwell mocked above. The platform is also screening its "Preferred" content, uploaded by the most popular video makers, and even that step has required hiring about ten thousand people.

But these moves are late and pretty modest next to the scale of the need, reflecting the tendency of platform companies to prioritize growth over the curation of their sprawling networks. For this reason, along with conspiracy-mongering content the platform has also become overrun with far-right extremist views, with huge numbers of heavily subscribed user channels tied to real-world violence. Figures like far-right "comedian" Steven Crowder, who was allowed to call socialists "f*gs" for years on the platform, and *Vox* correspondent Carlos Maza a "lispy queer" and a "gay Mexican." But since he did not specifically call for violence or doxing (the public release of personal information like some-one's phone number online), YouTube waited years to boot him from the platform.[75]

The far right has also benefited from the watch-time-maximizing recommendation algorithm, because its members are inclined to post longer videos, with inflammatory messages that tend to attract views over more mainstream content. And along with the far right's reliable emphasis on building commu-nity and thus more reliable viewers, it now dominates YouTube, dwarfing the leftist content makers. Meanwhile platform execu-tives tell the *New York Times* they were "obsessed with increasing engagement during these years" and "rarely considered whether the company's algorithms were fueling the spread of extreme and hateful political content."[76] A further tweak to the algorithm called "Reinforce" employed users' past views and interactions to suggest related subjects, and was hugely successful at increasing watch time—and at steering conventional right-of-center view-ers toward crazy fascist ranting.

Throughout this time, some YouTube staff proposed tighter vetting of videos in the recommendation algorithm, or limiting search results after a mass shooting to more mainstream news sources. Each time, the suggestions were shot down by manage-ment. A former senior manager told *Bloomberg*: "We were so in the weeds trying to hit our goals and drive usage of the site. . . . I don't know if we really picked up our heads."[77]

By the summer of 2019 the platform had become so notorious that YouTube finally announced a policy banning white supremacy, neo-Nazism, and other views from its video system, specifically "videos alleging that a group is superior in order to justify discrimination, segregation or exclusion." The company's often-changing policies and "whiplash-inducing deliberations" now also mean the algorithm will surface less content that is extremist or "borderline," the platform's term for videos that almost but don't quite break its new content rules.[78]

The far right has claimed ever since that it is being censored, even though as conservatives their whole economic position is that private property shouldn't be regulated by the government and that markets are competitive; so by their own logic, YouTube and Facebook should be free to "de-platform" them, leaving them the option to simply move over to the next giant content platform. Or alternatively, they could wake the fuck up. This issue of how much extremism should be allowed exposure in terms of space and time is as old as media, but the suggestion many are now making is that YouTube, with its content algorithms and its eagerness to meet Wall Street's revenue expectations, should not be making the call.

Then there's the apparently bottomless abyss of "weird YouTube." An unholy combination of the inconceivable vastness of YouTube's content and the control of recommendations and search results by attention-maximizing algorithms, weird YouTube is fueled by the profit incentives of a capitalist economic system that reward the platform with more viewer-hours, and content creators with splits of bigger ad dollars. Giant numbers of small content shops now apparently create insane numbers of baffling, computer-created, algorithm-pleasing content that is damn weird and plainly made just to get through the system's recommendations hoops and make people (including kids) watch a pre-roll. On the website *Medium*, James Bridle published a brief essay about the creepy and *off* world of kids' YouTube and the disturbing, nonsensical computer-generated cartoons of which kids now watch large amounts. His unpleasant review observes the "unconsciously-generated, emergent outcomes" of the platform and how the result, I think indisputably, is "industrialized nightmare production."[79]

Children and their media are such a potential point of vulnerability for the platform that the press reports Google is considering major changes to kids' content, including moving all children's content to the separate YouTube Kids app. And far more dramatically, some YouTube employees are reported to be arguing for disabling the recommendation algorithm for kids' content altogether, a gigantic change from the point of view of the platform's watch-time-maximizing business model.[80] Such changes would have been inconceivable for the platform a few years ago, but the company's hand may be forced by the abyss of weird YouTube, as well as other emergent properties of the algorithm.

Most horrifyingly, at some point the recommendation algorithm evidently realized that some users favored certain thematic features of videos, like children in various states of undress in uploaded home movies. Sure enough, the algorithm had managed to tease out the viewing habits of pedophiles, and as designed it recommend further (innocently uploaded) content with these themes. This was an inadvertent, or "emergent," property of the system, which meant "YouTube never set out to serve users with sexual interests in children—but in the end . . . its automated system managed to keep them watching," as the *New York Times* reported.[81]

By now, the incomprehensible scale of YouTube is such that Google is visibly struggling to govern it, and dragging its feet on adopting a "gatekeeper" role that sets rules on what's allowed on the platform. Due to the insane number of daily uploads, comprehensive human screening isn't possible, let alone economical—algorithms have been relied upon to filter out videos according to signals in their titles or other data, but these have very real limits. After a long series of fairly hilariously mismatched ad-video pairings (high-end cosmetics on ISIS beheading videos and such), the platform unilaterally raised the threshold for a YouTube channel to host ads to ten thousand views, a high bar—industry watchers estimate about 88 percent of all YouTube channels fall below that mark—that represents just 5 percent of total views. Then, in 2018, this threshold was raised further, now requiring channels to have at least four thousand hours of watch time and one thousand subscribers.[82]

The same hyper-focus on Wall Street–pleasing growth, rather than on policing the ocean of content on the platform, is something YouTube shares with Amazon and Facebook—and Google itself. It has even extended to the relatively stable Maps application, which has recently become heavily populated with fake listings created by businesses to put them in more local search results and bring in more business. This means people searching for products or emergency services can be steered to addresses where no actual business exists, due to phony listings by unscrupulous operators— but Google still collects a fee on the click if the company paid for its alleged locations to be promoted in an ad at the top of a Maps search listing. And as with Amazon and Facebook, the company is conspicuously reactive, not proactive—removing fraudulent listings when the national press asks about them, but not changing the profitable algorithms to prevent the problem in the future. And much like Amazon, as a remedy the company often recommends that real companies buy ads to keep their businesses on the first page of search results to avoid being pushed down by a swarm of phony listings. Analysts studying the platform estimate that Google Maps has about eleven million fake business listings at any one time.[83] The dark depths of modern platforms are diagramed in maps with their own terra incognita.

Cookie Monster

Big Tech has become notorious for its hoarding of its users' personal data, collected with huge breadth and down to minute detail. Facebook in particular is associated with this practice, especially after a series of major scandals involving the use of personal data (discussed in chapter 6). But Google is inarguably the greediest of these companies in its data collection, to an extent that can surprise even jaded users. After all, as noted above, the collection of data is a key part of the network effect of online search—more searches and click data mean more accurate searches, attracting more users and searches, in the familiar positive feedback cycle of network effects.

Google has vacuumed up user data from the start. As Pariser puts it: "Brin and Page were determined to keep everything: every Web page the search engine ever landed on, every click every user ever made. Soon its servers contained a nearly real-time copy of most of the Web. . . . The search-quality division at the company acquired a black-ops kind of feel: few visitors and absolute secrecy were the rule."[84]

A major step in this area was the 2004 release of Google's email service, Gmail. It caused a large stir itself when users learned that the free, high-storage email service featured on-screen ads that were targeted to the user through the scanning of the text of their emails. The scanning was conducted automatically by software algorithms similar to those used to filter out spam from inboxes, but the company was completely unprepared for the backlash, not realizing that their huge scale and power made such moves feel far creepier. However, the service had a crucial ancillary benefit for the company—it required a login. With that, Google could cross-reference people's email data with their search history on Google and YouTube (which also required a login to post video), along with precise location data from Maps—the beginning of its program to synthesize all its data into comprehensive individual profiles.

But the real turning point was the acquisition of the giant display ad agency DoubleClick, which brought pivotal changes to the company's "cookies." Cookies are pieces of software planted on your computer or phone by sites as you browse the web, recording where you've been for the purpose of presenting ads you're likely to be interested in. Cookies are now stupendously widespread—visiting a typical website like CNN installs an average of 64 of them, while Dictionary.com puts 223 cookies and other trackers on your computer, according to Pariser.[85]

Google's AdSense system had always used these cookies, but the escalation was dramatic. As *Wired*'s Steven Levy reported, through a corporate acquisition the company gained "an omniscient cookie that no other company could match." As a user browses, the cookie

> develops into a rather lengthy log that provides a fully fleshed out profile of the user's interests . . . virtually all of it compiled by stealth. Though savvy and motivated consumers could block or delete the cookies, very few knew about this possibility and even fewer took advantage of it.
>
> The information in the DoubleClick cookie was limited, however. It logged visits only to sites that ran DoubleClick's display ads, typically large commercial websites. Many sites on the Internet were smaller ones that didn't use big ad networks. . . . Millions of those smaller sites, however, *did* use an advertising network: Google's AdSense. AdSense had its own cookie, but it was not as snoopy as DoubleClick's. Only when the user actually clicked on an ad would the AdSense cookie log the presence of the user on the site. This "cookie on click" process was lauded by privacy experts. . . .
>
> Google now owned an ad network whose business hinged on a cookie that peered over the shoulder of users as it viewed their ads and logged their travels on much of the web. This was no longer a third-party cookie; DoubleClick *was* Google. Google became the only company with the ability to pull together user data on both the fat head and the long tail of the Internet. The question was, would Google aggregate that data to track the complete activity of Internet users? The answer was yes. . . .
>
> After FTC regulators approved the DoubleClick purchase, Google quietly made the change that created the most powerful cookie on the Internet. It did away with the AdSense cookie entirely and instead arranged to drop the DoubleClick cookie when someone visited a site with an AdSense ad. . . . Now Google would record users' presence when they visited those sites. And it would combine that information with all the other data

in the DoubleClick cookie. That single cookie, unique to Google, could track a user to every corner of the Internet.[86]

This means your online behavior is being tracked and logged, pretty much anywhere you go. The *New York Times* reports that a recent research paper found 74 percent of its sample of pornographic websites had Google trackers attached to them, often installed by the publishers to display DoubleClick ads or run analytics.[87] Amazingly, Brin called people's fears exaggerated and dismissed their claims about this mega-cookie being "more of the Big Brother type."[88] But even that might be putting a positive gloss on today's data hoarding—Lawrence Lessig, who has defended the company in areas like its book scanning, noted that in Orwell's book *Nineteen Eighty-Four*, when Big Brother was introduced, at least the characters "knew where the telescreen was. . . . In the Internet, you have no idea who is being watched by whom. In a world where everything is surveilled, how to protect privacy?"[89] Siva Vaidhyanathan calls our data crisis, in which Google and Facebook collect and trade our data and sell it off to unknown numbers of third parties, the "cryptopticon."[90]

In 2016, Google went even further by changing its terms of service (TOS). The change seemed positive at face value, asking users to activate new functions that would allow more control over their user data, and let Google show them more relevant ads. But what the change did was merge its tracking data with users' search history, and the personal information in Gmail/YouTube/Google+ accounts, into "super-profiles."[91] And Google wasn't done—beside using the mega-cookie to record users' browsing history, combined with their search logs and Gmail contents, Google "Now Tracks Your Credit Card Purchases and Connects Them to Its Online Profile of You," as a 2017 *MIT Technology Review* headline revealed. By contracting with third-party data firms that track 70 percent of all credit and debit card purchases, Google can now offer advertisers further confirmation of which ads are working, not just to the point of clicking but to the point of sale.[92]

With its new TOS, Google does let users view some of the data it holds on them, but it takes "an esoteric process of clicks," as Ken Auletta put it, and again most users are unaware of these issues in the first place even though they opted in, so most fail to ever view their data files.[93] Additionally, each Google service has its own privacy terms and settings, and they change without warning, so we have to be constantly vigilant for their changes and subtleties. And Google joins the tech community in its use of "dark patterns," repetitive tactics that wear down users into allowing data access.[94] And finally, even opting out of customization doesn't end the data collection, just the use of it to target ads to you—your movements, browsing, searching, emailing, and credit card buying are all still compiled. In 2017 Google announced it would soon stop the unpopular scanning of Gmail text to place ads—the catch was that the company had enough data on users from its super-profiles that it could now personalize them without the scanning.[95]

And for all its hoarding, the pile isn't even secure. Because of a glitch in their software, Google unknowingly allowed third-party developers designing applications for Google+ (their unsuccessful attempt at a social media platform to rival Facebook) to access private portions of user profiles. This included full names, email, gender, pictures, locations, occupation, and marital status—over a three-year period.[96] An internal memo indicates that as with Facebook's own developer data leaks, there's no way to know if the data was misused in any way. But, most important, Google learned of the issue in spring 2018 but refused to announce or disclose it, fearing "reputational damage" to itself. The episode only came to light after internal company communications were shared with the *Wall Street Journal*.

Whatever this company is, it rhymes with "shmevil."

Drone Striking

Google's labor force is well known for its lush perks, like free, healthy on-campus food options on top of median pay nearing

$200,000 a year.[97] But some, like Corey Pein, have identified the incriminating economics behind this generous-looking policy. In his book *Live Work Work Work Die*, he quotes a corporate recruiter who explains, "They might get a twenty-dollar steak, but with the extra time they've stayed at work, they've provided an extra two hundred dollars in value to their employer." Pein himself suggests that "the seeming lavish enticements were a way to attract profit-producing programmers, who were in exceedingly high demand, without offering higher salaries"—a pretty plausible-sounding idea.[98]

The Google workplace has other distinct perks. The company's in-house "chief cultural officer" seeks a "flat" corporate culture, and the workers are "smashed together" into teams and shared offices to advance a team feel.[99] Employees enjoy benefits like various high-quality cafes, on-staff masseuses, and a hirable errand-running service. Google's tech staff is said to recognize their work lives are "charmed."[100] Especially celebrated is the company's famous freely structured "20 percent rule," in which a Google engineer is free to work on any project they choose for the equivalent of a fifth of their worktime.

But the hiring process is notoriously long and detailed, requesting information back to individual undergraduate course grades, ranking applicants by the college they attended, and taking eight or more interviews over six to twelve months. This "whiff of elitism" tends to produce a workforce dominated by "brainy strivers from privileged backgrounds," as Steven Levy puts it.[101] Further, the celebrated 20 percent rule is misleading as well. It applies only to the computer science–trained staff, while the rest receive the benefit only at management's discretion. And "in practice, the self-directed labors often came in addition to a full week's work. Thus the company wide joke that such endeavors were actually '120 percent projects.'"[102] Indeed Eric Schmidt, in the book he wrote with Jonathan Rosenberg, himself says "20 percent time is more like 120 percent time, since it often occurs on nights and weekends," adding "we *don't* pay people for successful 20 percent projects. . . . We don't need to . . . the reward comes from the work itself."[103]

We should also remember that Google was found in court to have been one of the key players in the software engineer wage-fixing conspiracy organized by Apple's Steve Jobs. Schmidt's emails on illegally screwing the company's workforce are worth citing again. They began with "DO NOT FORWARD," and he added that he preferred to discuss the collusion "verbally since I don't want to create a paper trail over which we can be sued later?"[104]

And despite the claims of a "flat culture," there are well-recognized hierarchies among the company's eighty thousand workers. One is the privileging of company engineers, who write the actual code and configure the application interfaces that make the platform technology work. Levy observes they are "royalty" at Google, while those "without computer science degrees . . . weren't exactly second-class citizens, but definitely a lower class of citizens."[105]

However, the simple hierarchy of capitalist management is always present, even at cutting-edge tech giants that like to pretend they eliminate bureaucracy, as we saw with Amazon. And Google's "flat" workplace is actually a hilariously perfect example, as its HR arm developed an employee ranking system with no less than nine levels—eleven counting executives. Levy notes, "Some of the distinctions were vague. Often, Google didn't even share with employees what level they occupied on the ladder," which of course fits so so well with the company's alleged values of transparency and flatness.[106] Notably, at one point the founders noticed a new level of middle management appearing in the company's divisions as they grew, and they decided the company's engineers would no longer have managers. Instead the engineers would self-organize to fix problems and apportion resources, but the founders soon found the engineers preferred having managers carry the responsibility of coordinating and guiding the work of so many development projects. Brin and Page eventually relented and accepted the growth of a corporate bureaucracy to manage their great engineering forces, and what followed was, in Levy's words, "a corporate amnesia" about "Brin and Page's 2001 kill-the-managers caper."[107]

At the top of the system, the billionaire founders, who cleverly built useful software that exploited network economics at a time of rapid, publicly funded technological change, now lead lifestyles typical of the ruling class. Schmidt owns a yacht and a suite of private planes; Page, a $60 million yacht; executive Marissa Mayer, multiple homes including a penthouse suite at the San Francisco Four Seasons. The two cofounders own a pair of huge private planes, and they even obtained special permission to conveniently park them at the nearby NASA facility.[108] Spending less time in the office, the two and their families are often off to Africa or Alaska, or playing with elite toys like personal helicopters, Teslas, and sailboats. But, as Levy reports, "the key was keeping it on the down low. When someone failed to maintain that discipline, colleagues would note it," suggesting a culture of controlling phonies wanting to keep a poker face about their obscene wealth.[109]

This hierarchy extends to the company's great currency—data. In a memorable episode, a journalist for news site *CNET*, covering Google's vast data collection, gathered information on then CEO Eric Schmidt as a test case. His address, net worth, images of his home, political contributions, and other information were compiled, and despite his stumping for public acceptance of the company's data vacuuming, he had what journalists described as a "hissy fit." For publishing Schmidt's "personal information," *CNET* as a whole was cut off from getting answers from Google for a year.[110] And it wasn't even Schmidt's first time complaining about his data being accessible on the platform along with all of ours.[111] But of course Schmidt's data is no more public than yours or mine—*CNET* simply used Google's own services to essentially dox him. But unlike us, Schmidt had the power to create consequences for it.

Company cofounder and storied genius Larry Page himself also emerges as a bullying capitalist tyrant to stand alongside Gates, Jobs, and Bezos. After hearing carefully prepared presentations by exhausted engineers, Page has said, "You're wasting our time" before ordering their project killed. Other demos have been greeted by "I'd rather be doused with gasoline and set on fire than use your product," and, when an employee at a meeting suggested the company was going overboard against leaks in the run-up to the release of Android, Page shot back, "I think that's a decision for the team to make, not you."[112]

Google's executive team certainly made the decisions in the deep recession year of 2009, when even a quickly growing company found it economical to issue pink slips. Several hundred jobs in ads and a recruiting shop in Phoenix were axed, along with a whopping ten thousand contract workers—always the expendable front lines in layoffs. However, at the company's weekly venting session with management, called TGIF, the workforce complained, with one worker saying, "If we don't take care of them, shame on us as a company!" Ken Auletta reports that "Brin and Page said nothing, but associates said they were increasingly distressed by Google employees' sense of entitlement. This was a company, not a socialist paradise, and the Phoenix question—like the grumbling when Google pared cafeteria hours and no longer allowed employees to cart home dinners for the entire family—troubled them."[113]

But Brin and Page needn't be too troubled, thanks to a company stock structure granting them near-total control over major decisions. The company's somewhat-unusual two-tier stock structure gives the founders the ability to override conventional shareholders on decisions regarding most corporate affairs, including the appointment board members. So the firings went forward and front desk staff on the Google campus "suddenly disappeared, as swiftly and unceremoniously as Google deletes spam from its search rankings."[114]

But other issues among Google's staff soon arose, especially concerning the composition of the workforce. The tech industry is notorious for being dominated by men, especially white and Asian men. This is especially so at Google, where the Department of Labor sued the company after it refused to disclose pay data to confirm its compliance with equal opportunity laws, a requirement for government contractors like Google. Conducting its own analysis in 2017, the DOL found pay discrimination against women "pretty much across the entire workforce" and that "discrimination against women in Google is quite extreme, even in this industry."[115]

Google says that compensation is based on many factors including employees' HR rank, job, and performance rating, and that pay is settled by managers who don't have access to information about the employee's gender. Its own internal analysis found literally no pay gap across world operations.[116] However, like other tech behemoths it declines to release this compensation analysis, let alone the required raw data, and has aggressively acted to keep it secret. In 2015 a female Google engineer had posted a crowd-sourced spreadsheet on which employees could voluntarily share their salaries, with about 5 percent of workers participating, that showed visible disparities in pay.[117] She said managers retaliated against her in response and she soon left the company.

But the issue blew up when Google fired James Damore, another software engineer, who wrote a controversial memorandum that was posted to the company's internal communications systems. In it he claimed that inherent gender differences account for pay disparities, citing men's alleged ability to handle stress better than women, which thus accounted for women constituting only 31 percent of Google's staff and only one in five of its engineering and technical workers.[118] Google fired Damore, while saying the action was not taken because he had expressed unpopular views, but for doing so in a disrespectful fashion. This made Damore a hero in right-wing circles and outlets like *Breitbart*, but as a labor lawyer at UCLA told the *New York Times*, "There's no free speech in the private sector workplace." The company now faces dueling lawsuits, one from woman workers demanding equal pay and transparency regarding compensation, and one from Damore claiming he was unjustly fired. Of course, since it's not illegal to be fired on the basis of one's political views, the libertarian Damore (ironically) sued under California's more liberal labor law, which "prohibits employers from 'forbidding or preventing employees from engaging or participating in politics.'"[119]

But the politicization of Google's workforce has had the effect that literally every one of Google's recent efforts to not "be evil" have come from the increasingly organized workforce, not from company management. Consider China. The company's (partial) withdrawal from China has regularly been portrayed as an agonizing corporate decision to sacrifice access to a lucrative market rather than engage in state-demanded censorship. In the Chinese search market, beginning in 2006 Google arguably bested the state at censorship for a time, using its superior search technology; but in its defense, Google included an on-screen note letting users know if results had been censored. Since leaving the People's Republic of China in 2010, the company has been lustfully eyeing the country's enormous market and the huge growth of its domestic search engine, Baidu. But returning would surely mean a renewed commitment to a practice of slick censorship (and maybe no longer including in search results the company's previous notice that some results are being blocked), and thus hundreds of Google employees signed a 2018 petition demanding the company come clean about its planning for the company's new Chinese engine. Code-named "Dragonfly," the engine's secret development has incensed Google's outspoken workforce and led them to demand employee participation in ethical reviews as well as outside monitors. But to the commercial press, including the *New York Times*, the fact that Google is considering resuming its censorship role in China is "a sign of a more mature and pragmatic company"—and one less concerned aboutdoingevil.[120]

And the activism of Google's workforce isn't limited to participation in censorship overseas. Another petition with several thousand engineer signatures went to management after the revelation that the company was secretly working for Project Maven, a Pentagon program to develop artificial intelligence for military drones. While allegedly only for surveillance, it would also aid in the targeting capabilities of war machines responsible for the deaths of thousands of suspects without trial, along with numerous bystanders. The letter insisted, "Google should not be in the business of war" and should abandon its subcontractor status in the program.[121]

Google's management had gone to great lengths to conceal the nature of the program from its workforce, with one internal email from a head AI researcher advising that company PR and public statements "avoid at ALL COSTS any mention or implication of AI. . . . Weaponized AI is probably one of the most sensitized topics of AI—if not THE most. This is red meat to the media to find all ways to damage Google." The eminent author of the email noted she was speaking publicly about "Humanistic A.I." at the time in order to burnish the idea. But it was the company's workers who reacted volcanically, and Google ended up forced to host a debate on the issue, with so much interest among employees that the subject was debated not once but three successive times in one day so that workers around the world could watch. Brin, considered the most principled of Google's ranking figures, justified the company's involvement in the program by saying "it was better for peace if the world's militaries were intertwined with international organizations like Google rather than working solely with nationalistic defense contractors," according to the *New York Times*.[122] This is a pretty pitiful defense.

Soon opposition spread outside the company, with workers at other tech firms and professional tech societies signing petitions and making statements opposing the program, among them Page's own Stanford PhD adviser. According to a Google worker interviewed in the socialist magazine *Jacobin*, the company pushed the line "Ethics is complicated. Ethics is hard," but it was clearly eager to take the Pentagon's business. When a worker asked Brin what kind of voice workers had in making decisions like taking weapons work, he responded: "Letting you ask that question is the voice that you have. Very few companies would allow you to do that."[123] The worker notes: "Libertarianism is the ethos of the *leaders* of these big tech companies, not the rank and file. . . . We stood up because we believe workers should have a voice." The worker adds, "Organizing around Project Maven helped people realize that no matter how good their job is . . . they're still workers, not owners."

But the most impressive manifestation of Google's worker activism is definitely November 2018's full walkout of over twelve thousand employees, in protest of the revelation that Google had granted an enormous $90 million exit deal to Android unit leader Andy Rubin after finding he had been credibly charged with sexual harassment. Writer Angela Nagle, a maverick voice of the Irish left, had previously noted this tendency in the industry: "Tech companies may love the feel-good factor of intersectional feminism and diversity speak, but there are a few things they love more, such as tax avoidance and monopoly capitalism."[124]

Incensed by Rubin's golden parachute and informed by the struggles against Dragonfly and drone AI, as well as the #MeToo movement against sex harassment, the organizers united under the name Google Walkout for Real Change, observing that "these forms of marginalization function together to police access to power and resources. . . . Sexual harassment is the symptom, not the cause. If we want to end sexual harassment in the workplace, we must fix these structural imbalances of power."[125] The demands specifically included the same rights for contract workers, saying "the power structure . . . inherently diminishes" those temps and contractors, and is "rooted in the same foundation of inequality."[126] The walkout was as worldwide as Google's operations, with employees leaving work in California, London, and Singapore.

Google ultimately agreed to end its practice of forced private arbitration of sexual harassment and assault charges, which tend to require NDAs and often favor the employer and their great legal resources. In light of today's scrutiny of institutional sexism, unequal pay, and workplace discrimination, it should perhaps go without saying that the company shouldn't have changed its policy only when met with strikes and extensive public shaming. And notably, the company didn't address other demands by the workforce, like making its internal report on sexual harassment public, or its most pivotal demand—a board seat for an employee representative. Common in other developed countries, this limited measure of shared oversight was dismissed by CEO Sundar Pichai, who called it a decision for the company's board to make. Time and class struggle will tell.

A few months after these embarrassing walk-backs, Google quietly removed its "Don't be evil" motto from its corporate code of conduct. Schmidt had once called it a "cultural lodestar that shines over all management layers, product plans, and office politics."[127] But in 2015 Google's holding company, Alphabet, changed it to the wimpier "Do the right thing," and the dispensing of this cutesy shallow corporate bullshit was complete.[128] Now capitalist market incentives will openly determine who will be surfaced, and who submerged.

CHAPTER 6

Disgracebook

The trivial network
that moves the world

Many of us roll our eyes at the mention of Facebook, probably in response to the trivial nature of our friends' pointless posts, weird phony links, hyper-partisan bickering, and wonderful cat videos. But Facebook is the fifth-largest company in the world, after the other four tech giants dissected in this book, and it's a hugely important platform for many people. About 45 percent of Americans get news through it, and in large swaths of the developing world it's synonymous with the Internet itself. In June 2017 the US Supreme Court ruled that the government can't entirely ban even sex offenders from using social media like Facebook, since so much of society's politics and business is conducted there.[1]

Indeed, Facebook's colossal 2.1 billion user base is such a perfect example of network effects that it's literally a textbook case, picked by economics professors to illustrate the increased value of network services as more people use them.[2] Like the other tech giants we've reviewed, Facebook has its own disgraceful history of network monopoly and aggressive market power–mongering, and it has shown an enduring, cartoonishly casual treatment of two billion people's data. Some of its botches are finally weighing on the company, but as we'll see, the smart money is on Facebook's locked-in users staying put.

Creeps and Bounds

Facebook's origins are shrouded in controversy, with competing claims of who came up with the idea that became the platform. Various students at Harvard circa 2004 were interested in trying to develop an online social network, and the dispute over its creation would be made into a book and eventually a David Fincher movie. Despite its murky genesis, most everyone knows that credit ultimately gets attributed to Mark Zuckerberg, with his typical Harvard pedigree—the son of a dentist and psychologist who grew up with a nanny and attended the elite Exeter Academy.[3]

Zuckerberg had previously come to attention on campus with his creation of Facemash, which used ranking algorithms to display pairs of photos of students and allow site visitors to cast a vote for the hottest. Conceived as a campus-focused version of the then-popular HotOrNot.com, we know from an online journal post made at the time that Zuckerberg created Facemash while drinking beer after being dumped by a "bitch." Many of the pictures were obtained by hacking into the various campus residence houses and downloading their "facebooks," collections of photos of freshmen students. Zuckerberg's site asked: "Were we let in for our looks? No. Will we be judged by them? Yes." Luckily no one pursued an idea expressed in the journal to include farm animals for consideration alongside the freshmen.

So it could be said that Facebook's early success was driven by men's desire to be creeps. Zuckerberg was brought before the university administrative board for the hacking and privacy violations, but in line with the disciplinary actions often taken against privileged Ivy League students, the board let him off with a warning. However, the campus coverage of this affair brought Zuckerberg to the attention of a group of students attempting to establish an online social network, HarvardConnection. They eventually approached him to code it for them, which led to a major court case over whether Zuckerberg stole the idea from those students.

The short version of this gossipy origin story is that Zuckerberg had been hired informally, and after doing some work stopped communicating.[4] At any rate, Zuckerberg eventually settled with the other students in 2008, for amounts that speak to the money at stake—$30 million in cash and stock.[5] Other settlements would follow, including with another early cofounder who later sued over having his shares diluted.

But the endless contention misses important context. Communications scholar Tim Wu observes that the social network idea was very much in the air at the time, with Harvard's own residential computing head stating in mid-2004 that an "electronic facebook" for the campus was "a very high priority for the College. . . . We have every intention of completing the facebook by the end of the spring semester."[6] So between various Harvard students, Zuckerberg, and the university itself, it's clear that many people were thinking about the possibilities, and there wasn't a single flash of inspiration or solitary stroke of genius.

But Zuckerberg worked hard and quickly, and designed the site in an appealing minimalist style. The site became immediately popular after the publication of a profile in the campus paper, and it went on to benefit from the network effect in the most classic fashion: everyone wanted to join a network that their friends were on, and, as more and more users joined, the value of the network and its attractiveness to others grew and grew. Even though Zuckerberg's initial service had almost no functionality save the ability to create a profile and view others, its popularity skyrocketed, and soon the large majority of Harvard undergrads had joined—ten thousand users in about a month.[7]

Importantly, Thefacebook (as the service was originally known) in the early days was limited to Harvard, required the email address of a Harvard student or faculty member to create an account, and would only grow by gradually adding campuses with similar requirements. This worked to the platform's advantage in a number of ways—first, campuses are natural social units with extensive social networks, so it was a fortuitous starting point. Being limited to the campus also made it feel like a private network, easing students into the early step of sharing information on their online profile pages, similar to the paper ones the campus already maintained. As it expanded, its association with the flagship Ivy League school gave it useful prestige.

As the service became dramatically popular and expanded to other Ivy League campuses, Zuckerberg and his dorm-room partners struggled to keep up. Servers and network equipment were needed to host the site and handle the traffic, meaning thousands of dollars were needed to pay for it, and in the early period Zuckerberg resisted ads, thinking they would clutter the platform. A few were allowed, including Mastercard ads selling credit cards to college students, which was unsurprisingly successful. And raising near-term cash wasn't a huge obstacle, due to the economic background of the founders. Zuckerberg put in a couple thousand from programming jobs he'd held, his partners from wealthy backgrounds were able to invest tens of thousands, and of course Zuckerberg's parents kicked in, coming to a family investment of $85,000. The class basis of the service is worth remembering along with its creepy origins.

Zuckerberg used his elite connections with Exeter chums and others to get the site promoted at Stanford and Dartmouth, and each time the service was extended to another elite campus, membership would shoot up after just a few hours' coding.[8] As pure a case of network effects as can be found, Thefacebook definitely can't be credibly claimed to have succeeded over other online social networks because of its quality—to give just one example, in 2005 the customer support department for the entire platform was a single student at Berkeley, working part-time. At one point there was a backlog of 75,000 support requests from users, which grew to

150,000 before falling as the platform blew up and could afford more support.[9] Obviously, responsive service wasn't the driver of the site.

This was the same problem experienced by Friendster, the social networking site that was most similar to Thefacebook in its early days. It had a long head start over Zuckerberg, and often that is enough to become the enduring winner in network-based industries. However, Friendster couldn't keep up with its own network-driven growth, always behind in the race to catch up on server capacity, and in the end it collapsed under its own weight as pages took twenty seconds to load.[10] The great cost of "scaling," as it's known in Silicon Valley, is a real barrier to entry that Friendster failed to pass, but Thefacebook, with its frantic network investments, was able to clear it. Further, because of the controlled process of rolling out one new school's access at a time, it could grow rapidly yet in a somewhat-measured fashion, usually activating registration once the waiting list approached 20 percent of the student body.

The young Zuckerberg "used that word *dominate* all the time," an early visitor to their operation commented. Still it was the early days, and early exec Sean Parker found "Mark was actually very rational about the low probability of building a true empire."[11] However, they did know how building an empire could happen: Zuckerberg and his friends were very aware of "what economists call 'network effects,'" as a corporate biographer describes it, where "growth tends to lead to more growth, in a virtuous cycle."[12] Virtuous for a monopoly, anyway! So, as with Bill Gates and Jeff Bezos, but not Steve Jobs, their eyes were open to the economics working in their favor.

From 2004 some real money was coming in, primarily from Apple, which paid Facebook for a sponsored page, handing out a buck per group member per month, coming to over $50,000 monthly.[13] And by this time, Silicon Valley venture capitalists were taking notice, despite the company barely covering its rocketing server expenses. But huge growth is a magnet all its own for capitalists, and in early 2005 the service's users were growing by 3 percent daily.

Capitalist interest grew as the site added functionality like a "Wall" for the user or their friends to write on, which increased member engagement with the site. Users at Stanford reported, "I can't get off of it." "I don't study. I'm addicted." "Everyone's on it."[14] Music to the ears of advertisers! In the end, Accel Partners landed the investment, and it gave million-dollar bonuses to the founders. Following this investment, the recently renamed Facebook moved to a modern glass building and added the Photos app—a new functionality that demonstrated how pictures tagged with users could spread through the network and encourage the "Facebook trance" that the execs were already learning to feed. But it also led to Zuckerberg's conception of a "social graph" that represented the network of social ties and relationships among the members, which Facebook would exploit effectively once it developed its advertising-based business model.

At this point Myspace remained as the main challenger to Facebook, with four times its membership. It had survived the challenge of scaling well, but in summer 2005 it was bought by Rupert Murdoch's News Corp, which immediately blanketed it in ads. Along with Myspace's generally eclectic layouts, the site began to lose appeal—and load more slowly. These developments, along with Facebook's stunning growth, led the network effect to run in reverse for Myspace as users backed away from the service after seeing their friends do so.

Importantly, Facebook didn't reach its borderline-monopoly status just through network effects and Harvard name-dropping. Crucially, Zuckerberg and his friends had been reading up on business-school giants including Peter Drucker, the originator of the term "knowledge worker" and a symbol of refining corporate hierarchies, and they began using real predatory monopolist tactics. Consider the "surround strategy," used to take over the market at schools like Baylor University in Waco, Texas. The campus had its own local online social network, since there were numerous local startups in the firm's first years in the mid-2000s. Rather than open Facebook at that school and compete directly, the team prepared a list of colleges within a hundred miles of it and opened the service in those schools instead. As students piled into Facebook on those campuses, students at Baylor (and other schools where similar strategies were used) saw all their friends on a rival network, and the economics of it did the rest.[15] Soon the local network would be extinct, and Facebook would roll on to conquer new lands.

Indeed, Marc Andreessen, added to the board by Zuckerberg, suggested in 2009 that "it's too late for somebody to compete with Facebook on Facebook's turf."[16] He would know—he cofounded Mosaic, later Netscape, the first web browser widely used in the United States and which was famously crushed by Microsoft for resisting its monopoly in the browser wars.

Having activated open enrollment for everyone in 2006, Facebook finally surpassed Myspace in membership in 2008 as it went global. So, when reorganizing users' profile pages that year to encourage more sharing and network activity (for example, changing the "[User] is . . ." prompt for posts to "What's on your mind?"), the company internally referred to the change as "FB 95," referring to Microsoft's Windows 95, the product considered to have consummated Microsoft's drive to become a global monopoly.[17]

During this heady growth era, after Zuckerberg's friend and well-connected company executive Parker was arrested for suspected possession of cocaine, Zuckerberg gained total control over the board and the company's decisions, a position he maintained after the company's later initial public offering. As Parker put it, "That solidified Mark's position as the sort of hereditary king of Facebook."[18] And even today the company's official 10-K filings for investors note that the CEO holds an unusual amount of power even by corporate standards, observing, "[O]ur CEO has control over key decision making as a result of his control of a majority of the voting power of our outstanding capital stock." And "in the event of death, the shares . . . will be transferred to the persons or entities he has designated."[19] Parker wasn't exaggerating.

Former Zuckerberg adviser Roger McNamee says, "Decision making at Facebook is even more centralized than at Microsoft." He adds, "If you wanted to draw a Facebook organization chart to scale, it would look like a loaf of bread with a giant antenna pointing straight up. Zuck and Sheryl [Sandberg] are at the top of the antenna. . . . Everyone else is down in the loaf of bread. It is the most centralized decision-making structure I have ever encountered in a large company."[20] David Kirkpatrick's perspective on this model of control is that "Zuckerberg will almost certainly continue to rule over Facebook with absolute authority. He wants to rule not only Facebook, but in some sense the evolving communications infrastructure of the planet."[21]

As with the other CEOs profiled in this book, the power of bosses makes their personas important for the day-to-day realities of the workforce. Some friends of Zuckerberg's left the company, explaining that they "got fed up. . . . Working with Mark is very challenging," mainly due to his ambiguity.[22] Zuckerberg himself is a cipher to many who meet him, giving few reactions to conversations and listening blankly. During the company's all-out growth period in 2006, he was known for frequently fainting in the office, sometimes mid-meeting, until his sleep schedule and diet were brought under control. Andreessen compares him to Bezos (the temper-tantrum-throwing tyrant), Jobs (the abusive, blame-shifting incompetent), and Gates himself, who of course used his monopoly power to crush Andreessen's own firm in the 1990s.[23] It's unclear why Andreessen thinks this comparison is favorable.

The high point of Zuckerberg's enormous power and the childish, creepy misogyny that started his journey is his celebrated business card. Multiple sources describe his carrying (at least for some time) a pair of them—one reading "Mark Zuckerberg, CEO," and the other reading "I'm CEO—Bitch."[24]

The Feed

As Facebook rocketed upward, the service's functionality remained limited to viewing one another's profiles and vainly manicuring your own. But the pictures function demonstrated people's appetite not just for sharing but for being able to conveniently view all their friends' updates, which ultimately resulted in the News Feed. This is the now-familiar central landing place on the service where you view all posts or actions of friends, with the platform using algorithms to decide which items to display and what order to put them in.

The service was rolled out in fall 2006, along with the advent of the hugely successful open registration. But the Feed led to the biggest crisis Facebook had then faced, and like the far-bigger crises it would later confront, this one originated in user privacy. Previously, users felt they were sharing personal information only with their friends, and that their information was viewable only on their own wall. With the rollout of the Feed, it suddenly felt like everyone could see all of a given user's data—even though, as the company made clear in its response, nothing had changed, with the Feed only viewable by the same group of friends. What changed was the way the Feed brought to users' attention just how much they had exposed on the site.

Critical emails flooded the company, and huge new groups formed on the Facebook platform opposing the new feature. As they proliferated into the hundreds, some with hundreds of thousands of members, the company soon realized over 10 percent of the service's users were in organized opposition to its decisions.[25] Facebook hired security guards to escort staff members into the company building, and it responded in true capitalist fashion: condescension. "Calm down. Breathe. We hear you," read the blog headline Zuckerberg composed in response.

But patronizing bloggery couldn't hide the fact that the company would have to respond meaningfully to such a major revolt of the users, who after all generated nearly all of the site's content.

The internal debates foreshadowed issues surrounding Facebook's rise as an information hub—as Kirkpatrick recounts, "There were earnest debates in Facebook's conference rooms about whether they should simply block messages about the protest groups from showing up in people's News Feeds."[26] Zuckerberg vetoed this on grounds of "journalistic integrity." It was the first time the company would grapple with its growing power over the information people have access to, and it revealed the gun that remained in the site's hands.

In order to "quell the uprising," the company rolled out the first of many new privacy features that gave users some semblance of control over certain uses of their information. You could now opt out of having some actions reported to the News Feed, like photo comments or relationship status changes. Though these were small concessions, they were the first recognition of a threat Facebook continues to deal with: user content strikes. Since effectively all the platform's content is user-generated, the fact that sites like Students against Facebook News Feed grew to three-quarters of a million members in days showed that the service's convenient tools for organizing fans of the Apple Computer could also be used to organize opposition to corporate power.

And as Facebook's numbers rose into hundreds of millions and then billions of users, the content of the Feed became increasingly important. For among the flow of selfies, pictures of food, and wedding announcements, people were also sharing news. Naturally, news would be among those things users of a social network would be interested in sharing, but the site's exploding network growth meant that the news on the Feed, posted by friends or others, became a major source of popular information about world affairs. And problematically, this news was doubly curated, first by the interests of your online friends, and then by the algorithms of the company itself.

This has enabled the rise of the tech-mediated "filter bubble," where readers or viewers of news on tech platforms are exposed to items posted by their friends, or chosen by a service's algorithm based on what they've clicked on in the past. This tendency is very real—site algorithms are driven by "relevance," which is mainly established by what you've previously expressed an interest in. And, of course, our friends are more likely to have similar beliefs and views to us than the average person—surely an enduring fact through history. But now, because of these factors, many of us can accidentally end up exposed to nothing but views and news writing we agree with already, since everything else is filtered out.

Eli Pariser, who wrote the book on this subject, observes that this platform-enabled bubble is more serious than in previous eras, when people's views were largely limited to their real-world friends and their choice of newspaper or TV news. For one thing, the modern filter bubbles aren't visible to you—when you flick through cable news until you find an option relatively close to your views, or walk past library sections containing other ideologies, there is at least an indication that alternatives exist. But on tech platforms, like Facebook and Google, you may very well have no idea your search results are being personalized according to dozens of data points, or that your News Feed is tailored to what you've engaged with in the past.[27] This is particularly hazardous considering the availability of Facebook Everywhere, and its successor, the Pixel software, which have enabled sites across the web to port in the "Like" feature and other social media plugins. This allows a lot of off-Facebook activity to be logged back to your user account, and it potentially extends the company's echo chamber to the rest of the Internet.[28]

As the public increasingly uses these platforms to learn about the world, the tendency of bubbles to encourage partisan or hysterical information has heightened the spread of "fake news," which before the Trump administration's use of the phrase meant plainly false information that tended to spread quickly. A filtered Internet experience is dry tinder to this fire, as opposing sources that might debunk lies may be kept off-screen. The main approach to resisting fake news has been to affiliate with various "fact-checking" bodies, like the respected myth-debunking site Snopes, and to use their determinations to label posts.[29] For example, utterly false articles, such as those reporting Pope Francis's endorsement of the Trump campaign, get a "disputed" label. And more tellingly, the company has also begun to "surface" more coverage from various mainstream publishers, which means giving it a higher placement in users' Feeds.

But as the media watchdog group FAIR pointed out, if we were living under this system, in the nineteenth century, Ida B. Wells's anti-lynching news reports would surely never have appeared. That is to say that mainstream approval is mainly extended to news sources that don't disturb the commercial status quo, and that maintain a favorable climate for the influx of advertising dollars—a point explored in depth by a long list of leftists from George Orwell to Noam Chomsky.[30] The company has continued to experiment with its news settings, mostly in poor countries like Bolivia, Cambodia, and Slovakia, where small markets lower the risk in the company's eyes.[31]

Facebook later reported that articles tagged as "disputed" by fact-checking entities were clicked 80 percent less, raising the enormous power Facebook and its appointed fact-checkers have over the biggest information platform in the world.[32] This fact is now widely recognized—most vocally by the political right, which lit the reactionary corners of the Internet on fire with claims of conspiracy and anti-conservative bias after recent revelations by *Gizmodo* that some editors of Facebook's Trending Topics section curated it to limit conservative sources.[33] The company later fired the contract workers who altered pieces for political reasons, moving to a software-based approach, which "quickly led to the appearance of false stories in the box," according to the conservative *Wall Street Journal*.[34] This was the beginning of the right's antagonism to Big Tech, whose rise it happily supported for decades in the name of free markets.

Meanwhile, there arose a wave of research reports and statements from former company insiders suggesting that engaging with the platform was actively making people sadder. The Royal Soci-

ety for Public Health in the United Kingdom studied young people's use of various social media platforms including Facebook and
Instagram, finding they tended to encourage users to compare their
lives with others'.[35] And Facebook's former VP for user growth,
Chamath Palihapitiya, said he feels "tremendous guilt" over his
role in the company because the curated versions of ourselves we
upload tend to have negative effects on users, especially those pas-
sively viewing others' sunnier-than-reality versions of their lives on
the platform. Palihapitiya said the result is "ripping apart the social
fabric," and that his kids "aren't allowed to use that shit."[36]

In response to this fairly horrifying news, the company decided
to focus the platform more on "meaningful interaction," pivoting
its algorithm to show less posted content from businesses (including media) and more from friends. This meant plunges in traffic
for commercial websites and dire financial straits for many media
outlets. Over the course of 2017, news publishers' average referrals from Facebook fell from 40 percent to 24 percent, a crushing
drop.[37] Whether the change toward more shallow content from
friends and less shallow content from business is positive or not,
the point is that Zuckerberg and the board will decide how much
news we see on their platform. As *Wall Street Journal* reporters put
it, despite Facebook's resistance to playing "an even more active
role in deciding what content is acceptable on its site," it remains
"the most powerful distributor of media content on the web."[38]

One prominent left media editor, Nathan Robinson of the
socialist magazine *Current Affairs*, wrote frankly that since news-
stand sales now barely exist, and "almost all of our online traffic
comes from Facebook and Twitter . . . the sharing of our articles on social media is the engine of our growth." So one simple
change in Facebook's algorithms or a cheeky tweet that Twitter
decides violates its terms of service, and they can shut off links
to the site. "Instantly, we would lose a significant portion of our
audience, with no way to get it back."[39] For this reason Robinson
titled his essay "Why I Love Mark Zuckerberg and Can Never
Say a Word against Him."

Ad to Worse

From the earliest days developing the service, Zuckerberg was resistant to advertising. While his opposition was more aesthetic and not as intellectually elaborated as Google's founders', in its earliest years Facebook had very limited advertising. In discussions with early investor Peter Thiel, Zuckerberg agreed to put growing the user base above short-term monetization—much like tech leaders did during Amazon and Google's salad days.[40] But as the platform's network-fueled growth went vertical, servers worth millions of dollars had to be paid for and kept running. And as with Google, a project that began largely for its own merits, with profit as a relative afterthought, now faced a requirement set by the economic structure of capitalism—to become a commercial business so it could acquire the financial resources needed to grow. But even in its early days, the company promoted its "addicted" users to buyers of its limited early ads.[41]

In 2006 Google had a deal with Myspace to place ads on its site, and Facebook struck a little-remembered deal with Microsoft to do the same. This brought in significant cash to finance Facebook's galloping growth, especially since Microsoft, in its eagerness to compete with its archrival Google, agreed to money-losing rates, swinging Facebook from losses to a respectable profit.[42] In time Google began courting Facebook for its ad-placing business, and Zuckerberg soon moderated his views of ads, remarking, "I don't hate all advertising. I just hate advertising that stinks."[43]

But during the negotiations, Facebook's contact-importer function, which allowed new users to find their friends on Facebook by uploading their email address books, stopped working with Microsoft's popular Hotmail service, which steered emails Facebook was sending to spam folders. The contact importer was an important source of Facebook's frantic expansion, and the glitch caused the company's growth to slow up dramatically. Once the ad deal was struck, the importer started working fine with Hotmail again—meaning Microsoft had very likely turned to its classic tactic of purposefully creating incompatibilities with other software as a means of arm-twisting.[44]

But crucially, the deal also freed up some ad inventory with which Facebook could begin experimenting, especially in the area of micro-targeting. With its ocean of user data, Facebook could steer ads for different goods and services to quite-specific groups of users, with ads at first based on simple keywords users had written on their user profiles. The sheer volume of personal information users had entered into the platform allowed Facebook to take advantage of its network, providing enormous potential for micro-targeting.

And with the hire of Google advertising head Sheryl Sandberg, Facebook developed an online advertising business model that would satisfy a different market segment than Google's wheelhouse. Google's model for its gigantic ad business is based on finding and displaying ads to consumers already searching for them—those who have decided they want to buy a new smartphone or movie tickets or a pair of sneakers. This advertising "fulfills demand" in industry language, whereas Facebook's access to so much lifestyle and life-event data means it's better suited for ads that make you realize you'd like to buy something in the first place—for example, it could display ads for diapers and pediatric services to a user who recently posted that she was pregnant. This is called "creating demand" or the "soft sell" in ad circles, and it represents a far larger portion of the ad market than demand fulfillment—TV ads are demand creators, for example.[45] But despite this distinction, both companies focus on highly targeted online ad dollars, and thus they remain in competition over corporate spending.

Law professor Tim Wu observes in his absorbing book *The Attention Merchants* that Facebook was attractive to many users at first partially because it had few to no ads, unlike Myspace, which was packed with trashy-looking online come-ons. But once users were more locked in (and as the company needed a greater cash flow to finance infrastructure investments), it opened up the floodgates. Wu reviews the history of the ad-driven business model from radio to online platforms, founded on providing "free" entertainment or news in exchange for a few moments of your time, looking at or listening to commercials for companies whose payments for your attention provide the media business's revenue. In other words, he finds that while we may feel like customers of ad-based businesses, we are in fact the product, since our attention is sold to ad buyers.[46]

Soon Facebook had developed a large number of categories to slot its users into, allowing micro-targeting on a minute level just as the spread of high-speed broadband Internet service encouraged large numbers of people to go online, and the revenue model became an incredible success. Interestingly, among the early adopters of these targeted demand-generating ads were local businesses, taking advantage of the ease of the platform's targeting software and its simple credit card payment system. But national brands were on board too, and in time the ad model utterly dominated the company's revenue, coming to a whopping 98 percent of its income in 2017, according to its financial filings.[47] In Wu's description, "[T]he public became like renters willingly making extensive improvements to their landlord's property, even as they were made to look at advertisements . . . a virtual attention plantation."[48] Or as Sheryl Sandberg put it, for all the company's "connecting the world" rhetoric, "we have the business model. The revenue model is advertising. This is the business we're in, and it's working."[49] And Facebook's ad-based business model extended well outside the platform proper and into the rest of the web— for instance, planting "cookies" on your computer, thus creating those ads that creepily follow you around the Internet after you view a company's site an Amazon listing and leave without buying.

There have been snags—Facebook has a history of misstating, to its benefit, the viewership of posted video and other metrics. Recognizing the essential nature of its relations with its main customers, Facebook agreed to form a "measurement council" composed of its ad gurus, representatives of major commercial buyers, and ad industry executives.[50] However, Facebook maintains the power in the relationship, since it has the irreplaceable platform with two billion users and a galaxy of their personal and tracking-based information. So despite it all, the *Wall Street Journal* observes that "while marketers may be frustrated right now, few have actually left Facebook," and its ad business continues to generate $40 billion in yearly revenue—much like us, advertisers are locked into the platform. One ad exec with a prominent advertising firm says they must "play ball" with Facebook.[51]

The platform has reorganized its privacy functionality a number of times, showing users their various categories of personal information and allowing them to download it. But despite it all, company execs have stated publicly that users "largely haven't changed their privacy settings" despite even the uproar over developer data access triggered by the Cambridge Analytica scandal (see below).[52] This inertia may speak to user disinterest, or the feeling of futility given that the information is likely already out there for good, and network effects keep the users on the platform for the same reason they were already there—everyone else is there.

The Hands of f8

Since its creation, Facebook has been a platform—users are encouraged to create their profile content and upload photos and other media, while the company provides the attractive space of a popular social network. But in 2006 Zuckerberg also began looking seriously at the possibility of allowing outside software developers to create tools and games that would run on Facebook for its billions of users. As his fawning biographer and *Fortune* journalist David Kirkpatrick relates, "He wanted to do for the Web what Gates did for the personal computer," and "not only did Apple succeed at this masterfully with its Macintosh operating system, but it succeeded again, first with the iPod and then with its magnificent iPhone."[53] Zuckerberg in fact consulted with Gates, the adjudicated monopolist. Yikes.

This broader platform strategy was designed in part to definitively defeat Myspace, a company often held up as a claim that network effects don't necessarily favor incumbents, as it had a membership lead of many millions during Facebook's early days. However, it accepted large amounts of unappealing ads that cluttered the site, and at the time it had declared some independent applications wouldn't be allowed on the site, weakening its platform position.[54] Zuckerberg saw a chance to build out the platform, and additionally, to make itself distinct from Myspace in a way that would secure its social media dominance.

The open platform was formally inaugurated in 2007 at a new annual conference the company arranged, where third-party developers could show off their new applications and games. Perhaps ironically, in light of the huge privacy ramifications years later, the conference was named "f8"—it would turn out to be "f8-ful" indeed. Dozens of companies demonstrated apps at the first conference, and the event, along with the launch of the iPhone a month later, seemed to augur a new era of mobile applications.

Traffic on the site spiked yet again, to the point that Facebook had to actively borrow servers from other tech companies, and in time the company cocreated a dedicated data center for app partners.[55] Soon goofy, trivial games like FarmVille were hugely popular, and notifications from players to other Facebook users were stuffing system inboxes. By summer 2008 the havoc wreaked by these explosively popular apps and their ubiquitous links led the company to try to weed out the spammers and more obviously abusive apps by lowering their prominence in the News Feed. It encouraged users to file complaints and eventually implemented a rating system that led to a reduction in the chaos. Once the initial turbulence was stabilized, the move toward transforming Facebook into a platform proved hugely successful, and by 2009 app makers were bringing in around $500 million annually—almost as much as Facebook itself. At the time, a Facebook exec said, "We sort of stumbled our way through becoming good at dealing with developers."[56]

Did they? Throughout these years, a Wild West atmosphere had developed among the developers—not just independents making useful tools or fun games, but classic capitalists eyeing Facebook's gigantic trove of valuable targeting data. This was the environment that enabled the large-scale scraping of our personal information for which the company has now become notorious. The more or less open leveraging of our freely entered information to attract huge numbers of developers seemed to trouble even the *Wall Street Journal*, which in 2018 assessed that "Facebook was, for a time, a vehicle for exfiltrating massive amounts of data about its users to developers and data miners of every stripe," pulling data about users of the third-party apps as well as all their friends.[57]

Zuckerberg allowed the practice for several years, over which the company rose to rank among the top-five towering Big Tech companies. But Facebook began to fear the results of this policy and started reigning in developer access, especially to data about the friends of app users. And yet, the decision to stop this licentious approach to personal information was only taken after a consent decree with the Federal Trade Commission in 2011, following a suit filed by the Electronic Privacy Information Center (EPIC) after the company continued claiming users could keep their data private while routinely allowing it to be made public. The FTC required the company to provide app users with their privacy information and require consent before applications could pull more information beyond what they have set to "public" on their user profiles. And only in 2014 did the company tell developers to delete information about users' friends, effective in 2015; moreover, some companies got extensions, including Microsoft and Apple—making the latter's condemnation of Facebook's treatment of privacy sound pretty disingenuous.[58]

But by then, many applications had our data in their corporate hands, and some held onto it even after they were found out, as in the case of the now-infamous data analysis company Cambridge Analytica. The scandal involved the company lying about its use of the data it collected on tens of millions of people who participated in its personality quiz app, then retaining the data after Facebook demanded it be deleted. Amazingly, Facebook only became aware

Cambridge Analytica had held onto the data after a group of news agencies, including the London *Observer* and the *New York Times*, brought it to the company's attention. This shows the limited interest Facebook had in maintaining user control over personal information, in contrast to the consuming drive to become an open platform. A Columbia University professor observed, "For many years, Facebook was basically giving away user data like it was handing out candy," driving its platform to its current heights.[59]

The data-gathering apps themselves often indicated up front that any data collected would be for academic purposes, "but the fine print . . . may have told users it could be commercial," the *Times* reported. Such apps are able to pull all your address book's contacts' basic information and "likes" in under a second.[60] Hilariously, the company's open-platform era was given a passing grade in the area of user control of data by its outside auditor, the respected consulting firm PricewaterhouseCoopers, as late as 2017![61]

The company is now probing suspicious-looking developers, but Zuckerberg himself has conceded that it's impossible to find out where all the user data went and how it will be used, since the open period lasted several years, and after all, many of the companies running shady data-scraping apps through the period no longer exist.[62] Indeed, the scale of the platform is such that Zuckerberg has since openly referred to holding internal discussions about whether enough trained auditors exist in the world to audit all the apps now or formerly on the platform.

In the midst of the Cambridge Analytica scandal, the company also admitted that besides various classes of application-developing partners, Facebook also shared extensive user data access with more than sixty hardware companies, including Apple, Amazon, and Samsung. These companies were also exempted from the 2015 restrictions on friends' data, on the absurd grounds that the firms delivered the Facebook platform to mobile users and thus Facebook considered them essentially extensions of the company under the FTC's terms.[63] Notably, Facebook now expects to pay a fine to the FTC for this lapse, since it violates the terms of the 2011 consent decree. The company has indicated it anticipates a fine in the neighborhood of $3 to $5 billion, which sounds punishing, but the *Wall Street Journal* observed that "Facebook made over 11 times the high-end of that amount in revenue last year alone."[64]

The waves of bad press crashing into the company were accompanied by the backlash over the use of the platform in the 2016 US election. The campaign was an infamously divisive and trashy episode, and one of the most contentious aspects has been the revelation that foreign entities created groups and bought social media ads promoting themselves and related events in the United States. Typically, the accounts took contentious or extreme positions and seemed to have the effect of inflaming tensions among different social groups. Sometimes the accounts supported opposing events, in some cases even held on the same day—anti-immigration groups were supported along with Black Lives Matter.[65] These pages promoted or partially financed dozens of political events, and since then, positions outside mainstream political bounds are often alleged to be foreign backed—sadly, not a new phenomenon.

But most reporting on the subject has observed that the outside groups seemed to glom onto preexisting social groups and their movements, with the *Wall Street Journal* reporting they "often sought to work alongside legitimate groups organizing rallies and protests."[66] And after all the evidence we've seen of Facebook failing to anticipate the problems of its platform, it's maybe unsurprising that the company actually cut Russia out of its own (pre-controversy) report it published on the 2016 election. At the advice of its attorneys and policy team, its report was shortened by several pages and Russia-related material was removed, with the country's name appearing only in a blog post months later.[67]

Considering that a grand total of 290 Facebook and Instagram accounts were found to be connected to the St. Petersburg–based Internet Research Agency—a firm that receives Russian government support—and that a total of about $100,000 was spent on ads promoting these groups, this should be considered relatively small potatoes in the world of global election-influence intrigue.[68] The United States spends billions annually on international diplomacy and espionage to influence elections every year, and the US Chamber of Commerce and its members in the banking, pharmaceutical, and energy industries spend billions to manipulate American elections, making this hugely discussed outside spending look puny. Since then, Facebook has required that buyers of political ads include affiliation information that can be viewed on an ad display, and political regulation is now expected among the numerous government investigations of the company.

The scandals have added up, including recent reports of a giant security breach in which the personal data on thirty million users was stolen, ostensibly by spammers, reportedly leading Zuckerberg to tell his senior execs that Facebook was "at war," that he would act with less company consensus and that he would confront critics, including by hiring slimy political opposition researchers. Zuckerberg famously bought four houses surrounding his main mansion in Palo Alto for extra privacy, as nakedly ironic as that is. But the escalating backlash has also led to more animosity toward Silicon Valley billionaires, to the extent that company security expenses for Zuckerberg and his family reached $20 million in 2018, according to the *Wall Street Journal*.[69]

The company has reacted to the setbacks as most gigantic corporations would—by pouring cash into advertising that tries to reshape the associations people have with its brand. The company shelled out $382 million in 2018 and is sharply increasing that amount, including to pay for what the business press calls "apology ad" campaigns. (These numbers are enormous, though still well behind Amazon's unbelievable $1.84 billion annual spend).[70]

But the fallout of this parade of scandals, from selling off our data to build its platform to the Russia affair, have sufficed to finally penalize Facebook in a meaningful way, at least in the near term. Its stock price took a steep, headline-grabbing dive in summer 2018, representing the largest one-day loss of value for any

US company in history, after its report that user growth—while continuing—was slowing, as was growth in ad sales. The company had indicated this user trend would continue in the near term, leading to the headline-grabbing market drop. The price largely recovered after users failed to desert the service; platform lock-in has to date put a floor under the stock.

Yet even that same earnings report showed the network's enduring strength—revenue increased 42 percent from the previous year and profits leaped 31 percent from their already-high levels.[71] These kind of numbers normally cause giddy joy in the wealthy elite who own most corporate stock, so the fact that they caused the stock to skid may say more about how overheated equity markets have become than it does about the company's impending doom.

Valley of the LOLs

Despite its market swoon, Facebook remains firmly dominant in social media and the targeted ad market. Besides its main site, the company also controls Instagram, Messenger, and WhatsApp, each with over a billion users—gigantic in comparison with competitors Twitter and Snapchat, with under a half a billion users between them. Its subsidieries capture a whopping fifty minutes of the average American's day.[72] It holds tens of billions in cash and had a truly preposterous profit margin of 39 percent in 2017, according to its 10-K federal filing for that year. Like other fast-growing tech companies, it pays no dividends to its stockholders but is embarking on a large stock repurchase program of up to $6 billion.[73]

The company has real potential to flex this muscle in the future—Tim Wu observed in *The Master Switch* that "social-networking sites, Facebook first and foremost, stealthily aim to conquer by offering themselves as Web alternatives. Many forms of content that once stood independent on the Web . . . are now created instead on Facebook . . . unlike Web pages, Facebook pages are Facebook's property, and are deliberately not linked to the rest of the Web."[74] This walled garden is even more serious in the fast-growing markets of the developing world, where the company's Free Basics program, offered to users with simple phones and tiny budgets, gives Facebook total control over the user's access to the Internet, the ultimate walled garden.[75] The company is moving to open the service to kids under thirteen, following YouTube's steps to hook ever-younger users.

Defenders of the online monopolies rush to insist that new startup competitors could unseat them, as Facebook did to Myspace and Friendster in its early days. But like its Silicon Valley peers, the company is spending heavily to avoid that, prompting the *Wall Street Journal* to report that it has "an internal 'early bird' warning system that identifies potential threats." This of course helps the giant to follow in the monopolist footsteps of Microsoft and Amazon: closely observe competitors, mimic their products at a low price that loses money, and use existing network incumbency to utterly crush, or maybe buy, the startups.[76] The *Wall Street Journal*, despite claiming on its editorial page that disruptive tech startups can fix any social problem, recognizes that the giants "make it increasingly difficult for startups to compete and stay independent" without being "squashed by one of the behemoths." Apparently with no sense of irony, the *Journal* concludes that "Mr. Zuckerberg is sensitive to anything that might disrupt Facebook, even the teeniest startup."

This power could be checked by organized worker power, and as with the other tech giants profiled in this book, the terrain is only partially new. The company has had a reputation for a boys' club atmosphere—a notorious feature of the tech sector—as in the startup days, when the office ladies' room had a crude mural of hetero-fantasy lesbianism. When the company gained respectability after the VC investment, the mural was painted over.[77] For years there was only one woman working in the company's core engineering circle, and Zuckerberg handled sexual harassment charges by publicly embarrassing the offender in-office, with no follow-up.[78]

And to this day, women software coders at Facebook have their work rejected 35 percent more often than their male colleagues, confirming their widely held belief that women's coding work is subject to more scrutiny than men's.[79] In its reply to the company engineer who conducted the study, management stated that these findings simply reflected the ranks of engineers at the company—perhaps not itself realizing that this implies that women's "inferior" coding explains why they rise up the corporate coding ranks slower than men, raising its own questions.

In addition to the issues faced by white-collar workers, Facebook also has a more blue-collar segment of its workforce whose work conditions are comparable to that of Apple's Foxconn contractors or Amazon's warehouse workers. Facebook's content contractors are mostly temps with poor compensation, especially considering that they review about eight thousand posts daily, often screening them for violence, sexual abuse, cruelty to animals, and other twisted garbage from a human society with a warped economic system but free access to online services. This on top of their impossible task of cleaning up the platform's duplicate and persistent fake accounts.[80]

The *Wall Street Journal* reports that

> Facebook decided years ago to rely on contract workers to enforce its policies. Executives considered the work to be relatively low-skilled compared with, say, the work performed by Facebook engineers, who typically hold computer-science degrees and earn six-figure salaries, plus stock options and benefits. . . . Several former content moderators at Facebook say they often had just a few seconds to decide if something violated the company's terms of service. . . . Turnover is high, with most content moderators working anywhere for a few months to about a year before they quit or their assignments ended. . . . Former content moderators recall having to view images of war victims who had been gutted or drowned and child soldiers engaged in killings.[81]

A former monitor "rarely had time to process what he was seeing because managers remotely monitored the productivity of moderators"; another is suing Facebook, claiming that continuously viewing suicide and beheading videos caused her PTSD.

But of course, for platforms like Facebook and Google, the great majority of work for the platform is done for free, by the users. The great magnetic platforms attracting viewers create the incentive for us to produce video, create websites, and update our social media profiles while the platforms themselves merely keep the system running—and stalk us to refine their ads, to boot. Or consider Facebook's many translations of its site for markets around the world, which occurred through the use of software listing the words to be translated, and then allowing native speakers of those languages to nominate translations and then to vote on the best one. Through this system, the Spanish version of the site was created by users in four weeks, the German in two weeks, and the French in two days, costing the company almost nothing.[82]

So, since our "volunteer" user labor is a major part of the platform ecosystem, there's real gravity to the various semi-revolts among users down the years. Earlier I described the major uprising that accompanied the introduction of the News Feed itself, where at one point a full 10 percent of the platform's users were members of opposition groups, some of which reached many hundreds of thousands of members. But there have been numerous other revolts, including after the 2008 introduction of Beacon, a commercial alert system that announced purchases Facebook users made on partner websites like Netflix or Zappos. There was a drop-down menu that allowed users to opt out of sending the buying information to all their Facebook friends, but the users often failed to notice it and found themselves broadcasting their private purchases across the platform.[83] Again, tens of thousands joined protest groups as the company waited three weeks before even addressing the backlash to the abrupt, unannounced shift in how personal data would be treated. The platform then redesigned Beacon into a fully opt-in system, later allowing it to be shut off completely, which was among the opponents' major demands.

But the most famous user uprising to date involved the site's terms of service. Today many of the commercial relationships we enter into in capitalism are governed by TOS, which tend toward extensive detail and legalese that few users read, even though economists will tell you consumers make decisions with all the relevant data in mind. Facebook's TOS underwent a significant change in 2009, and indeed it was noticed not by a regular user but by the Consumers Union. The change occurred in the section granting Facebook a license to "use, copy, publish, stream, store, retain, publicly perform or display" your posted information and data. But the company had quietly removed a clause stating that this license would expire should you close your account and remove your content from the platform. This meant that even if you canceled your account, your data would remain in Facebook's hands, presumably to target marketing to you on the rest of the web.

Again, large Facebook groups opposing the change appeared, and in days they had hundreds of thousands of members. EPIC and other consumer entities were filing complaints with the FTC, and the mood was souring, until the CEO posted in the small hours that the previous TOS would be resumed temporarily. He then announced there would be a vote on a new "Statement of Rights and Responsibilities," with the catch that the vote would be binding only if 30 percent of users polled—which at that time would mean around 60 million people. In the end about 1 percent of that number voted.[84] However, Zuckerberg was able to express pride in his generous referendum offer—which he only extended after an outside group had caught the company's sneaky data-grab and the user base had begun aggressively organizing and put the fear of god into management.

But as the company has grown, partially replacing the public square as the venue for public discussion and debate, its decisions about the limits of argument have become hugely important, despite its long resistance to being forced into the role of the "arbiter of truth." The company can temporarily or permanently suspend accounts or simply downgrade them in the News Feed, allowing them to remain on the platform but keeping anyone from seeing their posts.[85] The policies have shifted almost continuously and are clearly subject to further change.

So far, the most public episode involving policing the platform is that of Alex Jones, the prominent conspiracy theory–mongering imbecile and host of a show on his site InfoWars. Known for feverish claims that 9/11 was committed by a government conspiracy, that fluoridated water is a mind-control plan, and that multiculturalism constitutes "white genocide," Jones seldom presents any evidence for his goofy claims and would thus simply be expected to have his content down-rated after fact-checkers found it failed to pass the laugh test. But crucially, Jones also has a long history of harassment and inciting violence; for instance, he publicly revealed the home address of a parent of a child killed in the Sandy Hook school shooting, after claiming the kids and parents were "crisis actors" hired by the state. He also frequently pantomimes firing guns on-air at figures he dislikes, actions Facebook cited in temporarily suspending his personal account. Following this move, Jones received bans—some temporary, others permanent—from Twitter, Apple's App Store, and Google's YouTube.[86]

Presently the company is working on an independent content-monitoring board that would operate partially separately from Facebook and as of this writing, develop hard rules that the company's multitude of moderators could use uniformly. But, the makeup of the board, how independent it would be, and how it would make decisions are all still up in the air, and the press reports "there has been little consensus of how [Facebook] should govern speech on its platform." Notably, the large number of scholars and speech advocates the company has consulted don't agree on the board's scope, with some academics and journalists suggesting the board should be free to debate the company's privacy policy or its algorithm for ranking posts. So far Facebook is resisting that role for the board, wanting it to focus on content governance only, while the company retains authority over the rest of the platform. Facebook hopes to release a "charter" that will detail the oversight board's rules on content, and the charter is expected to contain an appeals process through which a user can file a complaint if they feel a moderator has stifled their content unjustly. Zuckerberg explained, "If you're not happy after getting your appeal, then you can also try to appeal to this broader board or body," suggesting the structure is "like some of the higher courts in other areas."[87] Making the platforms more into a private government than ever.

Exactly where the line should be drawn is naturally a difficult question, as old as freedom of speech, but the absolutely essential point is that Mark Zuckerberg shouldn't be in charge of deciding. Having an obligation to serve the company's growth even while celebrating free speech, Facebook has followed a similar path to Google's, pushing any views outside the conventional political spectrum down in its rankings and visibility, whether they include any calls for violence or not. The media watchdog group FAIR observed the dark precedent being set by "de-platforming" the wretched testosterone-pill-selling idiot Jones, noting that it was immediately extended to banning—without warning—numerous left-wing Facebook pages that do not advocate bloodshed, including Occupy London and No Unite the Right 2, a group opposing large demonstrations by white nationalists. These abrupt disappearances were met with fairly large outcries, and soon the pages were back up, but again without explanation.[88] It suggests that Facebook's decisions about allowable content will be based on the commercial needs of itself and its advertisers, and the pressures of powerful states.

All of this lines up with a remark from a close company observer in Kirkpatrick's book: "Facebook can flip a switch and turn you off. Anybody. Anytime."[89] Power indeed!

As the company staggers from crisis to crisis, many users have come to a fatalistic view that "privacy is dead" and that their information is out of their hands for good. Perhaps that accounts for the popularity of a piece of business reporting that found the company has an alert that can tell users when private parts of their profiles, such as direct messages, have been accessed by a Facebook employee, typically for fixing bugs or reviewing platform issues. Regular users, however, do not see this alert, since it is available only for users who are themselves Facebook employees. The alert is known within the company as Security Watchdog, but company employees have their own internal term for it. They call it the "Sauron alert," after the nightmarish, all-seeing eye in the popular fantasy trilogy *Lord of the Rings*.[90]

Irony loves company.

CHAPTER 7

Neutralized

The defeat and victory of the telecom networks

Net neutrality is the principle that data should be treated equally by network operators like Internet service providers, the companies that transmit your online information through their cable or wireless services. This equality would eliminate practices like an ISP blocking access to a website run by a competitor, or discrimination in service, where companies that can afford it get access to "fast lanes" that deliver their data more efficiently, while smaller sites that can't cough up the money get relegated to slow lanes. The ISPs are the great companies of the telecommunications industry, including the giant cable and broadband companies like Comcast and AT&T, and the mobile cell service providers like Verizon, Sprint, and (again) AT&T.

On February 26, 2015, the Federal Communications Commission (FCC) made a headline-dominating decision to regulate Internet providers by a standard based on this principle, in a milestone for freedom of information and popular activism.[1] The business world's media reported that the decision was the outcome of opposing forces, both representing a "backlash."

The neutrality victory was driven by what the *Wall Street Journal* called a "public backlash"—its phrase for activist groups and engaged individuals unsatisfied by the FCC's earlier positions, which had favored the telecommunications industry.[2] In May 2014 the FCC issued a call for public comment—common for proposed new regulations—and it was swamped by the staggering volume of public comments filed—*four million*, with the press reporting that the "overwhelming majority of the comments supported common-carrier style rules," the central requirement of net neutrality.[3] But the conservative paper had previously observed that if the agency moved forward with this rare regulatory stance, it would also face a "telecom backlash" from Verizon, Comcast, and their trade association, which had won court cases against the FCC's previous efforts to impose some neutrality rules.[4] And with the advent of the Trump administration, they ultimately got their way.

However, this book's subject, the tech giants, have a shifting role in this political debate. Usually seen to be supportive of net neutrality, Silicon Valley's growing dominance is drawing it into the telecommunications industry, diminishing its support for the popular neutrality principles. This shift has the potential to reshape web access in the long run, and, thanks to Big Tech's pivotal role today, to fundamentally change online expression and freedom of information.

Bet the Net

A lack of net neutrality standards has two broad consequences. One has to do with the prices that ISPs charge for providing Internet access at reasonable speeds. ISPs could charge significant amounts to firms that can pay, creating an "artificial scarcity" in information markets and allowing ISPs to add a new revenue stream to their business model. "Artificial scarcity" describes markets where production technology allows for an abundant supply, plenty to satisfy the consumption needs of the whole market, but in which suppliers are able to restrict the amount produced. This often applies to markets characterized by intellectual property laws, like copyrights or patents, which limit lawful production to companies holding these licenses and thus possessing a monopoly.

Profits are elevated with higher prices, but this cuts off some part of the market from consumption, making the product or service "artificially" scarce. For example, without net neutrality an ISP might charge streaming video platforms like Netflix or Hulu for faster service, leading those firms to elevate their prices to an amount that some consumers can't afford. That means some consumers won't pay for the services, even though providing them would require invisibly small resources. And the telecoms aren't above it—a number of them already supplement their existing revenue streams by selling data about your web browsing habits, from your favorite sites to what health issues you search about, with AT&T being the leader in this market segment.[5]

The second consequence has less to do with relative prices and more to do with power. Having a degree of control over the flow of information through any medium, from phone service to TV to Internet access, grants a significant position of market power. The issue isn't as abstract as it sounds. In 2014, without any such regulation to prevent it, Comcast and other broadband providers deliberately "throttled"—restricted—the data transmission for the popular video-streaming service Netflix, frustrating thousands of subscribers waiting for their programs to load. To end the blockade, Netflix agreed to pay the broadband providers tens of millions of dollars a year. This was a significant trigger for elevated public awareness about neutrality principles, as the cable firms had gone too far—they had gotten between America and its TV.

It was a prominent episode but far from an isolated incident. Rebecca MacKinnon's book *Consent of the Networked* gives numerous other troubling examples, like when Verizon blocked text messages to supporters from the pro-choice organization

NARAL, with executives citing company policy to block "controversial or unsavory" content at their discretion. AT&T muted a portion of a Pearl Jam concert it livestreamed when front man Eddie Vedder criticized President George W. Bush.[6] Likewise, Comcast was found to be blocking use of the popular file-sharing service BitTorrent, including downloads of public domain content like the King James Bible.[7]

These relatively innocuous cases show the powerful potential of an unregulated, for-profit network. Broadband firms and ISPs could create a major new revenue stream by extorting content producers to pay up for faster speed service, and those unable or unwilling to pay could be neglected or, indeed, actively throttled. The cable and wireless firms would thus have major leverage over the flow of information through society.

But a lack of net neutrality has major potential ramifications for the politics of attention. Our news and commercial entertainment have long been developed in profit-centered institutions creating material that will not threaten the status quo. But as more "content" is delivered through online venues, the need for "content providers" to meet the demands of gatekeeping cable and cell phone companies adds an additional layer of profit priority for the products competing for our attention. A program may already be nonthreatening to the market model, may cross-promote a media conglomerate's other intellectual property, and may have an advertiser-friendly format. But Comcast or AT&T may require additional concessions, like favorable coverage or support for their future telecom consolidation plans, if they want to avoid paying a fee for adequately fast transmission. This represents yet another opportunity for major capitalist institutions to leave their fingerprints on commercial media products.

And the ability to limit streaming speeds of some sites or sources, in particular, represents a new weapon for these firms in the struggle over attention. Young Internet users, above all, are often guided to different sources by their ease of access, in addition to their prominence on the tech companies' platforms. The classic example of this is video streaming, where research indicates that the faster the online data speeds users grow accustomed to, the less time they are willing to wait to load a video. For users with fast fiber-based service, 80 percent abandon the video file after a delay of ten seconds, illustrating the potentially dramatic effects of paid prioritization on the capturing of user attention.[8] Further, sites critical of the telecom industry may be shunted from the attention of online users by telecoms lightly throttling access to them. It's hard to overstate the potential power the telecoms and their regional service monopolies hold without neutrality restrictions—our ubiquitous smartphones may give us instant gratification for information, but the power to provide that satisfaction could be used against industry critics, not by fully deleting them but by making their blogs take forever to load.

The business media found that these developments, plus the industry's earlier court victories, "made clear that broadband access providers face few limitations on terms they can seek in negotiations with content companies."[9] Tim Berners-Lee, considered to be the inventor of the World Wide Web, called this market development "a fundamental shift in power in the Internet economy," driven by the growth of residential ISPs like Comcast and their buying up of other "backbone" network-provider firms. Berners-Lee observed that this market concentration has made the ISPs into gatekeepers, a strong position since content lacks "any practical way to route around Verizon," as he put it. So rather than the net-neutral scenario—all data coming through the pipe should be treated equally—the possibility arises that "in a world where Netflix and Yahoo connect directly to residential ISPs, every Internet company will have its own separate pipe."[10] Which would also make regulation far harder, all due to what he calls the "growing power of the residential broadband providers" who appear to be conquering his invention.

Net neutrality activists argue that this potential power-mongering mess can be resolved through the FCC legally reclassifying the ISPs under Title II of the Communications Act of

1934. This is the regulation historically applied to "common carriers" relied on by the broader society, like the phone lines—under common carriage rules, if you dial your favorite pizza joint, AT&T can't connect you to another pizzeria that paid them money instead. The ongoing struggle to win this regulatory standard contains valuable lessons for social struggle and is shaped crucially by the economics of Silicon Valley.

Neutering Net Neutrality

The first of three rounds of fighting over neutrality began in December 2010 and was indicative of the FCC's long-standing reputation as a "captured" regulator. The FCC's chairman at the time, Tom Wheeler, was himself a former cable industry lobbyist, and unsurprisingly the FCC's first attempt at a neutrality policy was literally written by the industry.

This FCC order, in 2010, was prepared by lobbyists and attorneys for AT&T, Verizon, and Google, and it actually did ban the blocking and discrimination of data transmission. But a gigantic omission pointed toward the reason for the phone corporations' participation: the rule applied only to the "wired" Internet, meaning the part of service that comes through a fiber or cable line, not via a wireless signal. Liberal scholar Tim Wu, coiner of the term "net neutrality," observed in *The Master Switch*: "That enormous exception—AT&T and Verizon's condition for support of the rule—is no mere technicality, but arguably the masterstroke on the part of [the telecom firms]. It puts the cable industry at a disadvantage, while leaving the markets on which both AT&T and Verizon have bet their future without federal oversight."[11]

Wireless was then and remains the growth center of the industry, so this exemption meant AT&T and Verizon would be free to block, discriminate, and prioritize to their sleazy deal-making hearts' content. Still, the telecom companies overall found even this infringement on their corporate liberty to be too much to tolerate, and the major trade associations, including the United States

Telecom Association and the National Cable and Telecommunications Association, filed lawsuits immediately after the decision. The regulation, the Open Internet Order of 2010, was ultimately struck down in court in 2014, leading to the next round of the struggle.

Title II: The Quickening

To understand the second round of net neutrality confrontation, the lineup of corporate forces on either side of the issue must be reviewed. With the information industry's fast evolution, the lines shift quickly and need to be carefully analyzed. The most common picture puts the cable and wireless ISPs—primarily Comcast, Time Warner Cable, Verizon, and AT&T—on one side, opposed to net neutrality on account of their economic incentive to charge for fast-lane access to their data "pipes." On the other side, the platforms like Google, Facebook, and Amazon want to go on expanding their businesses without new tolls for net access.

This basic antagonism has indeed applied for some time, and it resurfaced in a 2014 open letter to the FCC—signed by dozens of tech firms, including titans like Google, Facebook, Amazon, Yahoo, and Twitter—opposing Chairman Wheeler's new scheme to allow "paid prioritization" and arguing against allowing "individualized bargaining and discrimination." The letter called the proposal "a grave threat to the Internet." This stance was enormously significant as it put major corporate weight on opposing sides, which in a capitalist society is often required before a subject can become politically contested.

However, the market and technologies have swiftly evolved, taking a turn when President Obama made his famous November 2014 video statement supporting Title II reclassification of the Internet—applying the common carriage rules of the phone industry to online systems. But at this exciting moment for the neutrality movement, the business press observed that the online giants left the handling of the response to the lower-profile Internet Association, one of their trade groups. The *National Journal*'s interpretation was that "aside from the letter, the big Web companies like Facebook and Google mostly stayed on the sidelines of the debate."[12] This "muted response" reflects the maturing of the online market and the growing market power of its largest firms.

Notably, Google was also moving toward becoming an ISP itself, with both its Google Fiber pilot projects in Austin, Texas, and the Kansas City metro area, and its piloted phone service, Google Fi.[13] These developments, though short-lived, meant the company was beginning to operate in both spaces of web content and web access, giving it conflicting allegiances in the debate. Indeed, after the Obama White House announced its support for common carrier rules, Google CEO Eric Schmidt told an administration official that the position was a mistake. Even worse, in the proposed 2010 rule written by industry, Google had agreed with Verizon that neutrality rules weren't even necessary on wireless systems. As a *Wall Street Journal* headline put it, "Google and Net Neutrality: It's Complicated."[14]

But once finally enacted in early 2015, the FCC's neutrality order decided to conspicuously "forbear" using the full regulatory apparatus of Title II, like price limits, keeping to a "light touch" approach that left more freedom to the industry. The policy also left open some neutrality-related issues, like how much ISPs like Comcast could charge content firms like Netflix to connect to high-capacity networks in the first place, although boosting or throttling that traffic would be prohibited.[15] But the main net neutrality provisions were confirmed, and the FCC in its short-lived rules frequently drew attention to the tsunami of public comments in justifying its decision: "Because the record overwhelmingly supports adopting rules and demonstrates that three specific practices invariably harm the open Internet—blocking, throttling, and paid prioritization—this order bans each of them, applying the same rules to both fixed and mobile broadband Internet access service."[16]

Among the several neoliberal objections to the common carrier designation was the Republican FCC commissioner Ajit Pai's claim that the agency's reclassification was unnecessary since "the

Internet is not broken. . . . There is no problem for the government to solve."[17] People waiting impatiently in 2014 for Netflix to load their TV shows when Comcast and other cable firms were throttling its bandwidth access might disagree. For their part, the cable and cellular ISPs claim that the threat of FCC interference will limit their infrastructure investments—meaning the networks will decrease their laying of cable and upgrading of cell towers. But this claim is somewhat implausible in view of the staggering fact that the network giants make an absurd *97 percent* profit margin on their bandwidth service, as *MIT Technology Review* reports.[18] This cartoonishly high profit rate means that any mild regulatory burden is unlikely to overcome the telecom industry's enormous incentive to expand the business and swim in profit. Experience with net neutrality in Europe and elsewhere has borne this out.[19]

The Empires Strike Back

The advent of the Trump administration amounted to a major setback for net neutrality, as it did for so many other important economic, social, and environmental policies. Trump appointed the leading Republican on the FCC, Pai, to head the agency, followed shortly by the announcement that the agency was reevaluating the Title II classification. Pai's main justification for doing so was his repeated claim that net neutrality was depressing investment in the telecommunications network, despite the absurd profit rates on broadband assets. Other observers noted that Comcast and other large broadband providers had continued to increase their yearly capital investments since the FCC's rules were issued.[20] But on December 14, 2017, the commission voted to overturn the Title II ruling, despite continued telecom investment and despite the lack of significant competition among the cable companies that supply the broadband for Wi-Fi.[21]

Exactly what this major reversal for freedom means as far as market conditions are concerned will take time to be revealed—but there are clues. Tech giants like Amazon already prominently sponsor Internet access in places that have always been exempt from neutrality rules, like coffee shops, in-flight airline services, and other places that provide web access as a perk. This means that users are steered toward the sites paying the sponsorship fee, although differences in permitted bandwidth aren't yet common. On mobile, the telecoms have been experimenting for some time with "zero rating," a practice of not counting use of certain partner websites or services against a data plan.[22] Alternatively, the *Journal* ponders cheap Internet service "subsidized by—and centered on—the internet giants themselves. This is how Facebook operates in vast swaths of the developing world, where users see the internet and the social network as one and the same."[23] The neutrality violations can be expected to expand over time, likely leading to poorer service for those less able to pay, and restricting the scope of the Internet to which they have access.

Once again, the Silicon Valley giants are broadly credited with opposing these steps toward ending enforcement of net neutrality, and once again their role is plainly exaggerated. While in 2010 the biggest online firms directly signed onto the effort, in 2014 they mostly left the role to their lower-profile Internet Association, and in 2016 their support was thinner still, so much so that some tech figures even argued that the reclassification wasn't necessary for effective neutrality.[24] The business coverage included headlines like "Web Firms Protest Efforts to Roll Back Net Neutrality," but reading the fine print reveals the companies involved were led by second-tier firms like Netflix, Reddit, and GoDaddy. And Netflix, itself the poster child for net neutrality, was "less vocal" on the subject after it worked out satisfactory commercial deals with the telecom giants to route its data. The *Wall Street Journal* bluntly reported that the company "says it is less at risk now that it is big enough to strike favorable deals with telecom companies. The company did just that, reaching several deals in recent years to pay broadband providers for ample bandwidth into their networks."[25] And "some big players," including Google and Amazon, "were content with relatively low-key efforts."[26]

During the neutrality debate, the smaller firms were purposely displaying the annoying spinning pinwheel that denotes slow-loading content as a warning against what a free hand for the telecom industry could mean. Meanwhile, Google couldn't be bothered to include the subject on the front of its hugely prominent search engine page, instead running a post on its relatively obscure policy blog. Amazon deployed a noncommittal button linking to the FCC comment facility, and Facebook CEO Zuckerberg posted that he supported Title II but was "open to working with members of Congress." Hardly aggressive stances.

Again, we must ask why. And the answer is plain: though these firms do rely on open access to the telecom industry's "pipes" of the Internet to deliver their oceans of free content to platform users globally, they are also themselves becoming ISPs, investing heavily in new cables and fiber services to bring content and their platforms' own services to users, even if the "last mile" to consumers is a telco.

As such, their interests are no longer directly opposed to the telecom giants; indeed, the interests of these once-antagonistic parties increasingly overlap.

Since the second round of net neutrality struggle, in which neutrality activists were dramatically victorious over the cell and cable companies, the tech giants have moved further in this direction. The business media describe the process behind this frequently, as when the *Journal* reported that in early 2016 Microsoft and Facebook were jointly investing in a transatlantic data cable to add redundancy to the networks their platforms rely on. Costing in the hundreds of millions of dollars, "only the very largest Internet companies have made the plunge" into digital infrastructure on this scale. The deal indicates "the biggest U.S. tech companies are seeking more control over the Internet's plumbing."[27]

Amazon has also invested in an undersea bundle of fiber-optic cables, and in late 2016 Facebook and Google announced major investments in a high-speed line between Los Angeles and Hong Kong.[28] In addition, Google is laying an incredible sixty-two-hundred-mile-long fully private cable from Los Angeles to its data center in Chile, part of efforts to catch up to Amazon and Microsoft in cloud computing. Fascinatingly, a Google cloud exec is reported to have claimed the company's telecommunications infrastructure "adds up [to] the world's biggest private network, handling roughly 25 percent of the world's internet traffic . . . without relying on telecom companies."[29] Except that now, it *is* a telecom company.

For years, all the tech giants have invested in their own high-speed data lines between major cities as well. These investments are also intended to ensure enough capacity to route information among the giants' enormous data centers. The business press suggests, amazingly, that "the investments have pushed aside the telephone companies that dominated the capital-intensive market for more than a century." The process is reminiscent of Rockefeller's money-gushing Standard Oil empire first conquering energy, and then taking over the rail lines carrying that energy.

The market developments make it easy to understand why the Big Tech firms are decreasingly confronting the telecom industry: they are increasingly entering the industry, and gaining an economic interest in the ability to prioritize data or penalize its flow depending on payment. This is a major long-term trend that will see the future blurring of the lines between tech and telecom, and largely explains Silicon Valley's declining commitment to net neutrality.

You and What Army?

Since the role of nominally open network-supporting corporations like Google turns out to be quite overhyped, there must be another factor to explain why telecom internet service was temporarily reclassified to "common carrier" status under Title II. It's not too difficult to identify—the commission received over four million comments on its proposed regulatory stance allowing "commercially reasonable" fast-lane treatment in 2014, with over 99 percent supporting strong net neutrality rules. The enormous volume of public comments repeatedly broke the FCC's comment facility, but was only the most dramatic component of the overall activist strategy that resulted in the victory at the commission. Considering the relative rareness of left-wing victories, and also the reversal of this policy under the Trump administration, these tactics are worth some attention.

One crucial dimension was the effective combination of online and offline organizing, especially relevant to an issue like this that directly affects the web environment. So while activists in groups like Free Press and the Electronic Frontier Foundation publicized the issue and steered alarmed web users toward the FCC comment system, organizers planned to increase the heat on public officials through "real life" actions.

Most dramatically, activists camped out in front of the FCC building in Washington, DC, an "occupy" tactic that ballooned from a pair of activists in sleeping bags to a tent city of dozens of people. This move was important, especially since the organizers prepared for the direct action through extensive training and awareness-raising. Malkia Cyrial of the Center for Media Justice told the valuable activist website *Waging Nonviolence*: "All along we've been doing a lot of education and advocacy, but at this point we're ready to take direct action against these companies and target members of Congress."[30] Likewise Kevin Zeese, an activist with Popular Resistance, named direct action as one activist strategy among many: "We don't like to occupy. . . . It's a tactic that we use very sparingly."

But the occupation—especially alarming to the FCC, which is accustomed to bureaucratic invisibility—played a critical role, since before 2015 the reclassification of ISPs as Title II common carriers had been dismissed as "politically impossible." As Zeese puts it, "When they say it's politically impossible, our job as activists is to make it politically doable." Demonstrations spread to regional FCC offices and the corporate headquarters of Comcast and Verizon. Of course, the main venue for organizing actions remained online, fitting for the subject and also reflecting the shift of civic engagement to web venues, for better or worse.

In 2017, Netflix, Reddit, and others reprised the "Internet slowdown" protest, showing the ubiquitous spinning "loading" wheel and playing an important role in reengaging activists from 2014. But the results were somewhat less dramatic than the previous round, perhaps owing in part to the diminishing support of the tech titans. However, an impressive level of public engagement was still reached as comments poured in at the FCC again, over the July–August public comment period. This forced the FCC to "rate-limit" submissions, in which tranches of comments were gradually submitted so as not to overwhelm their docket facility yet again.[31]

Notably, this time the level of comments soon spiraled out of control, reaching an absurd twenty-three million by the time of the repeal vote. It soon became apparent that many comments were being left by software on computers programmed to pour posts into the system, skewing against neutrality.[32] Many claimed to have been submitted by public figures, claims that were quickly demonstrated to be false; others were posted under the names of deceased or fictional people. A particular anti-neutrality email studied by the *Wall Street Journal*, starting with the same stuffy sentence, was posted at "a near-constant rate—1,000 every 10 minutes—punctuated by periods of zero comments, as if web robots were turning on and off. . . . The Journal examined those 'unprecedented regulator power' comments and found that duplicates of it exceeded any other comment. . . . The comment has been posted on the FCC website more than 818,000 times."[33] A report by telecom firms also found many of the mails were attributable to "FakeMailGenerator.com." On any side, it's a pity that by this stage the public comment process at the FCC and other public regulators' websites has now been heavily gamed.

Several of these tactics also echoed those used against other attempts to restrain the open web, like the copyright-mongering Stop Online Piracy Act in 2012, and the cable industry's attempts to persuade Congress to strip the FCC of its authority to stop paid prioritization in 2006. In the latter case, in one of the most impressive episodes of online social action, activists assembled an alliance of left-wing, right-wing, and overtly apolitical groups to oppose the measures, including some major online firms, consumer groups, MoveOn.org, Free Press, SEIU, the Christian Coalition of America, Gun Owners of America, the AARP, the American Library Association, and National Religious Broadcasters.[34] This broad coalition opposed the attempt by the cable and phone corporations to put up toll gates to reach their enormous networks. This activism was effective enough to kill the bills in Congress—no small feat.

In the end, the huge battles for net neutrality, and the major victory of getting the FCC to grudgingly support it despite major industry resistance, is a surprisingly happy if temporary chapter in a long story. The left has limited policy triumphs to celebrate these days, so this unvarnished, if short-lived, victory should not be forgotten. Four million commenters can't be wrong!

CHAPTER 8

Redefining R&D

*The state's unknown role in creating
the Internet and mobile tech*

The world-reshaping technology wielded by the corporations of Big Tech is usually considered to be the main justification for their power. Sure, they may be incredibly powerful and have unaccountable influence over our lives, but hey, they earned it—Gates and Jobs and Bezos and Page and Zuckerberg had to invent the technology, right?

Except they didn't invent it. The original name for the Internet was ARPANET, because it was developed by the US military's research arm and affiliated universities. The original address of Google was not google.com but google.stanford.edu, because it was developed in a publicly subsidized research campus. The original name for Wi-Fi was ALOHAnet, because the University of Hawaii struggled to network its island campuses and developed new radio technology to do it.

In fact, nearly *all* the scientific and engineering research that went into today's fancy high-tech products and services came from the public sector—primarily research universities and the military. Even a very brief survey of this history makes that abundantly clear and helps us see where resources could be best used to develop the science and technology of the future, and where the credit for today's platforms really belongs.

The Advent of ARPANET

Consider the chips themselves, the miniaturized processors that provide the computing power on the PCs and smartphones this book has described. In 2018 the Turing Award, given for achievement in the computer sciences and often considered the Nobel Prize of computing, went to professor Dave Patterson of the University of California, Berkeley, and professor John Hennessy at Stanford. In the 1980s these academics had codeveloped the reduced instruction set computer (RISC) chip, a more efficient processor that allowed for greater computing power. That chip architecture is completely ubiquitous on today's mobile processors, and even Intel chips have moved toward its simplified structure.[1] Today the two work for Google, Patterson as a researcher and Hennessy as an Alphabet board member, but their pivotally important original work occurred on public campuses with no near-term profit motive to harry them. In fact, the pivotal use of silicon to create modern semiconducting chips was first researched by public-private partnerships among the military, AT&T, Xerox, and others.[2]

The origins of the Internet and its most popular application, the World Wide Web, are somewhat better known. The system that would become the Internet first arose in the 1960s in response to twin needs of federal agencies: the desire of scientists to share access to then-scarce computer resources, and the US military's need for a decentralized, redundantly connected network that could survive a nuclear conflict—a major concern during the Cold War. The data-hungry world of espionage and counterinsurgency also played a major role from the early days. The project was taken up by the Advanced Research Projects Agency (ARPA), the Pentagon's main research arm.

The technology to provide these goals was eventually found in "packet switching," a means of sending information in which data or a message is broken down into packets with address information attached, sent through a communication network, and reassembled at its destination back into the original message. This technology had costs related to the need to include routing info on so many packets, but it made the system flexible and allowed for cheaper hardware.[3]

One difficulty was that in order to connect with each other, the research centers and military facilities had to use a huge variety of different computers and operating systems—this was before the standardizing effects of the IBM PC and the Microsoft operating system monopoly. But, if they could connect all these machines, it could eventually make the network stronger by bringing together so many different resources.

ARPA funded the leasing of communication lines from AT&T—which held a monopoly over US telecommunications until the 1980s—and organized the sprawling project. The first ARPANET computing installation to be connected was UCLA in September 1969, followed by the other early network nodes of UC Santa Barbara, the University of Utah, and the Stanford Research Institute. A good deal of technical details had to be painstakingly ironed out, yet decisions were mostly made through a consensus process among users and operators, and ARPA's funding gave it the ability to coerce holdouts who were using other technical standards.

Notably, in the early days of limited network use in the 1970s, computer user activism was common, including in the Users Interest Working Group (USING), which lobbied for more applications funding and other issues. But as Janet Abbate observes in her essential *Inventing the Internet*:

> Faced with organized action by users, the ARPA managers were evidently afraid that the network might slip out of their control. Members of USING were dissuaded from pushing their demands by ARPA program manager Craig Fields, who

made it clear that the authority to make plans for the network lay with ARPA, not with USING. . . . The fate of USING revealed the limits of ARPA's generally non-hierarchical management approach. Individual users or research teams had tacit or explicit permission to add hardware and software to the system; ARPA even gave financial support for some of these experiments. However, users as a group had no say in the design decisions or funding priorities of the ARPANET project. The ARPANET experience is a reminder that the efforts of individuals to build virtual communities are constrained by the realities of money and power that support the infrastructure of cyberspace.[4]

More and more scientists were using ARPANET to transmit data sets and gain access to computing power, analyzing seismic and weather data, modeling molecules, and advancing medicine. And packet-switching technology was being applied to other communications media, so by the 1970s ARPA was running three experimental networks—the wired ARPANET, the Bay Area radio-based PRNET, and the satellite-based SATNET.

It was only when ARPA successfully demonstrated interconnection of these different network systems that the Internet could be born. This would require devising technology for connecting them, called protocols, which had to be designed to run on many different computers and allow for an orderly flow of data between hosts. The solution, after prolonged design debate under ARPA's aegis, was a set of protocols knowns as the Transmission Control Protocol and Internet Protocol (TCP/IP), with the former arranging the flow of packets and the latter managing the articulation among the different networks—like information flowing through wired broadband connections to a radio signal for cell service. TCP/IP was well suited for the military, which eventually adopted it and thus gave it a great impetus to spread as an informal standard.

Notably, ARPA insisted that the protocols, as well as source code for the computers connecting the ARPANET and other crucial information, be publicly available and not the property of its primary contractors. And as Abbate comments, "Beyond Xerox PARC . . . there seems to have been no corporate participation in the design of the Internet."[5] Of course, in the United States a strong political tendency exists to privatize public goods as soon as possible, but, as another technology history recounts, "[i]ndeed, in 1972 the telecommunication giant AT&T declined the government's offer to take over ARPANET, the forerunner of the modern internet, on the grounds that it was not likely to make a profit."[6] IBM also turned it down.[7]

So it was ARPA that triumphantly carried out the first demonstration of the Internet, a network of networks, when on November 22, 1977, packets of data were broadcast from a traveling van on a California highway over PRNET, to an ARPANET gateway, into space through SATNET to Europe, and back via ARPANET to California. This proof of concept excited the technical community and spurred interest among many research and defense bodies, which joined the network and adopted its open protocols, often with ARPA help or funding.[8] In time the military insisted that all ARPA sites adopt these same protocols, which meant long hours reconfiguring host computers but helped further the technical standards for internetworking. The military also peeled off its network (MILNET) from ARPANET in 1983, putting the latter under civilian control and bringing university researchers back into dominating its user base.

In light of how the popular tech fairy tale presents a story of online tech arising from brilliant small business startups, it is hilarious that in reality, it was Colonel Heidi Heiden who ordered the commercialization of the technology. Nominally this was done so that there would then be multiple commercial suppliers of the networking tech, but market forces would soon lead to large regional monopolies. The privatization included a $20 million fund for computer manufacturers to port TCP/IP to their products, which Abbate openly calls "technology transfer," a term that today is more associated with Western companies condemning

Chinese government requirements that Western companies share tech secrets in exchange for access to China's giant market. But this current tech being forcibly transferred by China relies on public US research that was forked over to the business world decades ago, and unlike the Chinese, those companies were even paid for the privilege—"All the major computer companies took advantage of this opportunity, and by 1990 TCP/IP was available for virtually every computer on the American market."[9] Years later, the federal government's Office of the Inspector General concluded that the privatization program was polluted by conflicts of interest, with insiders retained to lobby for telecoms including MCI, and with no effort to seek competition.[10]

Indeed, Abbate's own rather apolitical book's summary leaves the conventional view dead in the water:

> The story of the Internet's origins departs from explanations of technical innovation that center on individual inventors or on the pull of markets. [ARPANET pioneers Vint] Cerf and [Robert] Kahn were neither captains of industry nor "two guys tinkering in a garage." The Internet was not built in response to popular demand, real or imagined; its subsequent mass appeal had no part in the decisions made in 1973. Rather, the project reflected the command economy of military procurement, where specialized performance is everything and money is no object, and the research ethos of the university, where experimental interest and technical elegance take precedence over commercial application.[11]

In the early 1980s, many more universities were connected to ARPANET via their computer science departments' phone-based connections, mainly through funding from the National Science Foundation (NSF), the major US basic science agency. ARPA helped fund these LANs (local area networks), too, while the NSF helped bring large regional networks of universities online and leased its own high-speed lines for a "backbone," creating a central network to manage the rising packet-switching traffic known as the NSFNET. The NSFNET overlapped with ARPANET for a time and shared costs, but by the time most universities were networked in the late 1980s, the ARPANET hardware and early configurations were showing their age. Twenty years is a long interval in computer science terms, and military overseers decided to retire it as obsolete, transferring the ARPANET nodes to the NSFNET, then formally dismantling it in February 1990.[12]

As use climbed through the 1980s, US telecom companies finally began taking an interest, and pressure rose to completely privatize the network, since private investment in commercial networks for companies, schools, or individuals had gradually spread in the wake of the pioneering ARPA and NSF networks. By the early 1990s, it was possible for the commercial spin-offs of the early contractors to take over since by then "a whole parallel structure of commercial TCP/IP networks had evolved."

In 1991 the NSF unveiled a plan for Internet service to be taken over by private firms—including some of the phone companies—which would be designated as Internet service providers. The argument was that the ISPs would inevitably provide better service and investment than government bodies since they would have to compete with each other and provide their own gateways to their network backbones. The transfer from NSFNET to commercial ISPs was effected on April 30, 1995, marking the end of US government ownership of the Internet's systems and infrastructure.[13]

But this vision of rich market competition quickly proved illusory when the cable ISPs went on a massive merger binge after deregulation in 1996, becoming great regional monopolies that would soon launch a crusade to undo net neutrality. It wasn't long before the Internet itself became dominated by a few gigantic online platforms, magnetically attracting users through the network effects we've seen demonstrated in case after case in this book. So, while the loss of control by authoritarian government institutions may sound appealing, the history comports with the main message of the authors of *Misunderstanding the Internet*, who found that early optimistic forecasts of the Internet's potential "all had one enormous error at their center. They failed to recognize that the impact of technology is filtered through the structures and processes of society. . . . In brief, the rise of the internet was accompanied by the decline of its freedom."[14]

The popular fairy tale of private geniuses driven by desires for personal gain leading to world-shaking innovation is even refuted in the case of Tim Berners-Lee, who is famous for developing the three main technologies that constitute the standard protocols needed for any user to get on the World Wide Web and access information. Working at a huge research institution that required an enormous amount of technical equipment to test fundamental particles, he developed a "memory aid" that allowed the creation of documents in which the act of clicking on a particular term could lead to other documents explaining that term. This technology became "hypertext," and Berners-Lee pioneered the acceptance of a decentralized protocol system for it. The lack of a central authority meant some could become "dead links," but that way the system would also be open to independent users.

Then came the encoding language (HTML) and the system for creating addresses for various sites and pages, each containing a universal resource locator, or URL. Berners-Lee also set up and wrote the software for the first computer "server" that made documents available to online users. Crucially, the European Organization for Nuclear Research (CERN) had adopted TCP/IP, so the web app could run on top of those protocols and be used by any user connected to the ARPANET/NSFNET.

Fascinatingly, there was another attempt at developing a global hypertext system similar to that created at CERN, but this was a private, market-based effort, and it occurred simultaneously with the military's failed attempts in the 1980s to get private corporations to take over the early Internet. Ted Nelson developed a project called "Xanadu," but as the press recounts, "Nelson wanted Xanadu to make a profit, and this vastly complicated the system, which never got off the ground. Berners-Lee, in contrast, persuaded

CERN to let go of intellectual property to get the Web airborne."[15] This was done in 1993, and while many mock Berners-Lee for not patenting the technology to become rich, his decision to release it publicly was typical of the scientific community's desire to broadly share information as part of the greater research enterprise.[16] It certainly created insane wealth for others who had useful platforms and fewer scruples.

Berners-Lee continued working with the early online giants—Microsoft, Sun, Apple—to maintain regular protocols on the fast-evolving early web to keep it from developing separate standards and becoming balkanized, with some sites requiring different browsers or other incompatibilities. Notably, as I mentioned in chapter 1, Berners-Lee is concerned that the World Wide Web's potential has been undermined since "some of its most successful inhabitants have begun to chip away at its principles. Large social-networking sites are walling off information posted by their users from the rest of the Web," and if that trend is not reversed, "the Web could be broken into fragmented islands."[17]

Getting Mobile on Its Feet

Consider the similar story of Wi-Fi, the modern world's favorite thing to both use and complain about. The local radio signals that allow mobile computing within range of a router at home or business are the principal means of Internet access today, and perhaps unsurprisingly, the technology was invented by a research university. Tech journalist Brian Merchant writes: "While wireless cell networks evolved from massive government-backed projects, the main way our phones get online began as a far-flung academic hackaround. Wi-Fi began long before the web as we know it existed and was actually developed along the same timeline as ARPANET." In the 1960s the University of Hawaii's various island labs couldn't communicate with the main computer in Honolulu. Scientists solved this problem using a pair of high-speed UHF channels to access off-site computing resources, launching "the project [that] would grow into the aptly named ALOHAnet, the precursor to Wi-Fi."[18] Notably, the project was partially funded by ARPA and the US Navy.[19]

On this same note, although Apple is the tech giant most associated with slick mobile technology, it arguably owes the most to public research. The famously sensitive multi-touch interface of the iPhone and later smartphone and tablet models owes an enormous amount to public research, despite Jobs's claims that the company originated it. Amazingly, the first screen surface able to detect multiple simultaneous finger movements was developed in the 1970s by an engineer at CERN, the same particle collider complex where Berners-Lee would later develop the Internet Protocols.[20]

Merchant notes that

> while Jobs publicly claimed the invention as Apple's own, multi-touch was developed decades earlier by a trail of pioneers from places as varied as CERN's particle-accelerator labs, to the University of Toronto, to a start-up bent on empowering the disabled. Institutions like Bell Labs and CERN incubated research and experimentation; which is to say that the government poured in hundreds of millions of dollars to support them.[21]

The idea for the touch-sensitive "capacitive screens" themselves, which take advantage of the human body's own ability to conduct electricity, arose in research by the Royal Radar Establishment, a UK military body, in the 1960s. The highly versatile multi-touch interface, allowing many different commands and actions from the user, was developed by a University of Delaware PhD candidate under an NSF-CIA research program. He later commercialized the technology, and the company was bought by Apple in 2005, two years before the first iPhone release.[22]

Together, these brushstrokes paint an overall picture that is pretty dramatic, one best observed by viewing the diagram below. It comes from a US government science-promoting body, the Office of Science and Technology Policy (OSTP), which in a February 2006 report on digital technology analyzed the iPod, Steve Jobs's celebrated mobile era–inaugurating smartphone predecessor. The diagram illustrates how the most impressive technical components, from the drive to the memory to the battery, were developed through public sector research. The complex LCD display was the result of research from the Department of Defense, the NSF, and the National Institutes of Health; basic research on processing radio signals was funded by the Army Research Office; the DRAM memory cache was developed by IBM with DARPA funding. The report observed that the iPod "illustrates the unexpected benefits of basic research. . . . The device itself is innovative, but it [is] built upon a broad platform of component technologies, each derived from fundamental studies in physical science, mathematics, and engineering."[23]

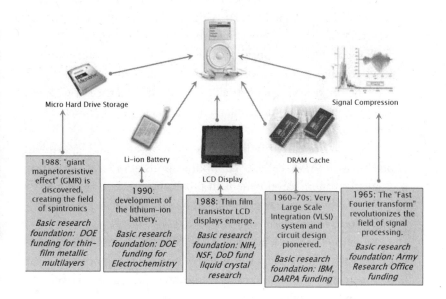

The Entrepreneurial State, by Mariana Mazzucato is by far the best consideration of all these issues, including the origins of the smartphone era. She observes that what makes a smartphone smart is its connection to the Internet and other online applications, which as we've seen rely completely on the networks created and nurtured over many years by ARPA and the NSF. But further, the Global Positioning System required for Google Maps and finding restaurants and bars was developed by the DOD in the 1970s for more accurate deployments of materiel and munitions. Only in the 1990s was the system released and quickly swamped with civilian use.

The attractive liquid-crystal displays, too, owe their existence to Cold War military investments, spurred by worries that the increasingly dominant Japanese suppliers of the 1980s lacked adequate capacity to meet US demand alone. So the Pentagon, eager for more sophisticated and interactive display technologies, organized an industry consortium working on flat-panel displays, with the breakthrough technology under development at consortium member Westinghouse. Mazzucato notes that "the research carried out at Westinghouse was almost entirely funded by the US Army."[24] But the company then shut down the program, leading the project head to appeal to a series of US computer giants—IBM, Compaq, Xerox, 3M—but it was turned down by all of them before receiving a contract from DARPA in the late eighties, enabling the development of later device displays. Further, the lithium-ion batteries essential to today's power-hungry devices have a similar story of early funding from the NSF and the Department of Energy.[25] Also, cellular communications standards, including the early system development to prove the concept, were heavily supported by European government investments in signal processing.[26] And so on.

Having checked a majority of the boxes of what makes a smartphone, Mazzucato lists nearly every functional component of the device, along with the public or military agency that developed it or funded its creation. It's an alphabet soup of public bodies—DOE, DARPA, NSF, CERN, Army Research Office, the Navy. Jobs sure was proud of his role in designing the device, but his engineers relied on decades of taxpayer-funded research at these agencies, whose investments created all the fancy tiny components of the slick device we use to navigate the world, communicate with our friends, and take pictures of our pets.[27]

Cheating at Monopoly

Beyond the basics, even the hardware and software technologies at the hearts of the Big Tech platforms themselves often derive from public work. Bill Gates's and Paul Allen's MS-BASIC operating system, which they sold to IBM and ended up dominating the global market for many years, was written in the BASIC computer language. This language was created by professors at Dartmouth in 1964 with funding from the NSF.[28] Later, Gates was filled with scorn that the public might oppose his use of this technology to monopolize computing.

And besides the background story of the smartphone multi-touch interfaces, Apple had even more fundamental roots in public-sector technology. The PARC research facility, from which Steve Jobs obtained the basics of the graphic user interface that became the Mac and later all computer interfaces, had several former ARPA researchers working on those display concepts. The prominent *Wired* journalist Steven Levy wrote, "This little-known branch of Defense was quietly kick-starting the computer revolution that would result in the Macintosh."[29]

The most visionary action that can be attributed to the world's richest man, Jeff Bezos, is that in the web's early days he was "doubling and tripling his bet on the Internet," as his biographer puts it.[30] A wily business move perhaps, but it amounts to recognizing a good opportunity to make money on technology developed by federal taxpayers over the 1960s, '70s, and '80s. Facebook's deferential corporate biographer David Kirkpatrick admits: "Something like Facebook was envisioned by engineers who laid the groundwork for the Internet. In a 1968 essay by J. C. R. Licklider and Robert W. Taylor, 'The Computer as Communication Device,'" the two essentially envisioned Facebook's basic social network.[31] They worked for ARPA.

And of course, Google itself, considered the most academically inspired of the megacaps, was originally google.stanford.edu, where it was developed through the state and federal tax funding of the state of California and the United States, which provided long-term research stability and freedom from the need to turn a short-term dollar. There, Page and Brin could state with detachment that "advertising funded search engines will be inherently biased towards the advertisers. . . . We believe the issue of advertising causes enough mixed incentives that it is crucial to have a competitive search engine that is transparent and in the academic realm."[32] Page's first research paper included the note, "funded by DARPA."[33]

But the secret origins of Big Tech in public research don't speak to how the tech is used once it's privatized. Google's search algorithms have been hugely elaborated since it became a private company, but once in the realm of the marketplace, technology evolves only in directions that engorge profitability. Data scientist Cathy O'Neil's distressing and digestible book *Weapons of Math Destruction* reviews details of harmful software algorithms, ones with no transparency or dynamic learning to improve on previous errors. She notes that "in the case of web giants like Google, Amazon, and Facebook, these precisely tailored algorithms alone are worth hundreds of billions of dollars." Yet "our livelihoods increasingly depend on our ability to make our case to machines. The clearest example of this is Google. For businesses, whether it's a bed-and-breakfast or an auto repair shop, success hinges on showing up on the first page of search results. Now individuals face similar challenges, whether trying to get a foot in the door of a company, to climb the ranks—or even to survive waves of layoffs."[34] O'Neil also notices that these harmful algorithms "tend to punish the poor. . . . The privileged, we'll see time and again, are processed more by people, the masses by machines."[35]

A similar story emerges with artificial intelligence, considered among the most advanced technological fields today. Merchant observes that "before Siri was a core functionality of the iPhone, it was an app on the App Store launched by a well-funded Silicon Valley start-up. Before that, it was a research project at Stanford backed by the Defense Department with the aim of creating an artificially intelligent assistant." That includes the spoken interface so associated with AI in the popular imagination: "As with much of the advanced computer research around Stanford then, ARPA was doing the funding. It would mark a decades-long interest in the field of AI from the agency, which would fund multiple speech recognition projects in the 1970s."[36]

The field is advancing through improvements in deep neural networks—computer algorithms modeled on the human brain that crunch data and attempt to learn to do different tasks. These most elaborate algorithms, however, will be corporate property, and corporations will resist divulging their proprietary code just as they already do for more conventional algorithms that sort search results and screen credit applicants. The *Wall Street Journal* observes: "For the corporations, the algorithms will be proprietary tools to assess your loan-worthiness, your job applications, and your risk of stroke. Many balk at the costs of developing systems that not only learn to make decisions, but that also explain those decisions to outsiders."[37]

This likely means that a powerful new tool will gradually emerge for the tech giants, and it will be developed as recklessly as the rivalry among the monopolists allows. The industry has tried to preempt serious government regulation by creating a number of proposed ethical guidelines backed by one or the other giant, including Microsoft, Intel, and the Information Technology Industry Council, which includes Google, Facebook, and Apple. It's of course unlikely these entities will propose anything that could limit their future profitable exploitation of the technology they're investing in today, but so far US administrations have been willing to allow self-regulation, and these guidelines are evidently intended to perpetuate that permissiveness.

Overall, however, the clear tendency is for publicly backed research entities, not private companies, to experience major technological leaps. Only states and publicly funded research institutions can support long-term basic scientific research, which by its nature is based on exploring the unknown and can never guarantee a genuine breakthrough will be the result, let alone a money-making one. Plus, the costs of scientific research and experimental engineering—including trained scientists and fancy prototyping equipment—are large.

Private institutions are under systemic and legal obligations to make money quickly to reward their capitalist investors; thus expensive, uncertain long-term research is inevitably harder and harder to justify as quarters tick by with few money-making breakthroughs to show for it. Small wonder, then, that the Internet, the web, the GUI, modern processors, Wi-Fi signaling, fundamental computer languages, and even Google itself arose from the academic or military research settings where steady funding is more or less assured and near-term stock prices don't drive whether projects get axed. The history is long—Guglielmo Marconi developed radio for the Royal Navy, Berners-Lee the web protocols for CERN. The OSTP notes, "Past DOD research has resulted in revolutionary technological capabilities such as radar, digital computers, wireless mobile communications, lasers, fiber optics, composite materials, the Internet (and other 'packet switched' networks), and satellite navigation."[38]

Mazzucato herself observes that private businesses dominate overall spending on research and development, responsible for 67 percent of the total. However, on *basic* R&D the exploration that takes place in more fundamental research areas with no immediate commercial return but that sometimes discovers basic new technologies—the federal government together with the university system hugely dominate at 72 percent.[39] Private companies appear to be more suited to shorter-term, applied research using basic discoveries and technologies developed by the public sector's basic R&D work.

The point, of course, isn't that the military should have discretion on where it spends its hundreds upon hundreds of billions of dollars each year, or that war is worth it for its high-tech spinoffs. The major role played by the Pentagon in US research funding means that there will be a bias toward research with potential military applications, a broad area but still a potentially limiting one—technologies with no clear military relevance will be at a disadvantage for limited funding dollars. Rather, the point is that the public sector is the natural space for scientific and technological research, providing the steady funding and also maybe imposing some popular constraints on what can be done with the tech.

Not only is technology too important to be left to the tech giants, it didn't even come from them in the first place.

CHAPTER 9

Leashing the Techlash

Tech's love-hate relationship

with politics

Big Tech had a long honeymoon, with users globally delighted by the convenience and versatility of modern tech platforms, from YouTube to Amazon Marketplace. Especially in the mobile era, with free or low-cost applications like Google Search and Facebook, consumers seldom saw any downsides to using these services, which undoubtedly provide major value for communication, work, and entertainment.

But every honeymoon's got to end sometime. Microsoft's antitrust trial and the guilty verdict on its monopolization of the web browser market started the process, but it escalated dramatically with the successive waves of revelations about the platforms' data policies, leaks of personal information, arm-twisting on carrying productivity apps, heinous labor conditions, and lax security protections against foreign election meddling. This bad press has piled up and definitely had an effect on the perception of the tech giants, and it's already leading to more government oversight.

By 2018 the tech megacaps had experienced so many scandals and embarrassments that press headlines referred to their regular responses as "the Tech Industry's Apology Tour."[1] Some speculated this would lead to user rebellions and state regulation—sometimes called the "techlash." But the companies' entrenched monopolies and oligopolies, fortified with network effects and "grooved-in" user habits, along with the giant mountains of data and lobbying cash on hand, may well put a leash on the techlash.

Trump l'Monde

It was so easy at first. For years, the high-tech sector was seen as a leading edge of economic innovation and a source of pride in American ingenuity. The web and other popular Internet applications remade society and created whole new industries not to mention enormous amounts of wealth. The United States' tradition of laissez-faire policy easily carried over to the new industries, and applied across the political spectrum. Back when Microsoft first faced investigations into its monopolies, then–Republican senator and later presidential candidate Bob Dole perfectly articulated the bipartisan response when he said: "A company develops a new product, a product consumers want. But now the government steps in and is in effect attempting to dictate the terms on which that product can be marketed and sold. . . . Pinch me, but I thought we were still in America."[2] US liberals and conservatives happily celebrated Big Tech well into the twenty-first century and the mobile era, with the business papers reporting that the "dominance" of "big online platforms . . . was made possible in part by a quarter-century, bipartisan Washington consensus backing rules and regulations designed mainly to foster their development."[3]

The bipartisan celebration of tech had a highly dark side, too, made most famous by the National Security Agency's secret

PRISM program, only revealed publicly when NSA contractor Edward Snowden leaked documents about the program in 2013. Inaugurated during the airless days of the Bush administration, PRISM took advantage of the incredible data hoarding of the platform giants. Supposedly intended to prevent terrorism, PRISM has taken advantage of a rubber-stamp oversight court to evidently vacuum up as much data as it feels like on nearly anyone. As *Surveillance Valley* author Yasha Levine writes, PRISM is "a sophisticated on-demand data tap housed within the datacenters of the biggest and most respected names in Silicon Valley: Google, Apple, Facebook, Yahoo!, and Microsoft. These devices allow the NSA to siphon off whatever the agency requires, including emails, attachments, chats, address books, files, photographs, audio files, search activity, and mobile phone location history."[4] Such complicated processes required significant participation by the tech companies themselves, to the extent that the *Guardian* reports the NSA paid the companies millions of dollars to cover their compliance costs.[5] The tech behemoths didn't see fit to inform their users about the program, even though it could potentially give the state an utterly complete picture of users' online activity, and in real time.

As Google rose to succeed Microsoft in the 2000s as arguably the most important of the platforms, it gradually followed the lead of other great corporations and opened up a lobbying shop in DC. It became famously close with the Obama administration, with numerous Google staff members working for the administration and its campaigns. *Wired* journalist Steven Levy records that "Google employees, through the company PAC, contributed more than $800,000 to his campaign, trailing only Goldman Sachs and Microsoft in total contributions."[6] That much money goes a long way toward undermining the separation of search and state.

Notably, the Federal Trade Commission, the national agency charged with monitoring and blocking monopolization or other abuses of trade, proposed a Do Not Track option for consumers in 2010. Modeled on the national Do Not Call list that legally bars telemarketers from calling listed numbers, it would have created an opt-out system preventing the collection of tracking data. Later the Obama administration developed a provisional Consumer Privacy Bill of Rights aiming to increase users' control of their data. Both were defeated amid heavy lobbying, mainly by Google and Facebook.[7]

The FTC also voted in 2012 not to charge Google with unfair practices. The investigation began after various third-party sites, like Yelp and LinkedIn, demanded that their content not be "scraped" by Google—making it appear directly on Google's search results and thus causing traffic to their actual sites to plummet. On its face, the case was quite suspicious, as Google was plainly a rising center of major power. But the Obama-era FTC vote was unanimous.[8]

Then, of course, came the administration of the nakedly racist, serial sexual-harassing, TV billionaire imbecile Donald Trump. A nation still reeling at his upset victory watched as the tech giants were invited to Trump Tower for a historic gathering to confer on the economy with representatives of the administration. Amazon, Google, Facebook, Apple, Microsoft, Oracle, Intel, IBM, and other platform giants all attended.[9] The meeting was favorable and led to typically bland press releases on commitments to innovation.

But Trump soon developed a significant antagonism with Silicon Valley, and as usual his hostility has been mainly about a personal grudge: namely the fact that the industry largely supported his opponent Hillary Clinton, who received $1.6 million from Google's political action committee (PAC) alone. Shortly after his meeting with the tech moguls Trump began to claim—on Twitter, with no attempt at providing evidence—that the platforms were all biased against him, that tech is utterly bereft of conservatives, and that Amazon pays too little in taxes and exploits the US Postal Service (that final claim is more plausible).

Most of these claims are hard to take seriously, considering that the tech execs have significant shared interests with conservative, pro-business political figures like those around Trump. As Jathan Sadowski wrote in *Jacobin*, the conference was relatively simple as "billionaires met to express their interests and discuss policy. . . . The executives didn't have to set aside their politics to talk business—their politics align with the new administration."[10] Above all, the prospect of a major corporate tax cut and a break on each company's gigantic overseas cash piles were magnetically attractive to the big corporations, and they got their wish in the 2017 Tax Act.

Sadowski's point was confirmed early in the administration, when it issued its first in a series of bans on travel for citizens of Muslim-majority countries, triggering large protests at airports nationwide. A *Wall Street Journal* reporter observed that when the administration "tightened the criteria for granting H-1B visas to temporary professional workers, it effectively favored Silicon Valley giants over outsourcing companies."[11] And *New York Times* reporting found that "the larger tech companies tended to be less forceful in their reactions to the executive order than the smaller ones," although "pressure had been building on companies to speak out against measures being endorsed by Mr. Trump. Some of that impetus came from employees, and some from activists."[12]

In fact, despite its usual love of the industry, the *Times* had to acknowledge that, as a headline put it, "Tech Opposition to Trump [Is] Propelled by Employees, Not Executives." It noted the companies are "vulnerable" to "the sentiments of their customers and employees, some of whom have more radical ideas in mind." Tech workers have formed activist groups like Tech Solidarity, which tries to provide IT help to people fighting the Muslim ban and other Trump policies, and the Tech Workers Coalition, which seeks to support labor and other organizing. One tech organizer said, "I want pressure from below to counterbalance the pressure management is already feeling from above."[13] As we saw with Google's occasionally principled moves of recent years, the main impetus for decency is from the workers, not the rich execs.

Claims that Big Tech has an anti-right-wing bias are also hard to reconcile with the fact that during the 2016 campaign, a number of Facebook workers complained that Trump's posts frequently violated the site's limits on hate speech, blaming national problems on various minorities. But Zuckerberg decided the importance of a national presidential candidate's speech overruled this requirement—speaking both to the power of Facebook's platform and to its tolerance of Trump's racist tirades.[14] Indeed, Trump was the biggest political advertising–buyer on Facebook in 2016, spending $274,000.[15] The campaign used the social network's targeting features extensively, often experimenting by running a dozen similar versions of an ad, testing which were most successful.

Other reasons for the political animus against Big Tech may be related to the claim by Steve Bannon, Trump's former chief strategist, that "two-thirds or three-quarters of the C.E.O.s in Silicon Valley are from South Asia or from Asia," which is both racist and incorrect, typical of Bannon's celebrated "strategizing."[16] But more likely, the main source of conservative antagonism toward tech is related to de-platforming, where a platform company, typically Facebook, Google, or Twitter, suspends a user's account or channel due to statements violating the terms of service. As discussed above, this isn't unheard of, especially for evidence-free, conspiracy-mongering huckster jerk-offs like Alex Jones, but the main victims have been leftists who have seen their most prominent sites dramatically downranked in Google's search results. Yet the right never forgets a grudge, and episodes like Facebook's short-lived curation of the News Feed to limit right-wing posts, and Jones's suspensions, will likely be enough to create right-wing ill will toward Silicon Valley until kingdom come.

But in the world of real policy, Google scored an early triumph in lobbying the Trump administration at the time it was considering nominating Utah attorney general Sean Reyes to head the FTC. Reyes had previously asked the commission to reopen its antitrust investigation of the company, and as the *Wall Street Journal* reports, "Google responded to the threat of potentially unfriendly policies from Mr. Reyes by engaging a squadron of GOP lobbyists to press the incoming Trump administration not to name him to the position," and succeeded.[17] It also freely contributed $285,000 to Trump's inauguration, as well as throwing money at reactionary gatherings like the far-right Conservative Political Action Conference (CPAC), plus donating heavily to right-wing institutions like the Heritage Foundation and the American Enterprise Institute.[18]

However, the main overlap because tech and Trump is the 2017 Tax Act, which dramatically reduced US corporate income tax and temporarily reduced middle-class taxes, but also contained a provision on overseas corporate cash. Historically taxed at a repatriation rate of 35 percent, firms will now mostly pay no US tax on international profit at all, but with the requirement of paying a 15.5 percent tax on the profits already piled up at the time of the bill.[19] Most of the Big Five tech platforms profiled in this book took advantage of this hugely lucrative change in the tax law, bringing home tens of billions for their share buybacks and dividends for the wealthy investors who own their stock. The towering overseas cash piles were an example of disruptive tech holding to older corporate practice—years earlier, when Google had been found to be funneling much of its business through a post office box in Bermuda in order to avoid $2 billion in yearly taxes, CEO Eric Schmidt responded to criticism by saying, "It's called capitalism."[20]

Of course, the Tax Act was sold to the public in the same way as the GOP's other tax cuts—the new money in businesses' hands would be used for new investment, creating jobs. But, as *Wall Street Journal* reporters observed on repatriating their money, "the nation's tech giants can now more freely dip into their stockpiles of overseas cash. They don't seem to be in any hurry."[21] The companies have been using low-cost borrowing to finance their data center investments and put cash into shareholders' hands, easily affordable for companies exploding with revenues. Most tellingly, Microsoft's chief financial officer told analysts, "When we have seen an opportunity to invest, we have not really waited for tax reform to do that." Despite right-wing claims that taxes are the obstacle to job creation, it turns out today's corporations are rich enough to work around them.

These policy victories speak to Big Tech's quick adaptation to the world of DC lobbying, aided by towering heaps of money. Tech lobbying has reached huge scales, with billions thrown at K Street influence-peddling douchebags to twist legislation to platform demands. From 2013 to 2018, only Boeing spent more on lobbying than Google, which internally describes its lobbyists and ex-diplomats as "foreign minister" and "ambassador."[22] The five tech titans are close behind, with each hurling 4 to 6 million bucks a year at warping US policy to their ends. While publicly entertaining the idea of some regulation, Facebook has lobbied behind the scenes to respond to its long list of heinous problems with its own promised software fixes, while Amazon has pushed to create a uniform national e-commerce tax code and to keep antitrust law limited to preventing monopolistic price hikes.

Despite this, Big Tech's political hand has been weakened by the much-commented-upon scandal of Russian interference in the 2016 and 2018 US elections—mainly by buying ads for controversial or divisive Facebook pages and YouTube channels. While American commenters have been shocked by these programs, by US standards this is a pretty mild level of interference, given America's long history of fixing overseas elections and overthrowing governments. I took this up in greater detail in chapter 6, but it's worth noting here that the United States has recently attempted the exact same strategy as a means to meddle in other countries, including Cuba. The *Miami New Times* reported that the US Office of Cuba Broadcasting, which produces programming opposed to the Communist regime, planned "to create non-branded local Facebook accounts to disseminate information," and that "budget documents suggest the OCB planned to spread U.S. propaganda through Facebook channels designed to fool Cuban users into thinking the information was coming from other Cuban users."[23] USAID was caught operating a phony "Cuban Twitter" platform also, the paper reports. But this is US propaganda, so the political mainstream considers this not to be an act of war, which is how hyperventilating liberals have described Russia's comparatively modest trolling.

Despite the shadow cast by possible future regulation, the tech giants appear to have reached a new pinnacle. Although they have disrupted many industries, tech platforms "haven't attacked banks," as business observers have put it, instead limiting their incursions to moves into accepting deposits, making loans, and other practices of commercial banking. One suggested reason why is that the great US megabanks are becoming major cloud-computing customers, making the tech giants wary of antagonizing such big customers.[24] And certainly cloud services are more profitable than retail banking, and as a result, when the platforms roll out new mobile payments services, they tend to do so in partnership with one or another of the gigantic banks providing the capital and back-end services. All this suggests Big Tech's true arrival: it is apparently reaching codominance of the economy with Wall Street.

Disrupted

And so it was that in June of 2019, the dam finally broke and even the investment-friendly US government, across its branches, at last began to turn on Big Tech. First, the Department of Justice and the Federal Trade Commission, which share jurisdiction of antitrust policy that targets monopolistic firms, announced they had negotiated to split up responsibility for future investigations of the tech giants, with Justice taking potential probes of Google and Apple, and the FTC taking Facebook and Amazon.[25] This represents a real threat to the platforms, as antitrust cases carry at least the theoretical possibility of firms being broken up, as the DOJ tried to do with Microsoft in the nineties, only calling off this goal during the appeals process.

Then, Congress got involved, with the House Judiciary Committee opening an investigation into the platform companies that looked into Big Tech's squelching of competition, with several other committee heads and senators threatening or planning hearings on a variety of aspects of the firms' business. Even cases that end up putting few restraints on Silicon Valley will still probably drag on for years, running up legal bills and creating bad PR for the industry.

And a number of US state attorneys general are organizing their own investigations, as they also have state-level antitrust laws similar to national ones, as when several state governments participated in the nineties-era DOJ antitrust action against Microsoft. The states are broadly seen to carry far less weight than the federal bodies, but the scale could grow—presently, between one and two dozen attorneys general are involved in discussions about bringing tech monopoly cases.[26] It's a real array of forces against the platform giants, despite the national political leadership waiting forty years into the platform era to get interested (the Microsoft case notwithstanding), typical of the famously pro-business policy leanings of the US government.

The companies vary in their exposure. Apple's public posture as the tech giant who cares about privacy doesn't spare it from the consequences of its own monopolistic sins, like when the trillion-dollar colossus lost a 2019 Supreme Court case that allowed an antitrust lawsuit to be brought against the company's control over the App Store, where iPhone users download games and applications. The company's hearty 30 percent slice of app sales, along with the conspicuous fact that Apple users spend nearly double the amount spent on Android apps—despite the latter serving a far-larger mobile market—led the justices to find that the suit can move forward.[27]

Investigations have found that Apple's own apps reliably appear at the top of searches in its store, a major advantage despite the fact that its applications often are notoriously unpopular (like Maps) and indeed are often barred from being rated, unlike third-party apps. For apps that generate subscription or sales revenue, Apple's appear first in 95 percent of store searches![28] The practice is similar to Google's and Microsoft's past efforts to steer results toward their other products in any gatekeeper role they gain from network effects.

Still, that's a smaller headache than the one Google is dealing with, although both are in an anxious scramble to shift some of their massive phone-production chains out of China to avoid the effects of the administration's clumsy trade war, with Apple asking its major suppliers to explore moving up to 30 percent of their production process from China to nations in Southeast Asia.[29]

Google and Facebook, with their data hoards and political baggage, are more at risk. Google's relentless disruption of industries to its advantage, from news to travel to e-commerce, have earned it a Microsoft-like enemies list. Indeed, nearly every company Google has stomped on in this book is lining up to brief or formally request DOJ action, including Yelp, Microsoft, TripAdvisor, Oracle, News Corp and other news publishers, and online ad buyers.[30] And while the FTC's 2012 investigation of Google saw some agency staff commenting that the company's products were popular, as well as pointing to their free cost, others observed its actions and mergers "likely helped to entrench Google's monopoly power over search and search advertising."[31]

Facebook has the biggest target on its back, with its successive giant scandals around election interference, its allowance of startlingly wide access to user data by developers, and its practice of buying or copying competitors. The press has reported that the company is expecting to have to hand over internal emails, including some from Zuckerberg himself, that suggest "senior executives didn't make compliance with the FTC order a priority." One is said to be an inquiry from Zuckerberg about one of the giant crowd of third-party apps the company allowed to be built for its platform, with the app claiming to have information on tens of millions of users, including personal details regardless of the privacy setting they chose. In the correspondence, Zuckerberg asked his lieutenants if it was possible the app developer really had collected so much data. That app was later suspended, but there was little effort to look into third-party privacy violations, and the company's main concern is that these and other emails will enter the public record (as many of Microsoft's most embarrassing monopoly-mongering messages did). Notably, internal company documents that were under US court seal but made available by the UK Parliament showed the company eagerly looked for ways to widen its access to user data without notification, and was able to track users' activity on other platforms.[32]

Likely due to this vulnerability, Zuckerberg has announced he is open to some form of regulation of consumer privacy and online political ads, along with ominous efforts to "define reasonable boundaries for public debate" on its platform, as the press puts it.[33] Facebook's goal is to be handed relatively light new rules that can perhaps be ignored over time, rather than serious antitrust action like a breakup that forces the company to sell Instagram, WhatsApp, or Messenger—a possibility made slightly more possible when company cofounder Chris Hughes wrote in the *New York Times* that the company ought to be broken up along these lines.[34]

The FTC finally imposed a $5 billion fine on Facebook in June 2019, which the agency hailed as an "unprecedented" penalty. But of course, the amount comes to about one-eleventh of the company's annual revenue, and the deal exempted Facebook's conduct prior to that fine from further legal action.[35] It also required the usual mild requirements, like an independent privacy-monitoring board and "privacy audits."

At the same time, the agency announced it was opening a new formal antitrust investigation into the company, as the techlash rolls on. But right away, there are unusual and not very encouraging signs that the US government is not being very aggressive—one being that the two of the platform giants that earn most of their revenue from targeted advertising will be investigated by two different agencies. Grouping Facebook and Google together would be the natural choice, with their similar profiling-based ad businesses, so separating those investigations suggests duplicated work.

Further, many insiders are calling less for breakups of the

giants and more for "behavioral" settlements, where companies are required to hold their different units at arm's length so as not to create unfair advantages over rivals. This is a bad sign, since this was the compromise reached with Microsoft, which was later found to have nakedly violated the terms, in part because it was in charge of monitoring its own compliance. This is a strong sign of lessons *not* learned from the industry's history of bucking antitrust regulation and the courts. Additionally, anti-monopoly law in the US relies heavily on proving a dominant firm has harmed consumers by raising prices, even though that's far from the only form of market power, and it's a test companies are especially likely to pass if they offer their products for free, as Google and Facebook of course do.

And even as national investigations grab headlines, you have to look seriously at the massive resources the platforms have to defend themselves. Gearing way up from the early days, when the public and policymakers were euphoric about tech, and policy issues could be an afterthought for the companies, Big Tech now includes some of the biggest lobbying spenders in the entire economy. The scale is incredible—Apple, Amazon, Google, and Facebook spent a total of $55 million on lobby shops in 2018 alone, with Microsoft just south of $10 million.[36] Among its team, Facebook now employs a pair of lobbyists who formerly worked for House Speaker Nancy Pelosi's office, including, incredibly, her former chief of staff. Even more staggering, the very head of the Antitrust Division at the DOJ itself, Makan Delrahim, worked as a contract lobbyist for Google in 2007. He now favors "a broad view" of Big Tech, with the press reporting that while in office, he "has favored middle-ground solutions."[37]

Hell, in May 2019 the industry's main lobbying organization, the Internet Association, gave its "Internet Freedom Award" to none other than the noted champion of online expression, Ivanka Trump. The *Wall Street Journal* relates that "the internet giants have learned from the hard lessons of Microsoft, which was caught flat-footed with a sparse lobbying presence in the 1990s when federal antitrust officials called for a breakup of the software giant."[38] Its headline was "Tech Giants Amass a Lobbying Army for an Epic Washington Battle," and it must be recognized the companies are sitting on the better part of half a trillion in cash.

For its part, Amazon is now "One of Washington's Most Powerful Players," as a *Journal* headline ran, with its PAC giving $637,500 in 2018, amusingly split evenly between Republican and Democratic candidates.[39] Some of that spending, of course, is to help maintain Amazon's giant government cloud computing contracts, from the CIA to the Pentagon. That's in addition to its huge spending on public policy and advocacy groups, including the conservative American Enterprise Institute and the Competitive Enterprise Institute, and the company reported in that year giving $10,000 or more to around forty-seven different groups and think tanks.

Indeed, all five of the Big Tech platform companies reviewed in this book now spend north of $5 million a year on lobbying activities. But Google has been far in the lead for years, spending around $15 million annually since 2011, and recently overhauling its DC influence shop in the face of the new potential investigations. As of 2018 the company had a hundred lobbyists spread over dozens of firms, bringing it the honor of the greatest lobbying spender in the United States that year. Like Amazon, it pours millions into friendly think tanks, university departments, and policy groups writing reports favorable to the company. Until 2018, Google's own DC lobbying operation was headed by a former Republican congresswoman.[40]

Further, tech now leans heavily into the other form of corporate investment in government influence: campaign financing. Today both political parties take in giant volumes of Silicon Valley cash, in part because, as the *New York Times* gracefully put it, "the progressive base has already soured on Wall Street, fossil fuel and pharmaceutical cash. Silicon Valley had been, until recently, one of the last relatively untainted wellsprings from which to draw campaign contributions." That certainly includes the more typical conservative, pro-business Democrats, like 2020 presidential front-runner Joe Biden, one of whose fundraisers was hosted by former Google CEO Eric Schmidt. In 2019 Pelosi held a congressional fundraiser luncheon at the home of Microsoft's chairman, who kicked in $50,000.[41]

And even the more liberal candidates like Senator Elizabeth Warren and leftists like Senator Bernie Sanders are major recipients of tech dollars for their campaigns—the biggest donor group for both is Alphabet, with Microsoft and other tech companies close behind.[42] And incredibly, despite the acidic opposition to immigration of all kinds by the Trump administration, large companies sponsoring educated tech works via the sought-after H-1B visa are getting applications approved at rates around 99 percent, according to the *Journal*, while smaller firms have far more petitions turned down.[43]

I should also add that not all outside companies want the online firms broken up. In particular, advertisers have indicated that breaking up Facebook and Google "could work against their interests," the business pages report, because "the technology giants have allowed them to reach huge audiences and target them efficiently." Indeed, a credit card company marketing exec has said, "I cannot walk away from scale"—no doubt bearing in mind the incredible data hoards allowing precision targeting.[44] However, ad buyers do have gripes with the platforms, especially since it's hard to tell if their ads placed with Google or Facebook have led to a given sale. They hope regulation will include "universal identifiers" attached to ad performance across platforms—a reform that would only help other giant corporations track us more effectively.

The confrontation between Big Government and Big Tech will likely drag on for years, and past history isn't very promising. But the threat of US regulation is also a late arrival on the scene, as the European Union has so far taken the lead in trying to rein in the giants.

Tech's Nemesis

The nations of the European Union have a reputation for a stronger regulatory apparatus than in the United States, although the differences are often exaggerated. The disparity is wider in tech, largely because the megacap platforms are US-based and have benefited from a purposefully light regulatory hand. Yet because of Europe's enormous market, its more aggressive approach has forced Big Tech to bend to its demands. The *Wall Street Journal* notes: "Europe's international influence stems from a confluence of factors, starting with its market size. Companies wanting access to the EU's 500 million potential consumers—one of the world's richest markets for products and services—must play by EU rules." And "in today's globalized markets many also seek to standardize internationally, for scale economies or other reasons."[45]

Consider Google's comparison-shopping searches, which have put the company's commercial listings at the top of its search results to the detriment of independent online shopping services. The EU brought down a large $2.7 billion fine on Google for the practice and demanded it change the displays, and it also cracked down on the company's practices regarding apps on phones running its Android operating system. Google requires handset makers to include several of its own apps, like Search, Maps, and YouTube, and to make its search and Chrome browser the phone defaults—almost perfectly mirroring Microsoft's practices on the OS it owned.[46] The EU met this move with an even bigger $5.1 billion fine, which is staggering by US standards. Yet as the *New York Times* observes, "Google hardly felt it," as it made $3.2 billion in profit that quarter *after* the fine, "shrugging off" this aggressive sanction.[47] Even the EU's regulations may not be enough to restrain Big Tech and its surging river of cash.

Other tech kingpins have been challenged by European competition standards, too—not least Amazon, which is also being investigated for unfair competition in response to its particular combination of its own retail and third-party merchants.

Because it often sells products in competition with its independent Marketplace sellers, it likely has access to information about pricing, sales, and production of those goods that the smaller independent sellers can't match.[48]

The EU's tax crackdowns have gotten more attention though, as the cartoonishly low tax rates paid by the most profitable firms on God's earth have proven intolerable, especially as most of Europe spent years in grinding recession with austerity programs that reduced public benefits. And because of the enormous size of the online platforms, small EU states like Ireland and Luxembourg have made special deals with them to attract their investments and employment, running up against EU prohibitions against "illegal state aid."[49]

Through complex tax-avoidance strategies that place the company's revenues in low-tax locations, many corporations today dramatically lower their tax bills and avoid kicking in for the huge amount of public goods and services they suck up. Google used a profit-shuttling method known as the "Dutch Sandwich" to reduce its overseas tax rate to 2.4 percent, racking up $3.1 billion in tax savings over 2007 to 2009 alone, *Bloomberg* reports.[50] Notably, the IRS actually approved this ludicrous arrangement in 2006.

Amazon had a similarly exploitative relationship with Luxembourg, while for many years Apple used another complicated scheme called the "Double Irish," paying a tax rate of between 0.005 percent and 1 percent on the entirety of its enormous European profits.[51] But again, Ireland's EU-forced efforts to recover the lost $15 billion-odd in tax revenue aren't likely to materially hurt the world's largest corporation—as the *Journal* reports, "Even if Apple is forced to pay the full penalty, it would make only a small dent in the company's $231 billion cash hoard."[52]

But the centerpiece of Europe's efforts to tame Big Tech is its suite of personal data and privacy laws, above all the GDPR—the General Data Protection Regulation. In contrast to the marketplace approach, the GDPR treats personal data in a fundamentally different way, seeing it as the personal property of individuals.

That means it has major requirements for the platforms—above all, they must ask user permission before using personal data, although that requirement doesn't prohibit them from collecting the data initially. Under this arrangement, users can ask companies what information they have on them, and request they delete it. To partially level the playing field against the huge corporations, the GDPR allows users to form class action–like bodies to file complaints, which have a regular but bureaucratic process with many steps to pursue cases. The companies must also take some steps to make it easier for users to change services, to avoid the "lock-in" common with online platforms. Amazingly, it further requires that terms of use must be in actual readable language, rather than legalese, and it has real enforcement teeth, with potential fines up to 4 percent of global revenue, meaning many billions of dollars for the tech giants.[53] It appears to be inspiring other enforcement mechanisms involving actual punishments, as in Australia, where a panel proposed a nuclear option for rule violation—policing the companies' actual algorithms.

But as often happens, some attempts to limit the power of gigantic corporations by regulating them have already been gamed to the benefit of the giants. Google, which the GDPR was designed to regulate, has actually insisted on a strict interpretation of it for its clients on AdSense, its program placing ads on independent websites. This actually helps Google maintain power over the online ad market, sinc,e besides keeping Google on the right side of the GDPR, the policy strengthens its hand against other ad-placing companies: Google's users are often more willing to click the consent option, since Google's huge suite of crucial services makes the bargain more attractive than for less-known sites. And as smaller online ad-space sellers struggle to get visitors to consent to the use of their data for tracking, more ad buyers are being directed by online ad markets like DoubleClick Bid Manager toward Google's own ad inventory, which is reliably in line with the data law.[54]

This means Google and Facebook are "leveraging their vast scale and sophistication as they seek consent from the hundreds of millions of European users who visit their services each day . . . setting an industry standard that is hard for smaller firms to meet," the business press reports.[55] Google now requires its ad-selling website and app-making clients to get consent for targeting from each ad-placing company they use; likewise, it demands its digital ad-placing competitors get consent for each possible company that might place an ad on them or be blocked from Google's services. This is a very high standard for Google and Facebook's much-smaller competitors, making the European ad business a sad business.

Facebook is seeing success in getting European users to approve of the use of their data for some targeted marketing, but also has to work around a prohibition on buying more personal data on users about their offline purchases. Yet even in Europe the company's revenue has continued to shoot up, partially because the decrease in daily users has been small, and only a minority of remaining users have opted out of targeted ads. This is perhaps because, as the *Journal* reports, "users who don't want to give Facebook access to their data must go through a few more steps before Facebook accepts their decisions, according to mock-ups of the permission screens. . . . Facebook hasn't built a way for users to decline to provide more data with a single tap."[56]

All of this suggests that even in the face of Europe's aggressive competition laws and data controls, the tech behemoths may be too great to be tied down by any law that leaves the power of their market platforms intact. So to see real limits of their power, we should turn to markets where the platforms themselves are barred or harnessed.

Watch on the Great Firewall

China has become a great bogeyman in the eyes of the West, with world news often dominated by horrified reporting on China's rapid economic growth, its rise as a world power, and its eager building of infrastructure in the developing world. The accounts accurately identify these recent moves as imperialist, but never with any reference to the far bigger and longer history of the Western countries' imperialism and global debt-fueled influence mongering.

The Chinese government remains highly authoritarian and, since it sits on another of the world's greatest markets for goods and services, has frequently dictated terms to Western companies, including the tech platforms. The latter have become justifiably notorious for participating in the state's wide-reaching censorship and surveillance network. Referred to as the Great Firewall, this network has a level of information restriction that is often typical of the developing world, but Western commentators, largely out of chauvinism, showcase it as uniquely evil.

Microsoft, for example, banned the word "democracy" from Chinese blog posts it hosts and, more flagrantly, created a special version of its operating system for China, "Windows 10 China Government Edition." It's also likely to submit its source code to the government, allegedly so the state can check for the "back doors" that Edward Snowden revealed were installed by US intelligence agencies.[57]

Apple has especially extensive relationships in China, as "substantially all" of its products are manufactured there, as its financial filings state. The conditions in the factories operated by its largest contractor, Foxconn, have already been noted. But it also relies on China as the second-largest market for its high-end phones and gadgets, and as such has made a long list of concessions to the state's surveillance needs. Some Chinese citizens and dissidents are able to evade the Great Firewall using VPNs, virtual private networks, that create the appearance that a web user is outside the country and thus allowed access to blocked content; however, to keep friendly relations with the state, Apple removed almost seven hundred VPNs from its App Store in 2017 alone.[58]

Worse, to comply with government demands Apple agreed to transfer the iCloud data of Chinese users to a domestic partner, meaning those users' data will be stored within China. This means the state will likely have extensive access to this information, and indeed could potentially seize the physical servers on which the data resides. Apple has also taken the additional step of storing the encryption codes for those user accounts in Chinese territory as well.[59] Cloud leaders Microsoft and Amazon have also transferred user data to Chinese partner companies, again to preserve market access.

Facebook, for its part, has experimented with censored versions of its social media platform in order to return to the country, which kicked it out in 2009. Other moves have so far been frustrated, from CEO Mark Zuckerberg's efforts to learn Mandarin to his stage-managed visits, during which he jogged through downtown Beijing without the protective pollution masks often worn by locals, creating a nice pro-China photo op but bringing little real result.[60]

But the most storied odyssey in the country is Google's, likely because of the contrast between the Western image of a pure-evil Chinese government and the company's ethical reputation. The company entered the market in 2006 with the creation of Google.cn, which required licensing that mandated Google would conform to state demands to censor results like "Tiananmen Square." But notably, Google's service included notices on its search results if some results had been blocked by government requirement.[61] The Chinese-language version of Google.com, on the other hand, ran from the United States and so was slow but uncensored, leading the government to frequently block it, along with other Google properties like YouTube and Blogger.

Google had to compete with Chinese search engine Baidu, which had more market share, but Google was favored by more educated, Western-oriented professionals. In order to carry out the censorship, Google as always used algorithms that could accomplish the whitewashing with limited human involvement, and, as tech journalist Steven Levy writes, the algorithms did "a scary-good job in preventing Chinese citizens from accessing forbidden information."[62] But the state still intermittently blocked or slowed Google.cn, would demand particular results be removed or searches cleaned up, and appealed to nationalism to give the censorship-accepting Baidu a popular edge over the foreign Google. As its participation in state censorship went on, the company drew increasing criticism in the West, as well as from the Chinese state media, which berated it for not stripping foreign news websites from its results. Finally, Google suffered a major hack targeting its crucial source code. As Levy relates, "What they stole was apparently so critical that Google never revealed its nature."[63] That was the last straw, and in 2010 the company closed Google.cn and directed traffic to its uncensored Hong Kong site, which the Chinese government continued blocking mainland users from reaching.

The episode is often held up as an example of Google holding to its high ethical standards despite strong monetary rewards for collaborating with the Chinese government. But the *Wall Street Journal* notes that "Google pulled its search engine only after Chinese hackers broke into its systems in search of source code. In other words, it fled an existential threat as much as an ethical dilemma."[64] Likewise, Ken Auletta observes that Google's participation in (and even exceeding of) Chinese censorship was yet another reason to be critical of the company's shady power, and thus Google's allegedly principled withdrawal from the country "was as much a business as a 'Don't be evil' decision."[65]

Attracted to China's giant market, the company has since endeavored to return leading it to recently develop another censored engine code-named "Dragonfly." The Google workforce's opposition to this and activism to stop it were discussed in chapter 5; at any rate, observers judge it unlikely that Google will be granted another search license there. The company still operates facilities in the country, including an AI lab, and of course works closely with phone manufacturers using its almost-universal Android mobile OS. Other Western tech giants have gone further, as when Yahoo provided the government with the identity of a dissident journalist, who was soon arrested. Worse, the data security company Cisco provided the Chinese government with the network tools to create the Great Firewall in the first place.[66]

Many writers have pointed out that censorship in China is less about utterly banning certain terms, although that does happen, as we've seen. It's more about manipulation of context and managing attention, keeping it attracted toward pop culture frivolity and cheap nationalism, to the detriment of hard-hitting dissident information. The attitude of the Chinese tech majors toward these issues is evident in the words of Alibaba head Jack Ma, responding to the question of whether his engine should include results from Chinese dissidents: "No! We are a business. . . . Shareholders want to make money. Shareholders want us to make the customer happy. Meanwhile we do not have any responsibilities saying we should do this or that political thing."[67]

The Chinese state has supported domestic tech giants of its own, keeping the US-based platforms at bay and at times abetting in the theft of Western technology. American commentators and the US government bitterly condemn this forced "tech transfer," but considering that said technologies were mostly developed by various US research agencies and then "transferred" to the private sector through privatization, a more sensible response is "easy come, easy go."

The giants of the People's Republic of China include Alibaba, colloquially known as China's Amazon, as well as search giant Baidu and the enormous Tencent, which dominates messaging and online games. The three heavies have strategic patterns somewhat parallel to the US platform giants, originating in different sectors and then trying to compete in limited areas where each feels they could claw away some market share. The Chinese companies also operate on the same scale as the Western ones, with the combined valuation of Alibaba and Tencent comparable to the total value of Facebook, Amazon, Google, and Netflix.[68] And following the US giants' lead, the companies purposefully create incompatibilities, such as blocking each other's links from working, making them unclickable. The American and Chinese platforms even sometimes strike deals among themselves, like when Google and Tencent reached a large patent-sharing deal.

World governments continue to endeavor to cope with the rising influence of Big Tech, with India taking similar steps to China's in demanding that the data of Indian users be stored in-country. India's telecom agency is also threatening Apple over its refusal to make the agency's spam-blocking app available on its prominent App Store.[69] Globally, dozens of countries are passing legislation to govern their citizens' use of tech platforms, including Japan, Malaysia, Brazil, and Colombia, which have advanced laws similar to Europe's privacy requirements.[70] As Facebook becomes the Internet for many impoverished users in the Global South and especially Africa, keeping it on track for finding another billion users may come down to its ability to block these privacy laws from taking hold in some of the world's poorest countries.

For years, the standard view has been that the greatest power centers in the world are national governments, with their abilities to tax, imprison, regulate, and invade. But Big Tech's mountains of cash, control over information, and planetary global networks may yet give them a run for their money.

CHAPTER 10

Share This!

Socializing the Internet

With our world seemingly hurtling toward catastrophe for several separate reasons, a movement to take control over the tech networks from their bullying douchebag CEOs could seem like a sideshow. But the total reliance of our economy, our social lives, and our attention spans on the tech giants and their online platforms raises the stakes.

Much of today's political momentum is apparently on the right, with borderline-fascist movements rising to power around the world. Many populations are groping for a response to these alarming developments, with some promoting the traditional pro-corporate, neoliberal political figures, like Hillary Clinton or Emmanuel Macron. But this centrist-rightist spectrum is now being challenged by an upsurge in leftward movement, sometimes centered on popular left figures like Bernie Sanders or Jeremy Corbyn. These figures are more critical of concentrated corporate markets, but the alternatives they offer remain within the realm of private ownership of large-scale capital, defined as capitalism.

By now, the parade of shameful power-mongering disgraces that is the Silicon Valley record suggests that the industry's power is out of control and should be challenged, limited, and per-haps stripped from them entirely. For all the world's breathless, cringey, sycophantically worshipful puff pieces on tech CEOs and their slick products and free services, the sheer scale of their economy-conquering, worker-abusing, all-knowing power is finally eclipsing their economic alibi. If our lives and economy now rely on these firms and their platforms, they are too import-ant to be left in the hands of the companies. A positive funda-mental change would be to bring them under the control of the people who make them run, and the users who create so much free content for them. An economic system where the economy and its productive capital are run by the workforce, known as socialism, can most definitely be achieved in the online economy.

Therefore, we should recognize an online socialism as a major priority for radical change, replacing the power wielded by the tech sector with democratic control over the Internet's crucial plat-forms. Online socialism would represent a movement to impose a form of popular representation on decision making about plat-forms, where the workers maintaining them and users making them fun decide how they will operate, rather than leaving it to a CEO to make sneaky terms of service changes in the dead of night. This would represent a major achievement in human liber-ation, owing to the platforms' pivotal role as a mode of modern human expression, information sharing, and enrichment. In fact, because of our widening dependence on web-mediated services, online socialism could be a leading edge in helping to socialize the broader economy—bringing the great corporate decisions that shape our lives, about investment and employment, under our actual control.

Socializing Silicon Valley means poses unique challenges and special opportunities. Markets that involve information, like traditional media and the tech platforms, reliably encoun-ter heightened resistance from defenders of capitalism. The wide extent of the companies' information-filtering capability adds a layer of complication, as does the global nature of these firms.

But the user-produced nature of much online content means the barriers to organization may be significantly lower than those in other industries. Further, the pivotal daily roles of these platforms suggest that a strong movement to socialize them could have a force multiplier, making it an especially fertile focus for leftist action. Strategies for socializing a sector aren't always worked out in detail, but plans are important, especially given the crucial importance of this industry. I'll attempt to briefly sketch out those strategies now.

User Disillusion

Envisioning a more radical network agenda today means moving well beyond mere anti-monopoly law and toward forms of public ownership and worker management of the crucial web platforms—those that are now accepted as essential for disseminating information, like YouTube, Facebook, and the smartphone operating systems. As labor and socialist history amply demonstrate, this is easier said than done, and a number of challenges present themselves, including ones common to information industries and others unique to the online sector. Not least among these is the particularly thorny question of exactly how the digital behemoths should be brought under democratic control.

Fundamentally, socialism in any part of the economy is about power, and who gets to make the important decisions about what will be invested in and how the economy will grow. Under capitalism, the great productive capital of the economy is private property, and investment and production decisions are made by businesses and the CEOs and boards who own them. Under socialism, workers make these decisions, usually understood to have goals of more equally sharing the goods produced and generally supporting other people, or "solidarity." Socialism is also thought of today with additional goals in mind, like improving work conditions and guaranteeing workplace diversity along racial, gender, and other lines, as well as taking environmental sustainability seriously rather than prioritizing near-term profit above all, as markets do.

So in a socialized economy, you would go to work and have access to the information about your business or workplace that the manager or boss currently keeps to themselves, and you and your coworkers would have to decide what to do in light of that information. Since the modern economy requires huge scales of production, both to produce enough goods and to achieve efficiencies like economies of scale, representation would be required—modern economic enterprises with tens of thousands of workers can't all meet and vote directly on everything. A socialist democracy could extend to economic decisions, through a system in which workplaces send delegates to attend decision-making meetings and report back on them, voting as the workplace itself votes, and being subject to recall if the schmoozing reps get too big for their britches and start bucking the will of the workers they represent.

This vision, of popular democratic processes making economic decisions, is the core idea of socialism, rather than the vision of a government takeover of industries, as it has been represented in the past. For online platforms, this would mean that users and the platform operators would share responsibility for developing the platforms, and do so toward shared, openly discussed goals rather than those settled on by an executive team striving for a Wall Street ad-clicks target. We users would actually be able to set what information we felt like sharing, what we do and don't want tracked for optimal platform experience, and share the decisions about how the platform should change its layout or functionalities.

Rather than picking up your phone and discovering a feature is no longer available, or that some information of yours has been tracked without your knowledge, or that an app no longer works on an updated operating system, you would know what changes were coming to the platform and would at least have a share in the process deciding on them. Any widely used platform should have a process where users and engineers jointly decide what new features should be developed, and how to implement them. Above all, your personal data would be considered your personal property, and you could readily opt in if you wanted more of the customization that the companies presently use to justify tracking you to every dark corner of the Internet. Today's product officers at Big Tech would be retired in favor of one or another democratic decision-making structure. Like socialism in any sector, we should bring an experimental attitude to the online sector, open to trying out and evaluating different organizational ideas and decision-making processes, but this is at least an idea of what online socialism could look like.

Proposals for democratizing the platforms are circulating, such as the call for platform cooperativism, advanced by Trebor Scholz and Nathan Schneider in their book *Ours to Hack and to Own*. They argue for co-op principles of "shared governance and shared ownership of the Internet's levers of power—its platforms and protocols. Democratic ownership and governance are the pillars of what *cooperativism* refers to."[1] These goals closely correspond to the broad ideals of online socialism.

State control, especially without a radical, society-wide process of democratization, is an unappealing option for the information network sector. The traditional saw of capitalism's reactionary defenders is that socialism inevitably means government control and a more authoritarian state, and this argument is often deployed with particular force in discussions about industries already prone to monopoly, like cable companies' broad empires and the entrenched networks around the online platforms. The aggressive virulence of this extremely common pro-business argument is undermined by the unflattering reality that these now-crucial tech monopolies clearly reveal that "free markets" rarely remain richly competitive. Instead, they result in markets concentrated into a few colossal companies, as in the tech industry or the other giants throughout the whole history of capitalism, like Rockefeller's titanic oil monopoly or Anheuser-Busch InBev's near monopoly in beer. So, even when the celebration of markets' alleged "freedom to choose" wouldn't pass the laugh test, the bit tyrants and their ocean of media supporters instead trash the idea of worker control, equating it to state totalitarianism.

Overcoming this argument requires the political sophistication to recognize the irrationally reflexive suspicion of public institutions in modern politics. This paranoia can be overcome if the left is willing to keep its focus on the question of power; indeed, the millions upon millions of public commenters in the various battles over FCC neutrality policy were significantly motivated by antagonism toward the enormous power centers of AT&T and Comcast. Most citizens are capable of seeing the towering power of the telecom empires, and the same is becoming true of the far-larger tech platforms, so this widely disseminated right-wing argument can be outflanked in organizing and education work.

Another challenge to socializing the Internet arises from the fact that unlike other networks (such as the railroads of the Gilded Age), digital networks are global in their extent, meaning any successful effort to socialize them will require coordinated international action by platform workers and users. This of course raises obvious problems of global activist articulation that are very familiar to veteran political and labor activists. Strategies for international organizing have historically included aggressive efforts to cultivate transnational organizational connections among labor and anti-capitalist movements, requiring significant institutional resources and sustained commitment. Campaigns to antagonize a corporate platform therefore require carefully planned solidarity with workers and users abroad to bring meaningful pressure on the platform owners, and indeed to mount the more dramatic coordinated actions needed for any political move aiming to bring the Internet under popular control. Some steps in this direction have occurred. For example, in the resistance against Amazon's labor practices in Europe, warehouse workers in Germany, Poland, and France have met to discuss how to coordinate across country borders, a necessary counter-strategy in a corporation where "orders can be shifted from one warehouse to another if problems arise," as a worker's account describes.[2]

A further implication is that any successful democratization of one or more of these platforms within a particular polity will represent only a piecemeal victory that would come under perennial sanction by the World Trade Organization or another body. One can readily imagine management in this sector responding with a capital strike, in which company owners, feeling threatened or otherwise displeased, shut down their enormous businesses, or pull their financial wealth out of a country, which can put colossal pressure on an economy.

In the tech sector, a capital strike could manifest in a move where the global architecture of a Google or Amazon refuses, out of ruling class indignation, to recognize a socialized portion of its system or be smoothly articulated, and suddenly links aren't connecting, orders aren't taken, and documents aren't intelligible. This speaks again to the desperate need for international cooperation.

As always, the greatest obstacle to socialist organization is the reaction from the powerful corporations in the industry. We can be confident that tech firms will react to existential challenges with aggression—the industry has already shown the true colors that lay behind its playful, cutesy nerd façade. The no-poaching wage-fixing conspiracy that Steve Jobs led and the industry's overexploitation of the white-collar and blue-collar sections of its workforce give us ample evidence of corporate greed and hostility to worker autonomy.

Beyond the usual firing of organizers on factory floors or in open-format office suites, online firms have a variety of levers of power to resist organization. Above all, these empires of capital can be expected to turn to propaganda, having overwhelming power to filter and shape the information that growing numbers of us go online for. This is a major obstacle, as citizens used to socially and politically engaging through Facebook cannot expect their News Feed to include many posts by "Socialize Facebook" group pages, nor can we expect Google Search to put "Socialize

Google" on the first page of results. The aggressive and deceitful actions of the cell carriers and cable companies in their fight to keep their broadband businesses free of net neutrality rules are probably suggestive of what can be expected, from heavy political lobbying to aggressive PR campaigns to well-funded minority civic groups willing to express "concern" that closely tracks the industry's own views.

Confronting this information-filtering power is surely the single-greatest challenge to socializing the Internet platforms and perhaps the broader economy. Counteracting the muscle that hub owners rely upon will require extensive reliance on both online and offline solidarity. The successful campaigns against the telecom firms, once again, prove that this broader solidarity agenda can be achieved. In 2015 and 2017, major online awareness campaigns, along with real-world sit-ins on corporate campuses and occupation of company and state offices, saw major successes and might do so again.

Further, we should recognize that the online giants' near-total ownership of our universe of personal private data will surely bear on any organizational drive to socialize the platforms. The larger part of the Valley's entire business model is, after all, built upon commercializing our personal data in a variety of ways, and it is utterly naïve to imagine the tech empires will confront a movement representing an existential threat to their wealth and network power without playing dirty. Movement leaders and ideological heads can confidently expect to be "doxed" by the platforms themselves, with their dirty laundry publicly aired in the cowardly anonymized-leak fashion, familiar to many veterans of movements for social justice. Skilled organizers could use the companies' clear responsibility for these fortuitously timed leaks to further undermine the credibility of the platforms' corporate owners, but of course this won't stop the damage from being done.

Any early projections like these about an emerging movement must also take into account the historic difficulty workers have encountered in drives to organize the professional ranks of software writers and hardware engineers, as existing groups like the Tech Workers Coalition have described. As I've reviewed throughout the book, these professional workers are well paid and mobile, not infrequently on something like their own terms. These conditions are certainly subject to change as market and political circumstances evolve, including for nonmarket reasons like state policy shifts. The Trump administration's crusade against immigration includes efforts to cut back the H-1B visa program, which allows employers in certain industries to sponsor the migration of workers with scarce technical skills. So far these steps have actually favored Big Tech, which had received very high levels of approval for its applicants, but stricter moves could shift labor market conditions in the sector, likely leading programmer salaries to rise, in which case the will to organize against employers may fall. Alternatively, salary ceilings may remain if temporary workers continue to be hired in higher numbers to defray the expense of fewer foreign workers. These changes could make the workforce more sympathetic to organization and unionization.

At the lower end of the wage and prestige scale, we have the frontline workers of the Silicon Valley money machine—the Foxconn contractors on Chinese factory floors, the Google content-checkers running content flags on YouTube, the low-wage sales force of the Apple stores, and the sweating subjects of the Amazon warehouse empire. Here the obstacles to organizing are more clear, as these are more traditionally exploitative work settings. This means classic union tools are called for, though surely they must be utilized in a more effective way than in recent years, as the union density numbers of the labor movement have continually fallen. Below I discuss in greater detail the ways organizing can be more effective, but the continuity of the challenges facing leftist organizing is pretty clear.

From a wide reluctance to promote public influence over information networks, to hoards of private information, to traditional anti-union tools, to control over the information filters we take for granted daily, Silicon Valley has plenty of means to resist organizing drives of all sorts. Having reviewed this grim toolbox, we can consider the unique opportunities to organizing in this sector.

Socialized Media

Despite the numerous major advantages held by the online giants, activists have certain assets in their struggle to bring the Internet under popular control. Given the growing importance of the online economy and its potential to serve as a lever to jump-start socialization of the broader economy, any advantages that may offset the bosses' high cards will be essential for our side to understand.

One advantage has materialized during the struggles for net neutrality: organizing has been aided by the fact that individuals spend more and more time in online environments, which for all its drawbacks does mean that the initiative required for contributing to the struggle is significantly reduced. Of course, online contributions—like blog posts, petition signing, regulator comments—are proportionately smaller as well; however, in some circumstances this can be compensated for by the resultant greater numbers. This dynamic was especially relevant during the neutrality battles because of the relative ease of filing FCC comments.

Naturally the issue of web access arouses particular passion among the extremely online, and the time and effort required to transmit a complaint to the FCC is plainly minute compared to one's contribution to taking over ownership of the major global online platforms. But the US telecom industry did put up a strong fight against Title II and still lost at least once, owing in part to the moral power and democratic weight of the four million neutrality-supporting public comments the agency received in 2015, and the yet-larger number in 2017. So, the relative ease of online engagement should be taken seriously and be part of modern campaign planning in any context. This dynamic is especially important considering the possibility, as yet unevaluated, that such low-initiative actions could be "gateway actions" drawing passive platform users into struggles that require both online and offline engagement.

It's relevant here to recognize this time-honored pattern of struggling for mild reforms and the way it leads to energized activism and emboldened demands. There are no shortage of "non-reformist reforms"—legal prohibitions and regulations that encourage further activism rather than stifle it through small concessions. The great media scholars James Curran, Natalie Fenton, and Des Freedman present a number of these reforms in their incredibly useful *Misunderstanding the Internet*. They include publicly owned broadband infrastructure, strict limits on the use of personal data by the tech firms, subsidies for journalism that has been displaced by platform economics, and the requirement that platform space be free of cookies and other invasive software.[3] Each of these proposals is a legitimate step forward, limiting the power of the tech giants and opening a little more space for privacy, journalism, and creator control.

But perhaps the most important advantage for organizers of online socialism is the reality that most of these tech giants employ relatively few workers relative to revenue, relying instead on user-generated content. From Facebook profiles to Google's YouTube to Apple's iTunes, content is in large part produced at no cost to the firm apart from the labor costs of the network managers and software engineers tasked with the maintenance of the platform. This immediately indicates that any project to lessen the power of tech monopolies will falter without major support from the great body of *users*, themselves demanding more control.

The dominance of user content has several specific ramifications for online organizing. The first to consider is the rather-unexplored possibility of significantly lower barriers to entry in radical campaigning. Consider the Herculean efforts required by labor organizers down the years to raise the consciousness of their fellow workers, to avoid workplace retaliation and illegal firings, and to navigate the reality of anti-union violence, all to organize workers into a bargaining unit that can campaign effectively. On today's online platforms, content creators are pivotal, so we must take seriously the major potential advantage of organizing users outside the intimidating presence of a boss in a conventional work hierarchy.

Plainly, any online organizing on the platforms themselves, as in the cases of Facebook pages calling for the platform's socialization, or YouTube channels criticizing Big Tech, is always subject to the companies' awareness and constant, detailed monitoring. However, because of the platforms' central economic role, activists have a plausible near-term expectation of hanging on to meaningful space for organizing against platform power. It must be appreciated that the barriers for achieving this are still significant, but a far cry from classic shop floor intimidation. Exactly what form an organization of online creators would take can be resolved in the organization process, and as always it should arise organically from those being organized—perhaps in the form of a creators' rights league, video producers' union, or online authors' guild. But this organizing must be based on a more radical conception than just winning a slightly better deal for the creators. The organizational ideology should be based on the simple recognition that the online firms have prospered gigantically through the advantages of their "donated" works and the extensive power they hold over these works, and that the proceeds and control should be vested in the hands of the originators and actual creative people rather than tech empires owned by the global 1 percent.

In light of the essential role played by user content, one very practical tactic suggests itself: user strikes. The various rebellions that have taken place on Facebook's platform show the potential of this tactic. For these platforms, an organized decision to withhold contributions of content by a large body of users could be just as painful as a strike by a traditional workforce—the value produced on social media derives entirely from the collective contributions each of us make when we post, contributions for which we get no compensation, while the CEOs and investors rake in historic profits. Like any strike, the pressure put on the companies will depend on how much of this exploited labor is withheld, and for how long, but the most critical metric among these firms is engagement—and if it falls thanks to some users purposefully boycotting, leading to other users engaging less as content declines, that means fewer eyeballs on ads and fewer links clicked. Gigantic amounts of money are created and lost quarterly as engagement on Facebook and Snapchat rises and falls—I expect in the future we will see that deliberate and sustained decreases in engagement can create real pain for these giants.

Further, a user strike offers advantages not found in a traditional one—the greatest of which is getting to avoid the burden of strikers' lost wages. Obviously, there would be other, partially compensating pressures, since using the platforms is often enjoyable and they often provide quite-essential services, as this book has argued. While third-party sellers on Amazon or creators of compensated video on YouTube would indeed take a potentially painful economic hit to contribute to the struggle, the rest of us would simply have to forego our streaming video and social media habits. Painful enough!

And full-on labor strikes among the workforce proper will still be essential, as demonstrated in the Google walkouts and Foxconn suicide strikes. Of course, this basic technique is nothing new, as strikes have for many years been part of the toolbox of the trade union movement and the radical left. In traditional labor strikes, workers refuse work on an organized basis in order to push their demands, such as for health care or pay increases from a company's rising profits. Because of the fundamental role skilled, experienced workers play in producing all the goods and services we consume, they have historically been able to wield surprising power against even the most gigantic companies, if they are well organized into unions or other bodies. As the escaped slave and public intellectual Frederick Douglass put it, "As the laborer becomes more intelligent he will develop what capital he already possesses—that is the power to organize and combine for its own protection," in order "to cope with the tremendous power of capital."[4]

The greatest form of labor strike is the "mass strike," where very large numbers of organized men and women strike for a broader social goal, like demanding the voting franchise or public health care. The prominent twentieth-century socialist Rosa Luxemburg wrote that "the mass strike" is "the method of motion of the proletarian mass," meaning it is the workers' most fundamental means of opposing capital and taking control of their lives into their own hands. Mass strikes require a good deal of preceding work and organization, as they "do not exactly fall from heaven."[5] But since the main obstacle to maintaining a mass strike of users is the nervous compulsion to check our phones—as opposed to the traditional striking obstacle of the nervous compulsion to eat—this tactic could be a useful and effective way of leveraging Silicon Valley's reliance on our donated labors.

Still, even within this somewhat more favorable organizing terrain, inherent limitations to these tools should not be underestimated. Major ceilings to this opportunity could include, first, making headway in swamped News Feeds, YouTube home pages, and Google search pages. These platforms are already bursting with plenty of abundant online content, and simply gaining attention for an important drive to organize users and workers will be an endeavor in itself.

Further, it will be a significant undertaking to persuade online users to put time into an uncertain effort to demand reforms, or indeed, major transfers of control or ownership. An often-noted feature of platforms is the tendency to take them for granted as handy venues for sharing all the posts and videos that make the web rich, and thus the traditional tendency to normalize the institutions of capital is very much an obstacle here.

Finally, there remain, of course, all the long-standing tools used by the great conglomerations of capital to legitimize their rule through various propaganda, which I have discussed in this chapter and throughout this book. The popular suspicion against big institutions and their profit obsession can be brought to bear, and of course, the firms themselves will attempt to turn it against whatever labor or radical organization is running the organizing campaign. These are classic contours of conflict between labor and capital, and can be expected to be particularly formidable since these firms have the major edge of the ability to filter information.

It's to be expected, should any movement against Big Tech show significant promise, that Google will rank activist sites lower in search results, Outlook spam filters will have their settings quietly adjusted to send activists' appeals into junk files, and Facebook will limit the visibility of these campaigns on News Feeds. The political question of how much influence the platform owners are allowed to exercise over campaigns to organize them must become a real political issue.

But these limitations do not obviate the reality that organizing and radicalizing online users still has conspicuously lower barriers to entry than are traditionally observed in classic labor organizing, such as it is. Savvy organizers and crafty activists can and should bring their creativity to bear in breaking through the online clutter and maneuvering around the limits that platform owners are sure to deploy.

In this, organizers and activists should be sure to highlight the reality that control of our self-created online content is increasingly limited, and on a fairly immediately visible basis. This extends from Facebook's ability to police our speech in posts on its platform, to Apple's efforts to push our work onto their cloud by omitting the universally accepted USB ports from their new laptops, to Amazon's control over your Kindle library. These transparently selfish moves by the Valley giants truly enrage people. People get pissed when platforms they have trusted with their life's work and private thoughts turn out to be utterly outside their control.

Many of us have direct experiences of this endlessly frustrating lack of control over our data and, freely created, and indeed donated content. This experience could be summarized by referring to radical communications scholar Robert McChesney: "Over half of the roughly 84 data categories Facebook collects about its users are not available for them to see."[6] Yet how many of us have even taken the time to read Facebook's policies regarding control of our data, even the fraction of it we *are* allowed to learn about?

The central role of user data in these platforms suggests some specific features for online socialism, as technology writer Evgeny Morozov explains in the *New Left Review*:

> It's primarily from data and not their algorithms that powerful companies currently derive their advantages, and the only way to curb that power is to take the data completely out of the market realm, so that no company can own them. Data would accrue to citizens, and could be shared at various social levels. Companies wanting to use them would have to pay some kind of licensing fee, and only be able to access attributes of the information, not the entirety of it.[7]

This kind of reconsideration of the nature of data would put significant autonomy back in the hands of platform users, and strip it from the giant platforms.

Again, none of this is to minimize the essential role of organizing the tech workforce. Well-planned campaigns with committed resources, coordinated international solidarity, an emphasis on strong numbers of experienced organizers, and a serious drive to engage the communities from which the workers come have proven to be enduringly successful for workers in more conventional settings, as Kate Bronfenbrenner and other labor scholars have shown.[8] Tactics along these lines, guided by the above principles, could go a long way toward overcoming the challenges to organizing the tech sector for democratic control.

Looking downstream to the data "pipes," there may be more than temporary utility to ensuring that opposition to net neutrality is permanently associated with the grotesquely unpopular Trump administration and its GOP appointees at the FCC. This would be in addition to its association with the widely disliked broadband empires of AT&T, Comcast, and Verizon. However, the recent price wars among these giants may temporarily limit consumer rage until a price leadership regime can be restored. A socialist campaign would recognize the power of these firms to control our information and online world, and would serve as a classic case for worker and user control.

So despite the major entrenched advantages held by the tech titans, there are legitimate tools in the hands of activists, organizers, and educators who can see the need for shared control over systems that affect all of us. Having considered the obstacles and advantages, what now can be projected about future struggles over the ownership and control of the Silicon Valley corporations and their platforms?

The Last LOL

It is a fact that online platforms have been superseded in the past, but only by fellow early-arrivers with moderately better software, as when Facebook displaced Myspace. The sole major exception to this limited pattern is AOL, the nineties-era Internet portal that became famous for introducing the United States to the web and for stuffing its physical mailboxes with free software discs. These allowed home PCs to get online through dial-up technology, where a modem could connect through a conventional household phone line. In the early years of the Internet, this for a time made AOL *the* main platform, and thus the object of the enormously expensive and unsuccessful AOL–Time Warner merger.

That platform's unusual loss of dominance owed to technological change, as the phone and cable companies developed broadband technology to send more data faster through phone lines, and then through cell signals and cable TV. As this new "broadband" service spread across the broad mass market from its early use on college campuses at the turn of the century, AOL's value utterly plummeted, until it came to be seen as a costly albatross around media conglomerate Time Warner's neck.[9] The role of entry point for the web shifted from that short-lived monopoly to the URL bar that allows any web address to be typed, but also to a limited number of dominant home pages run by the current majors—Google, Facebook, Microsoft's MSN.com, and Verizon's Yahoo.

But entrenched hubs that have grown into great established platforms seldom fall on their own, a historical precedent suggesting that the stock market's expectation of Big Tech's continued dominance looks like a pretty good bet. The worn-in role of these giant network hubs is the main basis for investors' enduring confidence in Silicon Valley, to the point that they now represent the five largest companies in the world by market value: Microsoft, Apple, Amazon, Google, and Facebook, respectively.[10]

Illusions around this reality are widespread, including some wildly deluded commentators who suggest that the new tech hubs are actually undermining capitalism. In a widely cited but grotesquely misguided article in the *Guardian*, Paul Mason suggested that "the giant tech companies . . . cannot last" because their "fragile corporate edifice [is] at odds with the most basic needs of humanity, which is to use ideas freely."[11] Mason's romantic idealism is apparently based on the popularity of sharing online media, and his column traveled widely on the notion that sharing a news article or YouTube video will lead to the crash of capitalism. This is difficult to square with the reams of documentation of Silicon Valley's legal and economic means of protecting its platforms. And if you're not convinced by this book, written by an economist on the political left, consider instead a November 2015 headline from the conservative *Wall Street Journal*: "Giants Tighten Grip on Internet Economy."[12]

It's possible the giants will seriously stumble despite their entrenched hub status—for example, through a crash in their stock values, which are extremely high (but arguably justified by the titanic profits and power the firms hold, and valuations aren't yet *as* out of control as they were during the 1990s tech bubble).[13] Another prospect is a major security hack or meltdown, which can't be excluded from the realm of possibility after revelations like Intel's 2018 disclosure that the core processor chips sold over the last decade to Amazon, Microsoft, Google, and Apple had security blind spots that could be hacked. This set off a race among the giants to ensure their huge server banks and software updates were patched, which could create major problems for a typical company but, as a corporate strategist said to the press, "when you control that much of the market and you're that prevalent with customers, you get away with it."[14]

And even the early signs of the emerging political techlash look modest—few official proposals of breakups exist. So, without a popular socialist takeover of this sector, the behemoths' dominance will probably last and they will also run the new technologies of augmented reality, virtual reality, and AI. Whatever the best plan is for developing these unprecedented technologies, it will be decided by those with custody of their development, which should probably not be the world's biggest profit-obsessed, power -mongering corporations. For God's sake.

That point applies more broadly—while no one can predict the future of technological evolution, any observer of the sciences will agree that among those making the most dramatic progress is biological technology—especially the use of genetic engineering and editing techniques. The potential ability of these new tools to alter human life is nearly inconceivable and may put today's electronics-based tech revolution to shame. The potential extension and improvement of life it promises is amazing, but it too will probably be under the control of a few nerdy brat billionaires using publicly developed technology—visible even now with the advent of innovative genome-editing tools like CRISPR-Cas9. Someday another economist will be writing a book about the *Bio Tyrants*. Obviously, the incredible potential power represented by this technology will be far more than the biotech entrepreneurs can be trusted with. This is capitalism.

Much like the rail tycoons on the nineteenth century, today's tech monopolists are fighting by using their platforms against one another. Amazon has refused to sell Google products that compete with its home speaker, or to make its Prime Video library functional on Google's Chromecast streaming device. Google retaliated by pulling YouTube service from Amazon's devices.[15] Amazon does carry Google's Pixel and buys its ad space, but it won't sell Apple's streaming device. The level of technology has changed, but what hasn't changed is our lives being held hostage to the ruling class's pissing contests.

Every day, thousands of young people are growing up with advanced technology in their hands that can bring them an ocean of information, games, video, and attenuated social interaction. The longer this essential technology, and the all-important network platforms around which it's built, are in the hands of huge corporations who care only for making their Wall Street growth targets, the more impoverished our lives will become and the harder the fight will be. The technologies of the Internet and its platforms are hugely valuable, and the potential of online socialism to develop them for human expression and education and entertainment is therefore enormous.

Already the tide is turning. The eminent Pew Research Center reported in 2019 that the proportion of Americans who hold broadly positive views of tech companies has fallen from around 70 percent to just 50 percent in just the last four years, with plunges across political party affiliation. Further, 55 percent of Americans said tech companies "have too much power and influence."[16] If Microsoft can come within a chip's width of being bisected by antitrust action, if Title II classification can at least temporarily become law over the heads of the telecom oligopoly, if Google and Facebook can be put on their economic heels by their inability to police their content empires, then Silicon Valley is *not* invincible. Global solidarity among tech workers and users can bring us an Internet that actually lives up to its hype, and indeed its potential. A socialized Internet, one that is actually under the control of all of us whose lives depend on it, can be won with online and offline activism. And online socialism could be a leading edge for socialism in the broader economy.

Each of us should contribute time and energy toward the activism and education required for this beautiful goal and the

spiritual changes in the social nature of humanity that it promises. If that goal were met, we could leave a far better world to
our kids than one in which their tiny wages go toward data plans
and tech toys that give them shallow entertainment and utterly
worthless semi-news, and above all leave them compliant subjects
of capital. We could give them a world of free men and women.

For all these reasons, and for the sake of all of us, we can't
allow the Internet platforms to remain the private property of the
online bitatorship. Today's technology raises legitimately difficult
questions, but the great mass of us users who have given the platforms most of their value should get to decide what the terms are,
not ruling-class CEO douchebarrels. The insistence from the far
right that it's the conservatives who are oppressed in this story
is a hard red pill to swallow, especially since in the early years
they opposed regulating the platforms in the first place. But a
movement this big means moving beyond conventional political
lines—for all the tendency of online entertainment and smartphones to drive us apart into our separate phones and bubbles,
our survival requires an online socialism that brings us together.

Irony loves company.

Notes

Load Screen

1. Michael Gordon and Ivan Nechepurenko, "U.S. Is Warned after It Downs Syrian Fighter," *New York Times*, June 19, 2017. The reference to the Gmail account has since been removed from online editions of the article.

Introduction: Bitatorship

1. David Dayen, "The Android Administration," *The Intercept*, April 22, 2016.
2. Jack Nicas and Rolfe Winkler, "Donald Trump Strikes Conciliatory Tone in Meeting with Tech Executives," *Wall Street Journal*, December 14, 2016.
3. Tyler Cowen, *Big Business: A Love Letter to an American Anti-Hero* (New York: St. Martin's, 2019), 100–101.
4. Don Clark and Robert McMillan, "Giants Tighten Grip on Internet Economy," *Wall Street Journal*, November 6, 2015.
5. Clark and McMillan, "Giants Tighten Grip," 143–44.
6. "Special Article: Microsoft and the Future: Busted," *The Economist*, November 13, 1999.
7. Clark and McMillan, "Giants Tighten Grip."
8. Charles Francis Adams, *Chapters of Erie* (Ithaca, NY: Cornell University Press, 1956), 11.
9. Matthew Josephson, *The Robber Barons: The Great American Capitalists, 1861–1901* (New York: Houghton Mifflin, 1934), 422, 392.
10. Josephson, *The Robber Barons*, 436–41.
11. Mina Kimes, "Railroads: Cartel or Free Market Success Story?," *Fortune*, September 13, 2011.
12. Christopher Mims, "Tech's Titans Tiptoe toward Monopoly," *Wall Street Journal*, May 31, 2018.

13. Simon London, "From Product to Platform," *Financial Times*, January 18, 2004.
14. Amy Harmon, "U.S. vs. Microsoft: The Overview; Judge Backs Terms of U.S. Settlement in Microsoft Case," *New York Times*, November 2, 2002.
15. London, "From Product to Platform."
16. Nicholas Carr, *The Big Switch: Rewiring the World, from Edison to Google* (New York: Norton, 2013), 139.
17. Arun Rao and Piero Scaruffi, *A History of Silicon Valley: The Greatest Creation of Wealth in the History of the Planet* (Palo Alto, CA: Omniware Group, 2013), 397, 398–99.
18. Richard Waters, "Google Changes Tack in Media' Swirling Universe," *Financial Times*, October 10, 2006.
19. Paul Krugman and Robin Wells, *Microeconomics*, 5th ed. (New York: Worth, 2018), 384.
20. Quentin Hardy, "The Web's Creator Looks to Reinvent It," *New York Times*, June 7, 2016.

Chapter 1: The Flaw of Gravity

1. Charles Francis Adams, *Chapters of Erie* (Ithaca, NY: Cornell University Press, 1956), 11.
2. Farhad Manjoo, "Tech's 'Frightful 5' Will Dominate Digital Life for Foreseeable Future," *New York Times*, January 20, 2016.
3. Farhad Manjoo, "Tech's Frightful Five: They've Got Us," *New York Times*, May 10, 2017.
4. "Daily Report: Seeking the Captive Consumer," *New York Times*, February 13, 2012.
5. John Gapper, "Steve Jobs' Legacy Is the Omniscient Tech Company," *Financial Times*, January 11, 2017.
6. Don Clark and Robert McMillan, "Giants Tighten Grip on Internet Economy," *Wall Street Journal*, November 6, 2015.
7. Jack Nicas, "They Tried to Boycott Facebook, Apple and Google. They Failed," *New York Times*, April 1, 2018.
8. "Everybody Wants to Rule the World," *The Economist*, November 29, 2014.
9. Rob Larson, *Capitalism vs. Freedom: The Toll Road to Serfdom* (Alresford, UK: Zero Books, 2018), chap. 1.
10. Albert-László Barbási, *Linked: How Everything Is Connected to Everything Else and What It Means for Business, Science, and Everyday Life* (New York: Penguin, 2003), 70–71.
11. Barbási, *Linked*, 83, 85–88.

12. Fragkiskos Papadopoulos et al., "Popularity versus Similarity in Growing Networks," *Nature* 489, no. 7417 (2012): 537–40.

13. Papadopoulos et al., "Popularity versus Similarity," 96.

14. Joseph Farrell and Garth Saloner, "Installed Base and Compatibility: Innovation, Product Preannouncements, and Predation," *American Economic Review* 76, no. 5 (1986): 940, 950.

15. W. Brian Arthur, "Competing Technologies, Increasing Returns, and Lock-In by Historical Events," *Economic Journal* 99, no. 394 (1989): 117, 127; see also Michael Katz and Carl Shapiro, "Network Externalities, Competition, and Compatibility," *American Economic Review* 75, no. 3 (1985): 425.

16. Steve Steinbereg, "Schumpeter's Lesson," *Wired*, January 1, 1998.

17. Christopher Anderson, "Doomonomics," *Financial Times*, May 25, 1996.

18. Tim Wu, *The Master Switch: The Rise and Fall of Information Empires* (New York: Vintage, 2011), 318–19.

19. Robert McChesney, *Digital Disconnect: How Capitalism Is Turning the Internet against Democracy* (New York: New Press, 2013), 132.

20. Arun Rao and Piero Scaruffi, *A History of Silicon Valley: The Greatest Creation of Wealth in the History of the Planet* (Palo Alto, CA: Omniware Group, 2013), 390.

21. "Free Does Not Live Up to Its Billing," *Financial Times*, July 1, 2009.

22. "E-Commerce: In the Great Web Bazaar," *The Economist*, February 26, 2000.

23. "Should Digital Monopolies Be Broken Up?," *The Economist*, November 29, 2014.

24. "Everybody Wants to Rule the World."

25. John Gapper, "When the Networks Bubble Over," *Financial Times*, March 30, 2011.

26. "Should Digital Monopolies Be Broken Up?"

27. Robert Bork and J. Gregory Sidak, "What Does the Chicago School Teach about Internet Search and the Antitrust Treatment of Google?," *Journal of Competition Law and Economics* 8, no. 4 (2012): 663–700.

28. Bork and Sidak, "What Does the Chicago School Teach?," 663.

29. Bork and Sidak, "What Does the Chicago School Teach?," 666.

30. Jack Nicas, "Google Searches Boost Its Own Products," *Wall Street Journal*, January 20, 2017.

31. David Brooks, "The Creative Monopoly," *New York Times*, April 23, 2012.

32. Barry Lynn, *Cornered: The New Monopoly Capitalism and the Economics of Destruction* (Hoboken, NJ: Wiley, 2010), 117.

33. Lynn, *Cornered*, 13.

34. Leonard Silk, "Antitrust Issues Facing Reagan," *New York Times*, February 13, 1981.
35. Brent Kendall, "Promised Monopoly Crackdown Fizzles," *Wall Street Journal*, November 7, 2015.
36. Alfred Chandler Jr., *Scale and Scope: The Dynamics of Industrial Capitalism* (Cambridge, MA: Harvard University Press, 1994), 23–24, 26.
37. Chandler, *The Visible Hand: The Managerial Revolution in American Business* (Cambridge, MA: Belknap Press, 1993), 375.
38. "How to Tame the Tech Titans?," *The Economist*, January 22, 2018.
39. Rob Larson, "The Economics of Net Neutrality," *Dollars and Sense*, July/ August 2015.
40. Matthew Josephson, *The Robber Barons: The Great American Capitalists, 1861–1901* (New York: Houghton Mifflin, 1962), 451.

Chapter 2: Macrosoft

1. James Wallace and Jim Erickson, *Hard Drive: Bill Gates and the Making of the Microsoft Empire* (New York: HarperCollins, 1992), 211.
2. Andrew I. Gavil and Harry First, *The Microsoft Antitrust Cases: Competition Policy for the Twenty-First Century* (Cambridge, MA: MIT Press, 2014), 157.
3. Wallace and Erickson, *Hard Drive,* 168.
4. Wallace and Erickson, *Hard Drive,* 233.
5. James Wallace, *Overdrive: Bill Gates and the Race to Control Cyberspace* (New York: John Wiley & Sons, 1997), 145–46.
6. Wallace and Erickson, *Hard Drive,* 120, 216–17.
7. Wallace and Erickson, *Hard Drive,* 213.
8. Gavil and First, *The Microsoft Antitrust Cases,* 155.
9. "Special Article: Microsoft and the Future: Busted," *The Economist,* November 13, 1999.
10. Wallace and Erickson, *Hard Drive,* 315–16.
11. Wallace and Erickson, *Hard Drive,* 252.
12. Tim Wu, *The Master Switch: The Rise and Fall of Information Empires* (New York: Vintage, 2011), 54.
13. Wu, *The Master Switch,* 279.
14. Albert-László Barabási, *Linked: How Everything Is Connected to Everything Else and What It Means for Business, Science, and Everyday Life* (New York: Penguin, 2003), 104.
15. Wallace and Erickson, *Hard Drive,* 23.
16. Wallace, *Overdrive,* 97.
17. Wallace, *Overdrive,* 390.

18. Wallace, *Overdrive*, 118.
19. Wallace and Erickson, *Hard Drive,* 99–101.
20. Wallace and Erickson, *Hard Drive*, 11.
21. Wallace and Erickson, *Hard Drive*, 38.
22. Wallace, *Overdrive*, 22–23; John Heilemann, *Pride before the Fall: The Trials of Bill Gates and the End of the Microsoft Era* (New York: HarperCollins, 2001), 125.
23. Wallace, *Overdrive*, 36–37.
24. Wallace, *Overdrive*, 45.
25. Wallace, *Overdrive*, 39.
26. Wallace and Erickson, *Hard Drive*, 398–99.
27. Wallace, *Overdrive*, 184.
28. Wallace, *Overdrive*, 266.
29. Wallace, *Overdrive*, 79.
30. Heilemann, *Pride before the Fall*, 17.
31. Heilemann, *Pride before the Fall*, 36.
32. Bill Gates, "Office Rendering" email, Plaintiff's exhibit 2991, *Comes v. Microsoft Corp.*, December 5, 1996.
33. Heilemann, *Pride before the Fall*, 112.
34. Heilemann, *Pride before the Fall*, 133.
35. Heilemann, *Pride before the Fall*, 113.
36. Gavil and First, *The Microsoft Antitrust Cases*, 82.
37. Gavil and First, *The Microsoft Antitrust Cases*, 100.
38. Heilemann, *Pride before the Fall*, 22.
39. Gavil and First, *The Microsoft Antitrust Cases*, 36.
40. Heilemann, *Pride before the Fall*, 64.
41. Heilemann, *Pride before the Fall*, 66.
42. Gavil and First, *The Microsoft Antitrust Cases*, 67.
43. "Bill Gates - Microsoft Antitrust Deposition - Highlights," YouTube video, November 2, 2018, www.youtube.com/watch?v=gRelVFm7iJE.
44. Heilemann, *Pride before the Fall*, 144–45.
45. Steve Lorh and Nick Wingfield, "When Mr. Gates Went to Washington," *New York Times*, April 14, 2018.
46. Randall Smith, "As His Foundation Has Grown, Gates Has Slowed His Donations," *New York Times*, May 26, 2014.
47. Heilemann, *Pride before the Fall*, 216–17.
48. US Department of Justice, "Justice Department Informs Microsoft of Plans for Further Proceedings in the District Court," press release, September 6, 2001.
49. Gavil and First, *The Microsoft Antitrust Cases*, 122–23.

50. Gavil and First, *The Microsoft Antitrust Cases*, 314.
51. Amy Harmon, "U.S. vs. Microsoft: The Overview; Judge Backs Terms of U.S. Settlement in Microsoft Case," *New York Times*, November 2, 2002.
52. Mary Jo Foley, *Microsoft 2.0: How Microsoft Plans to Stay Relevant in the Post-Gates Era* (Indianapolis, IN: Wiley, 2008), 125.
53. Stephen Grocer, "Microsoft, Peers Stage Rebound," *Wall Street Journal*, October 24, 2016.
54. Nick Wingfield, "Windows 10 Signifies Microsoft's Shift in Strategy," *New York Times*, July 19, 2015.
55. Wu, *The Master Switch*, 294; Arun Rao and Piero Scaruffi, *A History of Silicon Valley: The Greatest Creation of Wealth in the History of the Planet* (Palo Alto, CA: Omniware Group, 2013), 400.
56. Jay Greene, "Looks Who's Back! Microsoft, Rebooted, Emerges as a Tech Leader," *Wall Street Journal*, December 16, 2016; Steve Lohr, "Microsoft Buys GitHub for $7.5 Billion, Moving to Grow in Coding's new Era," *New York Times*, June 4, 2018.
57. Jay Greene, "Microsoft Expands Surface Lineup," *Wall Street Journal*, October 18, 2017.
58. Jay Greene, "Cloud Gains Lift Microsoft," *Wall Street Journal*, January 27, 2017.
59. Angus Loten, "Microsoft Narrows Gap with Amazon in Cloud," *Wall Street Journal*, August 2, 2018.
60. Jay Greene and Laura Stevens, "Rivals on Speaking Terms," *Wall Street Journal*, August 31, 2017.
61. Jay Greene, "Microsoft's Services Revenue Lifts Quarterly Results," *Wall Street Journal*, October 26, 2017.
62. Microsoft Corporation, Form 10-K, fiscal year ended June 30, 2016, p. 4.
63. Quoted in Nicholas Carr, *The Big Switch: Rewiring the World, from Edison to Google* (New York: Norton, 2008), 81.
64. Ted Greenwald, "Microsoft Unveils Virtual-Assistant Bot," *Wall Street Journal*, September 26, 2017.
65. Jay Greene, "Microsoft Downgrades Windows' Role in Cloud-Focused Reorganization," *Wall Street Journal*, March 29, 2018.
66. Tatyana Shumsky, "Stop Using Excel, Finance Chiefs Tell Staffs," *Wall Street Journal*, November 29, 2017.
67. Richard Waters and Hannah Kuchler, "Microsoft Held Back Free Patch That Could Have Slowed WannaCry," *Financial Times*, May 17, 2017.
68. Robert McMillan, "Microsoft Warns Of Bug in Windows," *Wall Street Journal*, May 16, 2019.
69. Waters and Kuchler, "Microsoft Held Back Free Patch."

70. Wallace and Erickson, *Hard Drive*, 38.
71. Tiffany Hsu, "Microsoft C.E.O. Says Tech's Progress on Gender Equality Is 'Not Sufficient,'" *New York Times*, September 26, 2017.
72. Bill Gates, "How to Keep America Competitive," *Washington Post*, February 25, 2007.
73. Jacqui Cheng, "Senators: Companies with 'Mass Layoffs' Shouldn't Hire More Foreign Workers," *Ars Technica*, June 7, 2007.
74. Paul Andrews, "Inside Microsoft—A 'Velvet Sweatshop' or a High-Tech Heaven?," *Seattle Times*, April 23, 1989.
75. Andrews, "Inside Microsoft."
76. Sarah Krouse, "The New Ways Your Boss Is Spying on You," *Wall Street Journal*, July 19, 2019.
77. Jay Greene, "Troubling Exits At Microsoft," *BusinessWeek*, September 26, 2005.
78. Wallace and Erickson, *Hard Drive*, 368; Stephen Satterwhite, "Here's to the Death of Microsoft's Rank-and-Yank," *Forbes*, November 13, 2013.
79. Wallace, *Overdrive*, 102, 104.
80. Sheera Frenkel, "Microsoft Employees Question C.E.O. over Company's Contract with ICE," *New York Times*, July 26, 2018.
81. Alan Hyde, *Working in Silicon Valley: Economic and Legal Analysis of a High-Velocity Labor Market* (Armonk, NY: M. E. Sharpe, 2003), 196–98.
82. Chris Benner, *Work in the New Economy: Flexible Labor Markets in Silicon Valley* (Malden, MA: Blackwell, 2002), 125.
83. Wallace and Erickson, *Hard Drive*, 417.

Chapter 3: The Apple Bitten

1. Owen Linzmayer, *Apple Confidential 2.0: The Real Story of Apple Computer, Inc.* (San Francisco: No Starch Press, 2008), 109.
2. Linzmayer, *Apple Confidential 2.0*, 20.
3. Adam Lashinsky, *Inside Apple: How America's Most Admired—and Secretive—Company Really Works* (New York: Business Plus, 2012), 126.
4. Steven Levy, *Insanely Great: The Life and Times of Macintosh, the Computer That Changed Everything* (New York: Viking, 1994), 74.
5. Lashinsky, *Inside Apple*, 75.
6. Levy, *Insanely Great*, 90.
7. Linzmayer, *Apple Confidential 2.0*, 4.
8. Linzmayer, *Apple Confidential 2.0*, 80.
9. Levy, *Insanely Great*, 125.
10. Linzmayer, *Apple Confidential 2.0*, 59–61, 93; Lashinsky, *Inside Apple*, 20.

11. Linzmayer, *Apple Confidential 2.0*, 88.
12. Linzmayer, *Apple Confidential 2.0*, 97.
13. Levy, *Insanely Great*, 224, 196.
14. Linzmeyer, *Apple Confidential 2.0*, 69.
15. Levy, *Insanely Great*, 194.
16. Levy, *Insanely Great*, 161.
17. Linzmayer, *Apple Confidential 2.0*, 169–71.
18. Quoted in Linzmayer, *Apple Confidential 2.0*, 245–48.
19. Linzmayer, *Apple Confidential 2.0*, 249.
20. Lashinsky, *Inside Apple*, 15.
21. Linzmayer, *Apple Confidential 2.0*, 247.
22. Linzmayer, *Apple Confidential 2.0*, 169.
23. Simon London, "From Product to Platform," *Financial Times*, January 18, 2004.
24. Lashinsky, *Inside Apple*, 24.
25. Adam Greenfield, *Radical Technologies: The Design of Everyday Life* (London: Verso, 2017), 28.
26. Tripp Mickle, "Apple Breaks Losing Streak, as Sales of iPhone 7 Shine," *Wall Street Journal*, February 1, 2017; Brian Merchant, *The One Device: The Secret History of the iPhone* (New York: Little, Brown & Co. 2017), 5.
27. Merchant, *The One Device*, 77–78.
28. Merchant, *The One Device*, 67, 97, 359.
29. Merchant, *The One Device*, 84–87.
30. Merchant, *The One Device*, 93, 70.
31. Merchant, *The One Device*, 189–90.
32. Merchant, *The One Device*, 59.
33. Greenfield, *Radical Technologies*, 19.
34. Greenfield, *Radical Technologies*, 297.
35. Apple, Inc., Form 10-K, fiscal year ended September 24, 2016, p. 9.
36. Lashinsky, *Inside Apple*, 130.
37. Betsy Morris, "Many Teens Check Their Phones in Middle of Night," *Wall Street Journal*, May 29, 2019.
38. David Benoit, "iPhones and Children Are a Toxic Pair, Say Two Big Apple Investors," *Wall Street Journal*, January 7, 2018; David Gelles, "Tech Backlash Grows as Investors Press Apple to Act on Children's Use," *New York Times*, January 8, 2018.
39. Merchant, *The One Device*, 174, 182.
40. Apple, Inc., Form 10-K, fiscal year ended September 24, 2016, pp. 5, 11.
41. Catherine Rampell, "Cracking the Apple Trap," *New York Times*, October 29, 2013.

42. Joanna Stern, "Ugh, Green Bubbles! Apple's iMessage Makes Switching to Android Hard," *Wall Street Journal*, October 18, 2018.

43. Fred Vogelstein, *Dogfight: How Apple and Google Went to War and Started a Revolution* (New York: Sarah Crichton Books, 2013), 6.

44. Betsy Morris, "What the iPhone Wrought," *Wall Street Journal*, June 24, 2017.

45. Vogelstein, *Dogfight*, 84, 129.

46. Vogelstein, *Dogfight*, 95.

47. Vogelstein, *Dogfight*, 117, 119.

48. Vogelstein, *Dogfight*, 124.

49. Walter Isaacson, *Steve Jobs* (New York: Simon & Schuster, 2011), 512.

50. Paul Barrett, "Apple's Jihad," *Bloomberg Businessweek*, April 2, 2012.

51. Vogelstein, *Dogfight*, 141.

52. Vogelstein, *Dogfight*, 185.

53. Timothy Martin and Tripp Mickle, "Phone Giants Ramp Up Rivalry," *Wall Street Journal*, April 2, 2017.

54. Tripp Mickle, "Apple's Cash Hoard Set to Top $250 Billion," *Wall Street Journal*, April 30, 2017.

55. Yasha Levine, *Surveillance Valley: The Secret Military History of the Internet* (New York: Hachette, 2018), 171.

56. Tripp Mickle, "Apple Touts New Privacy Features amid Scrutiny of Tech Giants," *Wall Street Journal*, June 3, 2019.

57. Vogelstein, *Dogfight*, 147.

58. Tripp Mickle, "Jony Ive Is Leaving Apple, but His Departure Started Long Ago," *Wall Street Journal*, June 30, 2019.

59. Josh Zumbrun and Tripp Mickle, "How Apple's Pricey New iPhone X Tests Economic Theory," *Wall Street Journal*, September 17, 2017.

60. Tripp Mickle and John McKinnon, "U.S., French Officials Question Apple over iPhone Battery Slowdowns," *Wall Street Journal*, January 9, 2018.

61. Tripp Mickle, "Apple Allays iPhone Worries, Adds $100 Billion to Buyback Plans," *Wall Street Journal*, May 1, 2018.

62. Tripp Mickle and Eliot Brown, "At Apple, One Ring to Bind Them All," *Wall Street Journal*, May 15, 2017.

63. Christina Passariello, "Steve Jobs Theater Debuts," *Wall Street Journal*, September 13, 2017.

64. Levy, *Insanely Great*, 141.

65. Levy, *Insanely Great*, 145–47.

66. Levy, *Insanely Great*, 95; Lashinsky, *Inside Apple*, 4.

67. Lashinsky, *Inside Apple*, 38.

68. Lashinsky, *Inside Apple*, 42.

69. Merchant, *The One Device*, 349.

70. Merchant, *The One Device*, 264.

71. Merchant, *The One Device*, 371.

72. Merchant, *The One Device*, 264–65, 270.

73. Andrew Ross Sorkin, "Apple's Tim Cook Barnstorms for 'Moral Responsibility,'" *New York Times*, August 28, 2017.

74. Merchant, *The One Device*, 273.

75. Merchant, *The One Device*, 310–11.

76. David Segal, "Apple's Retail Army, Long on Loyalty but Short on Pay," *New York Times*, June 23, 2012.

77. Mark Ames, "Revealed: Apple and Google's Wage-Fixing Cartel Involved Dozens More Companies, over One Million Employees," *PandoDaily*, March 22, 2014.

78. James Stewart, "Steve Jobs Defied Convention, and Perhaps the Law," *New York Times*, May 2, 2014.

79. David Streitfeld, "Court Rejects Deal on Hiring in Silicon Valley," *New York Times*, August 8, 2014.

80. Dean Baker, "Silicon Valley Billionaires Believe in the Free Market, as Long as They Benefit," *The Guardian*, February 3, 2014.

81. Merchant, *The One Device*, 377.

Chapter 4: Amazon's Smile

1. Sandra Garcia, "MacKenzie Bezos Owns $36 Billion in Amazon Shares. Now She Is Vowing to Give Away Much of Her Wealth," *New York Times*, May 8, 2019.

2. Brad Stone, *The Everything Store: Jeff Bezos and the Age of Amazon* (New York: Little, Brown, & Co., 2013), 52.

3. James Marcus, *Amazonia: Five Years at the Epicenter of the Dot.com Juggernaut* (New York: The New Press, 2005), 221.

4. Stone, *Everything Store*, 23, 57.

5. Stone, *Everything Store*, 31.

6. Stone, *Everything Store*, 37.

7. Nicholas Carr, *The Big Switch: Rewiring the World, from Edison to Google* (New York: W.W. Norton, 2013), 139.

8. Stone, *Everything Store*, 49.

9. Stone, *Everything Store*, 107.

10. Marcus, *Amazonia*, 182.

11. Marcus, *Amazonia*, 115.

12. "Primed," *The Economist*, March 25, 2017.

13. Stone, *Everything Store*, 115.

14. Sebastian Herrera and Sarah Nassauer, "The One Amazon Day Deal That Walmart and Target Can't Match," *Wall Street Journal*, July 15, 2019.

15. Herrera and Nassauer, "The One Amazon Day Deal," 303.

16. David Dayen, "Prime New World," *In These Times*, July 2019.

17. Laura Stevens, "Amazon's Profit Jumps, but Sales Growth Disappoints," *Wall Street Journal*, February 2, 2017.

18. Jack Nicas sand Karen Weise, "Anger at Big Tech United Noodle Pullers and Code Writers. Washington Is All Ears," *Wall Street Journal*, June 10, 2019.

19. Jon Emont, "Amazon Offers Sellers a Leg Up, with a Catch," *Wall Street Journal*, July 18, 2019.

20. Stone, *Everything Store*, 304.

21. Amazon.com, Inc., Form 10-K, fiscal year ended December 31, 2016, p. 14.

22. Matthew Dalton and Laura Stevens, "Why Amazon Still Has a Luxury Problem," *Wall Street Journal*, October 9, 2017.

23. Laura Stevens, "Amazon Snips Prices on Other Sellers' Items ahead of Holiday Onslaught," *Wall Street Journal*, November 5, 2017.

24. Vindu Goel, "Amazon, in Hunt for Lower Prices, Recruits Indian Merchants," *New York Times*, November 26, 2017.

25. Justin Lahart, "Why Wal-Mart Should Worry Amazon Investors," *Wall Street Journal*, November 16, 2017.

26. Stone, *Everything Store*, 288–89.

27. Stone, *Everything Store*, 289.

28. Amazon.com, Inc., Form 10-K, fiscal year ended December 31, 2016, p. 11.

29. Adam Liptak, "Supreme Court Clears Way to Collect Sales Tax from Online Retailers," *Wall Street Journal*, June 21, 2018.

30. Liptak, "Supreme Court Clears Way," 22.

31. Stephen Cohen, "Amazon Paid No US Income Taxes for 2017," *Seattle Post-Intelligencer*, February 27, 2018.

32. Stone, *Everything Store*, 167–69.

33. Marcus, *Amazonia*, 243.

34. Stone, *Everything Store*, 325.

35. Stone, *Everything Store*, 327.

36. Stone, *Everything Store*, 176–77.

37. Marcus, *Amazonia*, 53–54.

38. Stone, *Everything Store*, 233.

39. Marcus, *Amazonia*, 51.

40. Laura Stevens and Heather Haddon, "Amazon Acts First on Food Prices," *Wall Street Journal*, August 29, 2017.

41. Nancy Keates, "The Many Places Amazon CEO Jeff Bezos Calls Home,"

Wall Street Journal, October 5, 2017.

42. Marcus, *Amazonia*, 167–69.

43. Jonathan Taplin, *Move Fast and Break Things: How Facebook, Google, and Amazon Cornered Culture and Undermined Democracy* (New York: Little, Brown, & Co., 2017), 124.

44. Stone, *Everything Store*, 180–81.

45. Stone, *Everything Store*, 296.

46. Stone, *Everything Store*, 297–99.

47. Stone, *Everything Store*, 243–44.

48. Stone, *Everything Store*, 244.

49. Stone, *Everything Store*, 245.

50. Stone, *Everything Store*, 231.

51. Yasha Levine, *Surveillance Valley: The Secret Military History of the Internet* (New York: Hachette, 2018), 170.

52. Stone, *Everything Store*, 278.

53. Levine, *Surveillance Valley*, 278, 256.

54. Levine, *Surveillance Valley*, 280.

55. Packer, "Cheap Words," *New Yorker*, February 17–24, 2014.

56. Barry Lynn, "Killing the Competition," *Harper's*, February 2012.

57. Stone, *Everything Store*, 271–73.

58. Kirk Johnson, "5 Lessons Seattle Can Teach Other Cities about Amazon," *New York Times*, November 16, 2017.

59. Laura Stevens and Shayndi Raice, "Amazon Homes in on Tax Breaks," *Wall Street Journal*, October 20, 2017.

60. Nick Wingfield, "Side Benefit to Amazon's Headquarters Contest: Local Expertise," *Wall Street Journal*, January 28, 2018.

61. Laura Stevens, Shibani Mahtani, and Shayndi Raice, "For Amazon, a Grand Tour," *Wall Street Journal*, April 3, 2018.

62. Shayndi Raice and Laura Stevens, "In Their Push to Lure Amazon, Cities Face Unintended Demands," *Wall Street Journal*, March 15, 2018.

63. Heather Haddon, "Amazon Sells $1.6 Million in Whole Foods' Store-Brand Products in First Month," *Wall Street Journal*, September 29, 2017; Nick Wingfield, "Bit by Bit, Whole Foods Gets an Amazon Touch," *New York Times*, March 1, 2018; Greg Bensinger, "By Land, Air and Now Sea: Amazon Looks to Arrange Ocean Freight," *Wall Street Journal*, January 14, 2016; Laura Stevens and Erica Phillips, "Amazon to Deliver Air-Cargo Flights," *Wall Street Journal*, March 16, 2017; Greg Bensinger and Laura Stevens, "Amazon Takes Aim at UPS and FedEx," *Wall Street Journal*, September 28, 2016.

64. Carr, *The Big Switch*, 72.

65. Stone, *Everything Store*, 221.
66. Carr, *The Big Switch*, 74.
67. Angus Loten, "Microsoft Narrows Gap with Amazon in Cloud," *Wall Street Journal*, August 2, 2018.
68. "The Walmart of the Web," *The Economist*, October 1, 2011.
69. Ted Mann and Brody Mullins, "As Trump Bashes Amazon, the Government Relies on It," *Wall Street Journal*, April 5, 2018.
70. Jay Greene, "Tech's High-Stakes Arms Race: Costly Data Centers," *Wall Street Journal*, April 7, 2017.
71. Ted Mann and Brody Mullins, "Amazon's Rivals Fear They Will Lose Out on Pentagon's Cloud-Computing Contract," *Wall Street Journal*, April 12, 2018.
72. Steve Wasserman, "The Amazon Effect," *The Nation*, May 29, 2012.
73. Carr, *The Big Switch*, 235–36.
74. Robert McMillan, "Amazon Grapples with Outage at AWS Cloud Service," *Wall Street Journal*, March 1, 2017.
75. Nick Wingfield, "Miscue Calls Attention to Amazon's Dominance in Cloud Computing," *New York Times*, March 12, 2017.
76. Stone, *Everything Store*, 222.
77. Tripp Mickle and Laura Stevens, "Amazon Echo Prices Turn Smart-Speaker Market on Its Ear," *Wall Street Journal*, December 18, 2017.
78. Laura Stevens, "Amazon Alexa-Powered Device Recorded and Shared User's Conversation without Permission," *Wall Street Journal*, May 24, 2018.
79. Sarah Needleman and Parmy Olson, "Google Contractors Listen to Recordings of People Using Virtual Assistant," *Wall Street Journal*, July 11, 2019.
80. Betsy Morris, "Amazon Is Accused of Violating Kids' Privacy with Smart Speakers," *Wall Street Journal*, May 9, 2019.
81. Laura Stevens, "Amazon's New Echo Aims to Answer Age-Old Question: Does this Look Good on Me?," *Wall Street Journal*, April 26, 2017; Nick Wingfield, "Amazon Tries a New Delivery Spot: Your Car," *New York Times*, April 24, 2018.
82. Isabel Sterne, "Academic Research and Its Subjects, Both Now Pawns in Amazon's Empire," *The Technoskeptic*, Spring 2019.
83. Marcus, *Amazonia*, 17.
84. Stone, *Everything Store*, 49.
85. Stone, *Everything Store*, 43–44.
86. Stone, *Everything Store*, 73, 51.
87. Joe Allen, "Logistics' Two Fronts," *Jacobin*, March 28, 2017.
88. Stone, *Everything Store*, 89–90.

89. Stone, *Everything Store*, 336–37.

90. Marcus, *Amazonia*, 148.

91. Stone, *Everything Store*, 329.

92. Greg Bensinger, "Amazon Sues Executive Recently Hired by Target," *Wall Street Journal*, March 22, 2016.

93. Mac McClelland, "I Was a Warehouse Wage Slave," *Mother Jones*, February 27, 2012.

94. Spencer Soper, "Inside Amazon's Warehouse," *Morning Call*, August 17, 2015.

95. Georgia Wells, Rachel Feintzeig, and Theo Francis, "Amazon's Typical Worker Is in a Warehouse Making $28, 446 a Year," *Wall Street Journal*, April 22, 2018.

96. Stone, *Everything Store*, 161.

97. Amazon.com, Inc., Form 10-K, fiscal year ended December 31, 2016, pp. 58–59; Taplin, *Move Fast and Break Things*, 83.

98. Stone, *Everything Store*, 165.

99. Stone, *Everything Store*, 180.

100. Jennifer Smith, "A Robot Can Be a Warehouse Worker's Best Friend," *Wall Street Journal*, August 3, 2017.

101. Stone, *Everything Store*, 190.

102. Isobel Asher Hamilton and Ruqayyah Moynihan, "Amazon Reportedly Left Police in Spain 'Dumbfounded' by Asking Them to Intervene in a Mass Warehouse Strike and Patrol Worker Productivity," *Business Insider*, November 23, 2018.

103. Jana Kasperkevic, "Amazon to Remove Non-compete Clause from Contracts for Hourly Workers," *The Guardian*, March 27, 2015.

104. Matt Day, "Amazon Warehouse Envoys Rally to Tweet Upbeat Comments about Working Conditions," *Seattle Times*, August 23, 2018.

105. Clark Mindock, "Amazon Prime Day: Workers Strike across the Globe for Better Pay and Working Conditions at E-commerce Company," *The Independent*, July 15, 2019.

106. David Streitfeld, "What Happens after Amazon's Domination Is Complete? Its Bookstore Offers Clues," *Wall Street Journal*, June 23, 2019.

107. Brad Stone, "Amazon Erases Orwell Books From Kindle," *New York Times*, July 18, 2009.

Chapter 5: Being Evil

1. Jack Nicas and Juan Forero, "Google Will Put Servers in Cuba," *Wall Street Journal*, December 13, 2016.

2. Alexis Wichowski, "Net States Rule the World," *Wired*, November 4, 2017.

3. Tim Wu, *The Master Switch: The Rise and Fall of Information Empires* (New York: Random House, 2011), 296.

4. Ken Auletta, *Googled: The End of the World as We Know It* (New York: Penguin, 2010), 122.

5. Steven Levy, *In the Plex: How Google Thinks, Works, and Shapes Our Lives* (New York: Simon & Schuster, 2011), 229.

6. Levy, *In the Plex*, 21–22.

7. Auletta, *Googled*, 35.

8. Arun Rao and Piero Scaruffi, *A History of Silicon Valley: The Greatest Creation of Wealth in the History of the Planet* (Palo Alto, CA: Omniware Group, 2013), 397–99.

9. Auletta, *Googled*, 138–39.

10. Levy, *In the Plex*, 24–27.

11. Levy, *In the Plex*, 14.

12. Yasha Levine, *Surveillance Valley: The Secret Military History of the Internet* (New York: Hachette, 2018), 172.

13. Levy, *In the Plex*, 181–83.

14. Levy, *In the Plex*, 191–94.

15. George Geis, *Semi-organic Growth: Tactics and Strategies behind Google's Success* (Hoboken, NJ: Wiley, 2015), chaps. 1, 2, 5, 6, and 7.

16. Siva Vaidhyanathan, *The Googlization of Everything (And Why We Should Worry)* (Berkeley and Los Angeles: University of California Press, 2011), 133.

17. Shalini Ramachandran, "Google's 'Knowledge Panels' Might Think You're Dead. Or French," *Wall Street Journal*, May 31, 2019.

18. Jack Nicas, "Google Has Picked an Answer for You—Too Bad It's Often Wrong," *Wall Street Journal*, November 16, 2017.

19. "Personalized Search for everyone," Google blog, December 4, 2009, https://googleblog.blogspot.com/2009/12/personalized-search-for-everyone.html.

20. Eli Pariser, *The Filter Bubble: How the New Personalized Web Is Changing What We Read and How We Think* (New York: Penguin, 2011), 3.

21. Jack Nicas, "Ads Boost Alphabet, Fueled by Phone Use," *Wall Street Journal*, October 28, 2016.

22. Fred Vogelstein, *Dogfight: How Apple and Google Went to War and Started a Revolution* (New York: Sarah Crichton Books, 2013), 6.

23. Wu, *Master Switch*, 273; Jonathan Taplin, *Move Fast and Break Things: How Facebook, Google, and Amazon Cornered Culture and Undermined Democracy* (New York: Little, Brown, & Co., 2017), 249.

24. Levy, *In the Plex*, 41, 104.

25. Levy, *In the Plex*, 152, 145.

26. Levy, *In the Plex*, 331–32.

27. Vaidhyanathan, *The Googlization of Everything*, 19–20.

28. Vaidhyanathan, *The Googlization of Everything*, xiv.

29. Wu, *Master Switch*, 280.

30. Vaidhyanathan, *The Googlization of Everything*, 66.

31. Taplin, *Move Fast and Break Things*, 13.

32. Sam Schechner and Jack Nicas, "EU Targets Android's Dominance," *Wall Street Journal*, April 21, 2016.

33. Kate Conger, "Google C.E.O. Denies Allegations of Political Bias in Search Results," *New York Times*, September 21, 2018.

34. Charles Duhigg, "The Case against Google," *New York Times Magazine*, February 20, 2018.

35. Jack Nicas, "Google Searches Boost Its Own Products," *Wall Street Journal*, January 20, 2017.

36. Marc Tracy, "Google Made $4.7 Billion from the News Industry in 2018, Study Says," *Wall Street Journal*, June 9, 2019.

37. Daisuke Wakabayashi, "Trump Says Google Is Rigged, Despite Its Denials. What Do We Know about How It Works?," *New York Times*, September 5, 2018.

38. Robin Andersen, "Backlash against Russian 'Fake News' Is Shutting Down Debate for Real," *Extra*, November 29, 2017.

39. Brody Mullins and Jack Nicas, "Paying Professors: Inside Google's Academic Influence Campaign," *Wall Street Journal*, July 14, 2017.

40. Kenneth Vogel, "Google Critic Ousted from Think Tank Funded by the Tech Giant," *New York Times*, August 30, 2017.

41. Steve Lohr, "Antitrust Cry from Microsoft," *New York Times*, March 31, 2011.

42. Vaidhyanathan, *The Googlization of Everything*, 54.

43. Levy, *In the Plex*, 344.

44. Levy, *In the Plex*, 343–46.

45. Auletta, *Googled*, 23.

46. Sergey Brin and Lawrence Page, "The Anatomy of a Large-Scale Hypertextual Web Search Engine," Computer Science Department, Stanford University, January 1998.

47. Tim Wu, *The Attention Merchants: The Epic Scramble to Get inside Our Heads* (New York: Vintage, 2017), 264.

48. Wu, *The Attention Merchants*, 265.

49. Alphabet, Inc., Form 10-K, fiscal year ended December 31, 2017, pp. 5, 7.

50. Auletta, *Googled*, 21; George Orwell, "The Freedom of the Press," *Times*

Literary Supplement, September 15, 1972.

51. Vaidhyanathan, *The Googlization of Everything*, 60.

52. Pariser, *The Filter Bubble*, 151.

53. Pariser, *The Filter Bubble*, 41.

54. James Curran, Natalie Fenton, and Des Freedman, *Misunderstanding the Internet* (New York: Routledge, 2016), 63.

55. Levy, *In the Plex*, 104.

56. Richard Waters, "Microsoft in $6.2bn Ad Business Writedown," *Financial Times*, July 2, 2012.

57. Levy, *In the Plex*, 107.

58. Levy, *In the Plex*, 333.

59. Vaidhyanathan, *The Googlization of Everything*, 28.

60. Patience Haggin and Kara Depana, "Google's Ad Dominance Explained in Three Charts," *Wall Street Journal*, June 17, 2019.

61. Douglas MacMillan, "Google Will Block Spammy Ads (Just Not Many of Its Own)," *Wall Street Journal*, February 14, 2018.

62. Jack Marshall, "Google to Help Publishers Get Ready for Ad Filters," *Wall Street Journal*, June 2, 2017.

63. Alistair Barr and Rolfe Winkler, "Google's DoubleClick Outage Turns Internet Ad-Free for Over an Hour," *Wall Street Journal*, November 12, 2014.

64. Jack Nicas, "YouTube Tops 1 Billion Hours of Video a Day, on Pace to Eclipse TV," *Wall Street Journal*, February 27, 2017.

65. Geis, *Semi-organic Growth*, 66.

66. Auletta, *Googled*, 152–53.

67. Taplin, *Move Fast and Break Things*, 100.

68. Levy, *In the Plex*, 243.

69. Taplin, *Move Fast and Break Things*, 101.

70. Taplin, *Move Fast and Break Things*, 184.

71. Geis, *Semi-organic Growth*, 66.

72. Jack Nicas, "How YouTube Drives People to the Internet's Darkest Corners," *Wall Street Journal*, February 7, 2018.

73. Max Fisher and Katrin Bennhold, "As Germans Seek News, YouTube Delivers Far-Right Tirades," *New York Times*, September 7, 2018.

74. Jack Nicas, "YouTube Takes Aim at Conspiracies, Propaganda," *Wall Street Journal*, February 2, 2018.

75. Justin Anderson, "YouTube Continues to Selectively Enforce Its Terms of Service," FAIR, June 10, 2019.

76. Kevin Roose, "The Making of a YouTube Radical," *New York Times*, June 8, 2019.

77. Mark Bergen, "YouTube Executives Ignored Warnings, Letting Toxic Videos Run Rampant," *Bloomberg*, April 2, 2019.

78. Kevin Roose and Kate Conger, "YouTube to Remove Thousands of Videos Pushing Extreme Views," *New York Times*, June 5, 2019.

79. James Bridle, "Something Is Wrong on the Internet," *Medium*, November 6, 2017.

80. Rob Copeland, "YouTube Weights Major Changes to Kids' Content amid FTC Probe," *Wall Street Journal*, June 19, 2019.

81. Max Fisher and Amanda Taub, "On YouTube's Digital Playground, an Open Gate for Pedophiles," *New York Times*, June 3, 2019.

82. Jack Nicas, "YouTube Blocks Ads from Channels with Fewer Than 10,000 Views," *Wall Street Journal*, April 6, 2017.

83. Rob Copeland and Katherine Bindley, "Millions of Business Listings on Google Maps Are Fake—and Google Profits," *Wall Street Journal*, June 20, 2019.

84. Pariser, *The Filter Bubble*, 32–33.

85. Pariser, *The Filter Bubble*, 6.

86. Levy, *In the Plex*, 333–34.

87. Charlie Warzel, "Facebook and Google Trackers Are Showing Up on Porn Sites," *New York Times*, July 17, 2019.

88. Auletta, *Googled*, 185.

89. Auletta, *Googled*, 190.

90. Vaidhyanathan, *The Googlization of Everything*, 112.

91. Natalia Drozdiak and Jack Nicas, "Google Privacy-Policy Change Faces New Scrutiny in EU," *Wall Street Journal*, January 24, 2017.

92. Michael Reilly, "Now Tracks Your Credit Card Purchases and Connects Them to Its Online Profile of You," *MIT Technology Review*, May 25, 2017.

93. Auletta, *Googled*, 267.

94. Christopher Mims, "Who Has More of Your Personal Data Than Facebook? Try Google," *Wall Street Journal*, April 22, 2018.

95. Jack Nicas, "Google to Stop Reading Users' Emails to Target Ads," *Wall Street Journal*, June 23, 2017.

96. Douglas MacMillan and Robert McMillan, "Google Exposed User Data, Feared Repercussions of Disclosing to Public," *Wall Street Journal*, October 8, 2018.

97. Douglas MacMillan, "At Google's Parent Alphabet, Median Pay Nears $200,000," *Wall Street Journal*, April 27, 2018.

98. Corey Pein, *Live Work Work Work Die: A Journey into the Savage Heart of Silicon Valley* (New York: Metropolitan, 2017), 68.

99. Auletta, *Googled*, 18.

100. Auletta, *Googled*, 286.

101. Levy, *In the Plex*, 140–41.

102. Levy, *In the Plex*, 124.

103. Eric Schmidt and Jonathan Rosenberg, *How Google Works* (New York: Hachette, 2016), 227, 240.

104. James Stewart, "Steve Jobs Defied Convention, and Perhaps the Law," *New York Times*, May 2, 2014.

105. Levy, *In the Plex*, 130.

106. Levy, *In the Plex*, 260.

107. Levy, *In the Plex*, 158–59, 162.

108. Auletta, *Googled*, 334–35.

109. Levy, *In the Plex*, 157

110. Auletta, *Googled*, 136.

111. Levy, *In the Plex*, 175.

112. Levy, *In the Plex*, 171, 218.

113. Auletta, *Googled*, 273–74.

114. Levy, *In the Plex*, 257.

115. Sam Levin, "Google Accused of 'Extreme' Gender Pay Discrimination by Us Labor Department," *The Guardian*, April 7, 2017.

116. Georgia Wells, "Google Rebuts Claims It Underpays Women," *Wall Street Journal*, April 12, 2017.

117. Jack Nicas and Yoree Koh, "Google's 'Trust Us' Approach Doesn't Satisfy Pay Gap Skeptics," *Wall Street Journal*, June 24, 2017.

118. Daisuke Wakabayashi, "Contentious Memo Strikes Nerve Inside Google and Out," *New York Times*, August 8, 2017.

119. Allysia Finley, "OK Google, You've Been Served," *Wall Street Journal*, January 16, 2018.

120. Kate Conger and Daisuke Wakabayashi, "Google Employees Protest Secret Work on Censored Search Engine for China," *New York Times*, August 16, 2018.

121. Scott Shane, Cade Metz, and Daisuke Wakabayashi, "How a Pentagon Contract Became an Identity Crisis for Google," *New York Times*, May 30, 2018.

122. Scott Shane and Daisuke Wakabayashi, "'The Business of War': Google Employees Protest Work for the Pentagon," *New York Times*, April 4, 2018.

123. Ben Tarnoff, "Tech Workers versus the Pentagon," *Jacobin*, June 6, 2018.

124. Angela Nagle, "Silicon Intersectionality," *Current Affairs*, November 2, 2017.

125. Kate Conger and Daisuke Wakabayashi, "Google Overhauls Sexual Misconduct Policy after Employee Walkout," *New York Times*,

November 8, 2018.

126. Amie Tsang and Adam Satariano, "Google Walkout: Employees Stage Protest Over Handling of Sexual Harassment," *New York Times*, November 1, 2018.

127. Schmidt and Rosenberg, *How Google Works*, 65.

128. Kate Conger, "Google Removes 'Don't Be Evil' Clause from Its Code of Conduct," *Gizmodo*, May 18, 2018.

Chapter 6: Disgracebook

1. Issie Lapowsky, "The Supreme Court Just Protected Your Right to Facebook," *Wired*, June 19, 2017.

2. Paul Krugman and Robin Wells, *Microeconomics*, 5th ed. (New York: Worth, 2018), 384.

3. David Kirkpatrick, *The Facebook Effect: The Inside Story of the Company That Is Connecting the World* (New York: Simon & Schuster, 2010), 21–22.

4. Ben Mezrich, *The Accidental Billionaires: The Founding of Facebook: A Tale of Sex, Money, Genius, and Betrayal* (New York: Anchor Books, 2010), 123.

5. Kirkpatrick, *The Facebook Effect*, 84.

6. Tim Wu, *The Attention Merchants: The Epic Scramble to Get inside Our Heads* (New York: Vintage, 2016), 289.

7. Kirkpatrick, *The Facebook Effect*, 35.

8. Kirkpatrick, *The Facebook Effect*, 36–37.

9. Kirkpatrick, *The Facebook Effect*, 132–33.

10. Kirkpatrick, *The Facebook Effect*, 73.

11. Kirkpatrick, *The Facebook Effect*, 51, 53.

12. Kirkpatrick, *The Facebook Effect*, 143–44.

13. Kirkpatrick, *The Facebook Effect*, 102.

14. Kirkpatrick, *The Facebook Effect*, 118.

15. Mezrich, *The Accidental Billionaires*, 147; Kirkpatrick, *The Facebook Effect*, 101.

16. Kirkpatrick, *The Facebook Effect*, 312.

17. Kirkpatrick, *The Facebook Effect*, 303.

18. Kirkpatrick, *The Facebook Effect*, 148.

19. Facebook, Inc., Form 10-K, fiscal year ended December 31, 2017, p. 18.

20. Roger McNamee, *Zucked: Waking Up to the Facebook Catastrophe* (New York: Penguin Press, 2019), 155, 144–45.

21. Kirkpatrick, *The Facebook Effect*, 319.

22. Kirkpatrick, *The Facebook Effect*, 269–70.

23. Kirkpatrick, *The Facebook Effect*, 166, 320.

24. Mezrich, *The Accidental Billionaires*, 249.

25. Kirkpatrick, *The Facebook Effect*, 190.

26. Kirkpatrick, *The Facebook Effect*, 191.
27. Eli Pariser, *The Filter Bubble: How the New Personalized Web Is Changing What We Read and How We Think* (New York: Penguin, 2011), 9–10.
28. Pariser, *The Filter Bubble*, 39.
29. Deepa Settharaman, "Facebook Steps Up Fake-News Fight," *Wall Street Journal*, August 4, 2017.
30. Laura Flanders, "Could Ida B. Wells Have Exposed Lynching on Your Newsfeed?," *Extra*, May 9, 2018.
31. Sheera Frenkel, Nicholas Casey, and Paul Mozure, "In Some Countries, Facebook Fiddling Has Magnified Fake News," *New York Times*, January 14, 2018.
32. Brendan Nyhan, "Why the Fact-Checking at Facebook Needs to Be Checked," *New York Times*, October 23, 2017.
33. Farhad Manjoo, "Can Facebook Fix Its Own Worst Bug?," *New York Times Magazine*, April 25, 2017.
34. Nathan Olivarez-Giles, "Facebook Turns Screws on Fake News," *Wall Street Journal*, January 26, 2017.
35. Christopher Mims, "Zuckerberg's Dilemma: When Facebook's Success Is Bad for Society," *Wall Street Journal*, January 7, 2018.
36. James Vincent, "Former Facebook Exec Says Social Media Is Ripping Apart Society," *The Verge*, December 11, 2017.
37. Benjamin Mullin, "One Website's Facebook Apocalypse Is Another's Opportunity to Shine," *Wall Street Journal*, January 12, 2018.
38. Deepa Seetharaman, Lukas Alpert, and Benjamin Mullin, "Facebook to Overhaul How It Presents News in Feed," *Wall Street Journal*, January 11, 2018.
39. Nathan Robinson, "Why I Love Mark Zuckerberg and Can Never Say a Word against Him," *Current Affairs*, January 3, 2018.
40. Kirkpatrick, *The Facebook Effect*, 177, 271.
41. Wu, *The Attention Merchants*, 296.
42. Kirkpatrick, *The Facebook Effect*, 178.
43. Kirkpatrick, *The Facebook Effect*, 175.
44. Kirkpatrick, *The Facebook Effect*, 238–44.
45. Kirkpatrick, *The Facebook Effect*, 259.
46. Wu, *The Attention Merchants*, 12.
47. Facebook, Inc., 10-K for fiscal year ended December 31, 2017, p. 9.
48. Wu, *The Attention Merchants*, 301.
49. Kirkpatrick, *The Facebook Effect*, 273.
50. Mike Shields, "Facebook Says It Found More Miscalculated Metrics," *Wall Street Journal*, November 16, 2016; Lara O'Reilley and Suzanne

Vranica, "Marketers Say Facebook's News Feed Update Will Be 'Nail in the Coffin' for Organic Posts," *Wall Street Journal*, January 12, 2018.

51. Sapna Maheshwari, "Facebook's Current Status with Advertisers? It's Complicated," *Wall Street Journal*, Aril 18, 2018.

52. Stu Woo and Sam Schechner, "Facebook Doesn't Expect Revenue Impact over Privacy Concerns," *Wall Street Journal*, April 12, 2018.

53. Kirkpatrick, *The Facebook Effect*, 217, 218.

54. Kirkpatrick, *The Facebook Effect*, 222.

55. Kirkpatrick, *The Facebook Effect*, 227–28.

56. Kirkpatrick, *The Facebook Effect*, 232, 231.

57. Christopher Mims, "Facebook's Identity Crisis Looms," *Wall Street Journal*, March 20, 2018.

58. Deepa Seetharaman and Kirsten Grind, "Facebook Gave Some Companies Special Access to Additional Data about Users' Friends," *Wall Street Journal*, June 8, 2018.

59. Sheera Frenkel and Kevin Roose, "Zuckerberg, Facing Facebook's Worst Crisis Yet, Pledges Better Privacy," *Wall Street Journal*, March 21, 2018.

60. Matthew Rosenberg and Gabriel Dance, "'You Are the Product': Targeted by Cambridge Analytica and Facebook," *New York Times*, April 8, 2018.

61. Nicholas Confessore, "Audit Approved of Facebook Policies, Even after Cambridge Analytica Leak," *New York Times*, April 19, 2018.

62. Deepa Seetharaman, "Zuckerberg Says Facebook Probe into Apps Won't Uncover All Data Abuse," *Wall Street Journal*, March 22, 2018.

63. Nicholas Confessore, Cecilia Kang, and Sheera Frenkel, "Facebook Back on the Defensive, Now over Data Deals with Device Makers," *New York Times*, June 4, 2018.

64. Laura Forman, "Facebook May Be Tough Beast for Regulators to Tame," *Wall Street Journal*, June 4, 2019.

65. Deepa Seetharaman, "Russian-Backed Facebook Accounts Staged Events around Divisive Issues," *Wall Street Journal*, October 30, 2017.

66. Deepa Seetharaman and Robert McMillan, "Fake Facebook Accounts Latched On to Real U.S. Protest Groups," *Wall Street Journal*, August 2, 2018.

67. Robert McMillan and Shane Harris, "Facebook Cut Russia from Report on Election," *Wall Street Journal*, October 6, 2017.

68. David Kirkpatrick, "Facebook Sees Little Evidence of Russian Meddling in 'Brexit' Vote," *New York Times*, December 13, 2017.

69. Robert McMillan and Jeff Horowitz, "Tech Backlash Puts Silicon Valley on Edge," *Wall Street Journal*, May 10, 2019.

70. Alexandra Bruell, "Facebook to Boost Ad Spending as It Tries to Restore

Reputation," *Wall Street Journal*, June 14, 2019.

71. Sheera Frenkel, "Facebook Starts Paying a Price for Scandals," *New York Times*, July 25, 2018.

72. Christopher Mims, "How Facebook's Master Algorithm Powers the Social Network," *Wall Street Journal*, October 22, 2017.

73. Facebook, Inc., Form 10-K, fiscal year ended December 31, 2017, pp. 42, 26.

74. Tim Wu, *The Master Switch: The Rise and Fall of Information Empires* (New York: Vintage, 2011), 298.

75. Jonathan Taplin, *Move Fast and Break Things: How Facebook, Google, and Amazon Cornered Culture and Undermined Democracy* (New York: Little, Brown, & Co., 2017), 144.

76. Betsy Morris and Deepa Seetharaman, "For Tech Innovators, Facebook Looms Large," *Wall Street Journal*, August 10, 2017.

77. Kirkpatrick, *The Facebook Effect*, 118, 129.

78. Kirkpatrick, *The Facebook Effect*, 132, 136.

79. Deepa Seetharaman, "Facebook's Female Engineers Claim Gender Bias," *Wall Street Journal*, May 2, 2017.

80. Facebook, Inc., Form 10-K, fiscal year ended December 31, 2017, p. 4.

81. Lauren Weber and Deepa Seetharaman, "The Worst Job in Technology: Staring at Human Depravity to Keep It Off Facebook," *Wall Street Journal*, December 27, 2017.

82. Kirkpatrick, *The Facebook Effect*, 277.

83. Kirkpatrick, *The Facebook Effect*, 247–50.

84. Kirkpatrick, *The Facebook Effect*, 307–10.

85. Farhad Manjoo, "What Stays on Facebook and What Goes? The Social Network Cannot Answer," *New York Times*, July 19, 2018.

86. Kevin Roose, "Facebook and YouTube Give Alex Jones a Wrist Slap," *New York Times*, July 27, 2018.

87. Deepa Seetharaman and Jeff Horwitz, "Facebook's Effort to Build an Internal Court for Content Is Far from Simple," *Wall Street Journal*, June 27, 2019.

88. Alan MacLeod, "That Facebook Will Turn to Censoring the Left Isn't a Worry—It's a Reality," FAIR, August 23, 2018.

89. Kirkpatrick, *The Facebook Effect*, 327.

90. Deepa Seetharaman, "Facebook's Double Standard on Privacy: Employees vs. Everyone Else," *Wall Street Journal*, May 3, 2018.

Chapter 7: Neutralized

1. Rebecca Ruiz and Steve Lohr, "F.C.C. Approves Net Neutrality Rules,

Classifying Broadband Internet Service as a Utility," *New York Times*, February 26, 2015.

2. Gautham Nagesh, "Net-Neutrality Proposal Faces Public Backlash," *Wall Street Journal*, July 14, 2014.

3. Ruiz and Lohr, "F.C.C. Approves Net Neutrality Rules.

4. Ryan Knutson and Thomas Gryta, "FCC Likely to Catch Telecom Backlash," *Wall Street Journal*, January 8, 2015.

5. Sarah Krouse and Patience Haggin, "Internet Providers Look to Cash In on Your Web Habits," *Wall Street Journal*, June 27, 2019.

6. Rebecca MacKinnon, *Consent of the Networked: The Worldwide Struggle for Internet Freedom* (New York: Basic, 2012), 116–17.

7. Ben Collins, "Comcast Now Says It Will Not Sue FCC," *Daily Beast*, February 26, 2015.

8. S. Shunmuga Krishnan and Ramesh Sitaraman, "Video Stream Quality Impacts Viewer Behavior," University of Massachusetts, November 14, 2012.

9. Shalini Ramachandran, "Netflix to Pay Comcast for Smoother Streaming," *Wall Street Journal*, February 24, 2014.

10. Timothy B. Lee, "Comcast's Deal with Netflix Makes Network Neutrality Obsolete," *Washington Post*, February 23, 2014.

11. Tim Wu, *The Master Switch: The Rise and Fall of Information Empires* (New York: Vintage, 2011), 288–89.

12. Brendan Sasso, "Despite Fierce Opposition from the Major Internet Providers, the FCC Is Poised to Seize Expansive New Regulatory Powers," *National Journal*, February 5, 2015.

13. Alistair Barr, "Google Strikes an Upbeat Note with FCC on Title II," *Wall Street Journal*, December 31, 2014.

14. Alistair Barr, "Google and Net Neutrality: It's Complicated," *Wall Street Journal*, February 4, 2015.

15. Ramachandran, "Netflix to Pay Comcast."

16. Federal Communications Commission, *In the Matter of Protecting and Promoting the Open Internet*, Report and Order on Remand, Declaratory Ruling, and Order, March 12, 2015, p. 7.

17. Ruiz and Lohr, "F.C.C. Approves Net Neutrality Rules.

18. David Talbot, "When Will the Rest of Us Get Google Fiber?," *MIT Technology Review*, February 4, 2013.

19. Mark Scott, "Dutch Offer Preview of Net Neutrality," *New York Times*, February 26, 2015.

20. Miriam Gottfried, "Don't Get Too Excited about the FCC's New Rules," *Wall Street Journal*, April 16, 2017.

21. Cecilia Kang, "F.C.C. Repeals Net Neutrality Rules," *New York Times*, December 14, 2017.

22. John McKinnon and Ryan Knutson, "Want to See a World without Net Neutrality? Look at These Old Cellphone Plans," *Wall Street Journal*, December 11, 2017.

23. Joanna Stern and Christopher Mims, "Tech That Will Change Your Life in 2018," *Wall Street Journal*, December 27, 2017.

24. John McKinnon, "Web Firms Defend Net Neutrality as GOP Takes Aim," *Wall Street Journal*, April 13, 2017.

25. Drew FitzGerald, "Netflix Backs Away from Fight over Internet Rules Now That Traffic Is Flowing," *Wall Street Journal*, December 13, 2017.

26. John McKinnon and Douglas MacMillan, "Web Firms Protest Efforts to Roll Back Net Neutrality," *Wall Street Journal*, July 12, 2017.

27. Drew FitzGerald, "Facebook and Microsoft to Build Fiber Optic Cable across Atlantic," *Wall Street Journal*, May 27, 2016.

28. Drew FitzGerald, "Google, Facebook to Invest in U.S.-China Data Link," *Wall Street Journal*, October 12, 2016.

29. Drew FitzGerald, "Google Plans to Expand Huge Undersea Cables to Boost Cloud Business," *Wall Street Journal*, January 16, 2018.

30. Jay Cassano, "How Activism Won Real Net Neutrality," *Waging Nonviolence*, February 26, 2015.

31. "Net Neutrality Breaks Records," Fight for the Future, July 13, 2007.

32. James Grimaldi and Paul Overberg, "Lawmakers Seek Checks on Phony Comments before 'Net Neutrality' Vote," *Wall Street Journal*, December 13, 2017.

33. James Grimaldi and Paul Overberg, "Millions of People Post Comments on Federal Regulations. Many Are Fake," *Wall Street Journal*, December 12, 2017.

34. Lawrence Lessig and Robert McCheseny, "No Tolls on the Internet," *Washington Post*, June 28, 2006.

Chapter 8: Redefining R&D

1. Cade Metz, "Computer Chip Visionaries Win Turing Award," *New York Times*, March 21, 2018.

2. Mariana Mazzucato, *The Entrepreneurial State: Debunking Public vs. Private Sector Myths* (London: Anthem, 2013), 94–95.

3. Janet Abbate, *Inventing the Internet* (Cambridge, MA: MIT Press, 2000), 17–19.

4. Abbate, *Inventing the Internet*, 95.

5. Abbate, *Inventing the Internet*, 127.

6. James Curran, Natalie Fenton, and Des Freedman, *Misunderstanding the Internet* (New York: Routledge, 2016), 51.
7. Mazzucato, *The Entrepreneurial State*, 104.
8. Abbate, *Inventing the Internet*, 131–32.
9. Abbate, *Inventing the Internet*, 143.
10. Corey Pein, *Live Work Work Work Die: A Journey into the Savage Heart of Silicon Valley* (New York: Metropolitan, 2017), 124.
11. Pein, *Live Work Work Work Die*, 145.
12. Pein, *Live Work Work Work Die*, 194–95.
13. Pein, *Live Work Work Work Die*, 199.
14. Curran, Fenton, and Freedman, *Misunderstanding the Internet*, 33, 76.
15. Robert Wright, "The Man Who Invented the Web," *Time*, June 24, 2001.
16. Curran, Fenton, and Freedman, *Misunderstanding the Internet*, 54.
17. Eli Parsier, *The Filter Bubble: How the New Personalized Web Is Changing What We Read and How We Think* (New York: Penguin, 2011), 217–18.
18. Brian Merchant, *The One Device: The Secret History of the iPhone* (New York: Little, Brown, & Co., 2017), 190–91.
19. Abbate, *Inventing the Internet*, 115.
20. Merchant, *The One Device*, 70–72.
21. Merchant, *The One Device*, 9.
22. Mazzucato, *The Entrepreneurial State*, 101–3.
23. Office of Science and Technology Policy, "American Competitiveness Initiative: Leading the World in Innovation," February 2006, 8.
24. Mazzucato, *The Entrepreneurial State*, 106–7.
25. Mazzucato, *The Entrepreneurial State*, 108.
26. Merchant, *The One Device*, 188–90.
27. Mazzucato, *The Entrepreneurial State*, 109.
28. James Wallace and Jim Erickson, *Hard Drive* (New York: HarperCollins, 1992), 23.
29. Steven Levy, *Insanely Great: The Life and Times of Macintosh, the Computer That Changed Everything* (New York: Viking, 1994), 43.
30. Brad Stone, *The Everything Store: Jeff Bezos and the Age of Amazon* (New York: Little, Brown, & Co., 2013), 161.
31. David Kirkpatrick, *The Facebook Effect* (New York: Simon & Schuster, 2010), 66.
32. Parsier, *The Filter Bubble*, 31.
33. Yasha Levine, *Surveillance Valley: The Secret Military History of the Internet* (New York: Hachette, 2018), 147.
34. Cathy O'Neil, *Weapons of Math Destruction* (New York: Crown, 2016), 29, 115.

35. O'Neil, *Weapons of Math Destruction*, 115.
36. Merchant, *The One Device*, 228–29.
37. Heidi Vogt, "Artificial Intelligence Rules More of Your Life. Who Rules AI?," *Wall Street Journal*, March 13, 2018.
38. Office of Science and Technology Policy, "American Competitiveness Initiative," p. 11.
39. Mazzuczato, *The Entrepreneurial State*, 60–61.

Chapter 9: Leashing the Techlash

1. Farhad Manjoo, "Apple Shuns the Tech Industry's Apology Tour," *New York Times*, June 4, 2018.
2. James Wallace, *Overdrive: Bill Gates and the Race to Control Cyberspace* (New York: John Wiley & Sons, 1997), 269.
3. Jacob Schlesinger and Jeff Horwitz, "Tech Backlash Frays Cozy Ties to Washington," *Wall Street Journal*, July 26, 2019.
4. Yasha Levine, *Surveillance Valley: The Secret Military History of the Internet* (New York: Hachette, 2018), 190–93.
5. Ewen MacAskill, "NSA Paid Millions to Cover Prism Compliance Costs for Tech Companies," *The Guardian*, August 23, 2013.
6. Steven Levy, *In the Plex: How Google Thinks, Works, and Shapes Our Lives* (New York: Simon & Schuster, 2011), 319.
7. David Streitfeld, Natasha Singer, and Steven Erlanger, "How Calls for Privacy May Upend Business for Facebook and Google," *New York Times*, March 24, 2018.
8. Daisuke Wakabayashi, "Missouri Opens Antitrust Investigation into Google," *New York Times*, November 13, 2017.
9. Jack Nicas and Rolfe Winkler, "Donald Trump Strikes Conciliatory Tone in Meeting with Tech Executives," *Wall Street Journal*, December 14, 2016.
10. Jathan Sadowski, "Silicon Valley for Trump," *Jacobin*, December 21, 2016.
11. Greg Ip, "A Wary Tech Sector Is Booming in the Land of Trump," *Wall Street Journal*, April 25, 2017.
12. David Streitfeld, Mike Isaac, and Katie Benner, "Silicon Valley's Ambivalence toward Trump Turns to Anger," *New York Times*, January 29, 2017.
13. David Streitfeld, "Tech Opposition to Trump Propelled by Employees, Not Executives," *New York Times*, February 6, 2017.
14. Deepa Seetharaman, "Trump's Posts Fuel Discord in Facebook Ranks," *Wall Street Journal*, October 22, 2016.

15. Sheera Frenkel, "The Biggest Spender of Political Ads on Facebook? President Trump," *New York Times*, July 17, 2018.

16. Streitfeld, Isaac, and Benner, "Silicon Valley's Ambivalence."

17. John McKinnon and Brody Mullins, "Google's Dominance in Washington Faces a Reckoning," *Wall Street Journal*, October 30, 2017.

18. Cecilia Kang, "Google, in Post-Obama Era, Aggressively Woos Republicans," *New York Times*, January 27, 2017.

19. Douglas Macmillan, "Tech to Size Up Tax-Law Impact," *Wall Street Journal*, January 31, 2018.

20. Corey Pein, *Live Work Work Work Die: A Journey into the Savage Heart of Silicon Valley* (New York: Metropolitan, 2017), 127.

21. Douglas MacMillan and Jay Greene, "Tech Giants Are in No Rush to Spend Overseas Cash," *Wall Street Journal*, February 5, 2018.

22. Rebecca MacKinnon, *Consent of the Networked: The Worldwide Struggle for Internet Freedom* (New York: Basic, 2012), 7.

23. Jerry Iannelli, "U.S. Government Has Plans to Spread Hidden Facebook Propaganda in Cuba," *Miami New Times*, August 21, 2018.

24. Telis Demos, "Why Amazon and Google Haven't Attacked Banks," *Wall Street Journal*, April 26, 2018.

25. Cecilia Kang, David Streitfeld, and Annie Karni, "Antitrust Troubles Snowball for Tech Giants as Lawmakers Join In," *New York Times*, June 3, 2019.

26. John McKinnon, "Google, Others Now Draw State Scrutiny," *Wall Street Journal*, June 8, 2019.

27. Brent Kendall and Tripp Mickle, "Apple Loses Bid to End App Antitrust Case in Supreme Court," *Wall Street Journal*, May 13, 2019.

28. Tripp Mickle, "Apple Dominates App Store Search Results, Thwarting Competitors," *Wall Street Journal*, July 23, 2019.

29. Yoko Kubota and Tripp Mickle, "Apple Explores Moving Some Production Out of China," *Wall Street Journal*, June 20, 2019.

30. Ryan Tracy and Valentina Pop, "Google's Enemies Gear Up to Make Antitrust Case," *Wall Street Journal*, June 24, 2019.

31. Brent Kendall, "Justice Department Is Preparing Antitrust Investigation of Google," *Wall Street Journal*, June 1, 2019.

32. John McKinnon et al., "Facebook Worries Emails Could Show Zuckerberg Knew of Questionable Privacy Practices," *Wall Street Journal*, June 12, 2019.

33. Jeff Horwitz and Deepa Seetharaman, "Facebook's Zuckerberg Backs Privacy Legislation," *Wall Street Journal*, June 26, 2019.

34. Chris Hughes, "It's Time to Break Up Facebook," *New York Times*,

May 9, 2019.

35. Mike Isaac and Natasha Singer, "Facebook Antitrust Inquiry Shows Big Tech's Freewheeling Era Is Past," *New York Times*, July 24, 2019.

36. Center for Responsive Politics, "Microsoft Corp," www.opensecrets.org /lobby/clientsum.php?id=D000000115&year=2018.

37. Brent Kendall, "Antitrust Cop Balances Tech Issues," *Wall Street Journal*, July 8, 2019.

38. Cecilia Kang and Kenneth Vogel, "Tech Giants Amass a Lobbying Army for an Epic Washington Battle," *New York Times*, June 5, 2019.

39. Brody Mullins, Laura Stevens, and John McKinnon, "How Amazon Became One of Washington's Most Powerful Players," *Wall Street Journal*, June 20, 2018.

40. Brody Mullins and Ted Mann, "Google Drops Lobbying Firms as Government Scrutiny Grows, *Wall Street Journal*, June 13, 2019.

41. Shane Goldmacher and Stephanie Saul, "Democrats Take Aim at Silicon Valley. They Take Its Cash, Too," *New York Times*, June 6, 2019.

42. Ted Mann, Chad Day, and Julie Bykowicz, "Democrats Rake in Tech Donations," *Wall Street Journal*, June 8, 2019.

43. Louise Radnofsky, "New Gatekeeper on Legal Immigration Sets a Tougher Tone," *Wall Street Journal*, July 8, 2019.

44. Suzanne Vranica and Alexandra Bruell, "Advertisers Are Wary of Breaking Up Google and Facebook," *Wall Street Journal*, June 20, 2019.

45. Daniel Michaels, "Hot U.S. Import: European Regulations," *Wall Street Journal*, May 7, 2018.

46. Adam Satariano and Jack Nicas, "E.U. Fine Google $5.1 Billion in Android Antitrust Case," *New York Times*, July 18, 2018.

47. Jack Nicas, "Google Shrugs Off $5.1 Billion Fine with Another Big Quarter," *New York Times*, July 23, 2018.

48. Sam Schechner and Valentina Pop, "EU Starts Preliminary Probe into Amazon's Treatment of Merchants," *Wall Street Journal*, September 19, 2018.

49. James Kanter, "E.U., Citing Amazon and Apple, Tells Nations to Collect Tax," *New York Times*, October 4, 2017.

50. Jesse Drucker, "Google 2.4% Rate Shows How $60 Billion Is Lost to Tax Loopholes," *Bloomberg*, October 21, 2010.

51. Sam Schechner, "Apple Takes a Step on Payment of Back Taxes to Ireland," *Wall Street Journal*, April 24, 2018.

52. Robert McMillan, "EU Demand Adds to Challenges for CEO," *Wall Street Journal*, August 31, 2016.

53. Adam Satariano, "What Europe's Tough New Data Law Means for You,

and the Internet," *New York Times*, May 6, 2018.

54. Nick Kostov and Sam Schechner, "Google Emerges as Early Winner from Europe's New Data Privacy Law," *Wall Street Journal*, May 31, 2018.

55. Sam Schechner and Nick Kostov, "Google and Facebook Likely to Benefit from Europe's Privacy Crackdown," *Wall Street Journal*, April 23, 2018.

56. Deepa Seetharaman, "Facebook Provides a Preview of Its Privacy Makeover," *Wall Street Journal*, April 18, 2018.

57. Jonathan Vanian, "Microsoft Just Built a Special Version of Windows for China," *Fortune*, May 23, 2017.

58. Yoko Kubota, "Apple Pulls Illegal Apps Targeted by Chinese State Media," *Wall Street Journal*, August 20, 2018.

59. Robert McMillan and Tripp Mickle, "Apple to Start Putting Sensitive Encryption Keys in China," *Wall Street Journal*, February 24, 2018.

60. Paul Mozur, "China Said to Quickly Withdraw Approval for New Facebook Venture," *New York Times*, July 25, 2018.

61. Levy, *In the Plex*, 280.

62. Levy, *In the Plex*, 284.

63. Levy, *In the Plex*, 309.

64. Andrew Browne, "Beijing's Dream Is a Nightmare for Apple," *Wall Street Journal*, August 9, 2017.

65. Ken Auletta, *Googled: The End of the World as We Know It* (New York: Penguin, 2010), 339.

66. Levy, *In the Plex*, 284.

67. Eli Pariser, *The Filter Bubble: How the New Personalized Web Is Changing What We Read and How We Think* (New York: Penguin, 2011), 139.

68. Li Yuan, "Tech Titans Wage War in China's Next Internet Revolution," *Wall Street Journal*, December 21, 2017.

69. Newley Purnell, "India Looks to Curb U.S. Tech Giants' Power," *Wall Street Journal*, August 13, 2018.

70. Paul Mozur, Mark Scott, and Mike Isaac, "Facebook Faces a New World as Officials Rein in a Wild Web," *New York Times*, September 17, 2017.

Chapter 10: Share This!

1. Trebor Scholz and Nathan Schneider, eds., *Ours to Hack and to Own: The Rise of Platform Cooperativism, a New Vision for the Future of Work and a Fairer Internet* (New York: OR Books, 2017), 12.

2. Amazon Workers and Supporters, "'Stop Treating Us Like Dogs!'—Worker Resistance at Amazon in Poland," *Pluto Press Blog*, www.plutobooks.com /blog/worker-resistance-amazon-poland June 23, 2019.

3. James Curran, Natalie Fenton, and Des Freedman, *Misunderstanding the*

Internet (New York: Routledge, 2016), 207–8.

4. Frederick Douglass, in Philip Foner and Yuval Taylor, eds., *Frederick Douglass: Selected Speeches and Writings* (Chicago: Chicago Review Press, 1999), 676–78.

5. Rosa Luxemburg, in Helen Scott, ed., *The Essential Rosa Luxemburg* (Chicago: Haymarket Books, 2008), 141, 147.

6. Robert McChesney, *Digital Disconnect: How Capitalism Is Turning the Internet against Democracy* (New York: New Press, 2013), 152.

7. Evgeny Morozov, "Socialize the Data Centers!," *New Left Review*, Jan/Feb 2015, 45.

8. Kate Bronfenbrenner and Robert Hickey, *Blueprint for Change*, Office of Labor Education Research, Cornell University, 2003.

9. Tim Wu, *The Master Switch: The Rise and Fall of Information Empires* (New York: Vintage, 2011), 262–63.

10. Jonathan Taplin, "Can the Tech Giants Be Stopped?," *Wall Street Journal*, July 14, 2017.

11. Paul Mason, "The End of Capitalism Has Begun," *The Guardian*, July 17, 2015.

12. Don Clark and Robert McMillan, "Giants Tighten Grip on Internet Economy," *Wall Street Journal*, November 6, 2015.

13. Corrie Driebusch and Ben Eisen, "Nasdaq Crests 7000 as Tech Giants Roar into 2018," *Wall Street Journal*, January 3, 2018.

14. Ted Greenwald and Jack Nicas, "Intel Wrestled with Chip Flaws for Months," *Wall Street Journal*, January 5, 2018.

15. Jack Nicas, "Google Pulls YouTube from Amazon Devices, Saying It Isn't Playing Fair," *Wall Street Journal*, December 5, 2017.

16. Pew Research Center, "Americans Have Become Much Less Positive about Tech Companies' Impact on the U.S.," Fact Tank: News in the Numbers, July 29, 2019.

Index

"Passim" (literally "scattered") indicates intermittent discussion of a topic over a cluster of pages.

About the Author

Rob Larson is Professor of Economics at Tacoma Community College and author of *Capitalism vs. Freedom* and *Bleakonomics*. He writes for a number of venues including *Current Affairs, Dollars & Sense,* and *Jacobin*.

About Haymarket Books

Haymarket Books is a radical, independent, nonprofit book publisher based in Chicago.

Our mission is to publish books that contribute to struggles for social and economic justice. We strive to make our books a vibrant and organic part of social movements and the education and development of a critical, engaged, international left.

We take inspiration and courage from our namesakes, the Haymarket martyrs, who gave their lives fighting for a better world. Their 1886 struggle for the eight-hour day—which gave us May Day, the international workers' holiday—reminds workers around the world that ordinary people can organize and struggle for their own liberation. These struggles continue today across the globe—struggles against oppression, exploitation, poverty, and war.

Since our founding in 2001, Haymarket Books has published more than five hundred titles. Radically independent, we seek to drive a wedge into the risk-averse world of corporate book publishing. Our authors include Noam Chomsky, Arundhati Roy, Rebecca Solnit, Angela Y. Davis, Howard Zinn, Amy Goodman, Wallace Shawn, Mike Davis, Winona LaDuke, Ilan Pappé, Richard Wolff, Dave Zirin, Keeanga-Yamahtta Taylor, Nick Turse, Dahr Jamail, David Barsamian, Elizabeth Laird, Amira Hass, Mark Steel, Avi Lewis, Naomi Klein, and Neil Davidson. We are also the trade publishers of the acclaimed Historical Materialism Book Series and of Dispatch Books.